SAGITTARIUS ♐
The Archer
(Nov. 22–Dec. 21)

Ruling planet JUPITER ♃

The procrastinator with great ability and ideals who is intense, warm, and communicates well.

SCORPIO ♏
The Scorpion

The secretive, forceful organizer whose hallmark is individuality. One plays the game to win, not draw.

LIBRA ♎
The Scales
(Sept. 23–Oct. 22)
Ruling planet
VENUS ♀

The natural fighters for justice who battle for the underdog, but prefer gentleness and peace. Indecisive.

The analytical, practical person who may be shy, but with an affinity for contradiction.

VIRGO ♍
The Virgin
(Aug. 23–Sept. 22)
Ruling planet
MERCURY ☿

The vital, creative person with personal magnetism, charm, and an aura of sexuality—"You live for love."

LEO ♌
The Lion
(July 23–Aug. 22)
Ruling planet SUN ☉

The secure, family person who accumulates wealth and is a good cook, but is moody and ultrasensitive.

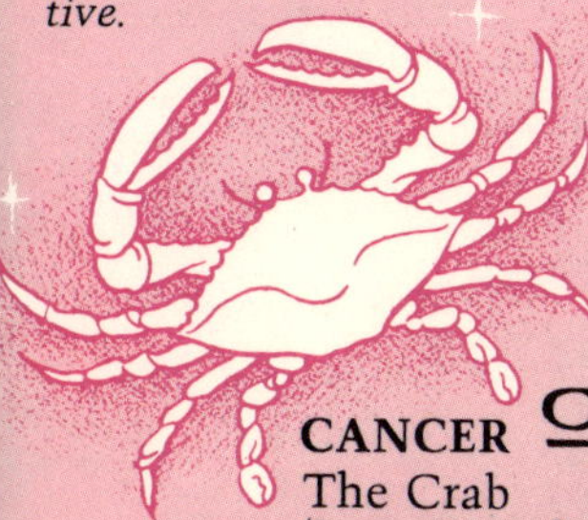

CANCER ♋
The Crab
(June 21–July 22)
Ruling planet MOON ☽

This is a basic solar chart with the stars, planets, and signs in fixed positions. The reader should keep in mind that over the centuries the zodiacal signs and constellations have ceased to coincide exactly, due to the precession of the equinoxes. Therefore, there are varying degrees of differences between the constellations and the signs, depending upon the date.

OMARR
Astrology and the Man

Books by Norma Lee Browning

OMARR: ASTROLOGY AND THE MAN
PETER HURKOS: I HAVE MANY LIVES
MILLER'S HIGH LIFE (with Ann Miller)
THE HONORABLE MR. MARIGOLD (with Louella Dirksen)
THE PSYCHIC WORLD OF PETER HURKOS
THE OTHER SIDE OF THE MIND (with W. Clement Stone)
JOE MADDY OF THE INTERLOCHEN
CITY GIRL IN THE COUNTRY

OMARR
Astrology and the Man

NORMA LEE BROWNING

DOUBLEDAY & COMPANY, INC.
Garden City, New York
1977

"Horseplayer's Horoscope," and Certified Statement by Harry Egner, reprinted from the May 1974 issue of *Argosy*. All rights reserved, copyright © 1974 by Popular Publications Inc.

"Astrology on Trial," reprinted from James Crenshaw article on the Kay Loring astrology/fortunetelling case, which appeared in Fall 1966 issue of *Fate* magazine. Used by permission of the author.

Excerpts from and condensation of article of May 1960 issue of the *Florida Medical Association Journal* on postoperative hemorrhaging by Dr. Edson J. Andrews. Used by permission.

"The Kennedys," reprinted from Sydney Omarr's articles that appeared in the December 22, 1974, and January 12, 1975, issues of *The National Tattler*. Used by permission.

"The Astrologer Seen Through the Eyes of a Friend," by Henry Miller, reprinted from *Sydney Omarr's Astrological Guide for 1973*, copyright © 1972 by Sydney Omarr. By arrangement with The New American Library, Inc., New York, New York.

Excerpts from *Sydney Omarr's Astrological Guide for 1974*, copyright © 1973 by Sydney Omarr. By arrangement with the New American Library, Inc., New York, New York.

Condensations from *Astrology and You*, by Sydney Omarr, adapted and reprinted by permission of the author and his agents, Scott Meredith Literary Agency, Inc., 845 Third Avenue, New York, New York 10022.

Excerpts from *Medical Astrology*, copyright © 1971 by Omar Garrison. Published by arrangement with Lyle Stuart, Inc.

ISBN 0-385-04443-7
Library of Congress Catalog Card Number 73-11628

Printed in the United States of America
First Edition

ENDPAPER CHARTS BY JOHN MORRIS

PALM CHARTS IN CHAPTER 18 DRAWN BY MEL KLAPHOLZ

This book is devotedly dedicated to
my favorite Aquarian, the only man in
my fifth house, my husband, who bore up well
during my astrological sojourn with Sydney,
who is everywoman's favorite Leo.

Norma Lee Browning
(Sagittarius)

Acknowledgments

In retrospect, I am awed and totally mystified that I could have written this book. I simply don't believe a word of it. I think Sydney Omarr merely mesmerized me while my Saturn was on his moon in the ninth house and this is what came out of our planetary affliction.

But Dr. John LaCorte, a brilliant young philosophy professor and specialist in the mantic arts, assures me it's all true. And he ought to know. He was there throughout all our taping sessions, and although at times I'm sure he was as mesmerized as I was, he at least had the advantage of knowing what Sydney was talking about and the patience to explain to me such basic astrological nomenclature as fiery and earthy triplicity, the lunar low, and grand trine.

Both John and Sydney are fiery Leos, and believe me, working with two Leos at a time is a handful even for a hardy, thick-skinned fiery Sagittarian. Sydney has about as much patience as a snapping turtle. So it was left to John to soothe my frazzled nerves with tranquilizers of Neil Diamond records and then carry on the course of instruction with all sorts of zodiacal charts, graphs, models, and pictures drawn especially for my edification. Following Sydney is like trying to latch onto the tail of a comet streaking across the sky. John LaCorte was my navigator in this celestial chase, as well as my chief censor, critic, boo-boo catcher, and interpreter during the preparation of this book. Without him I would probably still be stalled by Mercury in retrograde. I owe him a very special debt of gratitude.

My special thanks also to Mike Kanter, former proprietor of the once famous Kanter's magic shop, in Philadelphia, where Sydney spent most of his time as a boy. Mike played an important role in Sydney's early life and spent a great deal of time recalling for me some of the episodes included in this book, for which I am grateful.

I am indebted also to Herbert Scott, owner of radio station

WPAZ, in Pottstown, Pennsylvania, who gave Sydney his first break as a newscaster and let him talk about astrology on the air (horrors!); to Merv Griffin, whose popular TV show frequently features the wit and wisdom of Sydney Omarr (Merv is one of Sydney's most fervent fans); to Paul Solomon, talent co-ordinator of the Merv Griffin Show; to Joseph Chrenko, insurance executive and a special friend of Sydney's; to Dr. Alvin Bickel of Philadelphia; to authors Henry Miller and Jess Stearn, newspaperman Jimmy Crenshaw, TV's Rona Barrett, and astrologers Carl Payne Tobey and Ruth Hale Oliver. All these have been most generous with their time in granting interviews and providing material that has been invaluable in painting a word picture of Sydney Omarr, a man whom they obviously adore. My thanks to all of them for their contributions to this book.

With special appreciation for the palm-print photographs by William Margulies, American Society of Cinematographers; and to artists Vince Cameron and Diane Ehlers for their illustrations.

And from both of us an extra-special word of appreciation to our editors, Larry Ashmead and Eve Roshevsky; our agents, Reece and Dorris Halsey (for their patience!); our editorial and research assistants, Vera Servi and Pam Gallagher, and secretarial girl Friday Lois Kaufman.

Norma Lee Browning
Palm Springs, California
December 1, 1975

Contents

Introduction: The Astrologer Seen Through the Eyes of a Friend BY HENRY MILLER 11

THE OMARR-BROWNING CONJUCTION

1. *Mercury Goes Retrograde* (HOW IT ALL BEGAN) 19
2. *Astrology for Beginners* 27

THE MALEFICS: HOW THEY MESS UP THE WORLD

3. *The Winner Loses* (WATERGATE: CAPRICORN WITH PLUTO IN THE TENTH) 39
4. *Jupiter and Saturn Conjunction* (THE MYSTERIOUS DEATH CYCLE OF PRESIDENTS) 47
5. *It Was a Pluto 22 Year* (AND THE WORST IS YET TO COME) 58

WHO IS SYDNEY OMARR?

6. *Pluto Revisited: a Born Winner* 71
7. *Peck's Bad Boy in the Magic Shop* 83
8. *Jupiter in His Fifth* 96
9. *Army Astrologer* 103
10. *Thought Dial* 108

ASTROLOGER TO THE STARS

11. *Leo in Lotusland* 123

12. *Latching onto the Stars—Celestial and Cinematic* 128

13. *The Kennedys* 146

14. *Resident Astrologer on TV* 151

SCIENCE VERSUS ASTROLOGY

15. *Astrology on Trial* 173

16. *The Great Debates* 194

17. *Astrology and Religion* (TO EACH HIS OWN) 206

18. *Medical Astrology* (THE MOON AND YOU) 213

HOW TO DO IT YOURSELF: WITH ASTROLOGY

19. *How to . . . and When to . . .* (THE ANSWERS ARE ALL IN THE SKIES) 237

20. *How to Pick a Mate* (GETTING THE YIN-YANG OF YOUR LOVE STRAIGHT IN THE FIFTH HOUSE) 246

21. *How to Pick a Horse* (THE HORSEPLAYER'S HOROSCOPE) 260

22. *How to Pick a Pet* 275

23. *How to Cook with Astrology* 282

24. *How to Dress by Astrology* 288

CODA . . . NUMBER NINE . . . AN END OR A BEGINNING

25. *What Does the Future Hold?* 303

Introduction

The Astrologer Seen Through the Eyes of a Friend

by Henry Miller

You should know immediately, dear reader, that your favorite astrologer, Sydney Omarr, is human, all too human. Like most of us he is susceptible, vulnerable, even gullible at times. He can make mistakes, just like any other mortal. He craves love, recognition, approval, and will even accept a bit of flattery if it hails from the right source. Sometimes he reminds me of a big child who wants attention and affection. Above all, I think that he wants to know that his words make sense, that they are heeded, and that they do some people some good.

Like most interesting individuals he is a bundle of contradictions. He can be gentle and tough, timid and aggressive, shy and arrogant, strangely unsure of himself at times and then preposterously certain that whatever he says or does is right, absolutely right. It all depends on whom he is up against. With his friends he is extremely humble, kind, helpful, generous. With an adversary, particularly in the realm of astrology, he is obdurate, unflinching, merciless, but always fair, always cool as a cucumber, and always ready to forgive. He lives astrology twenty-four hours of the day, which is to say in his dreams as well as in his waking hours. He is bitter only toward supposedly intelligent people who are narrow-minded and prejudiced, who scoff at astrology without knowing anything about the subject.

One of his chief laments is his inability to do more for a client than merely indicate the nature and the possible solution of a problem. He himself sees so clearly what needs to be done or not to be done. He is never reconciled to the fact that seeing and doing are quite separate things. Yet he knows that astrologers cannot always help themselves, that they behave like fools at times, and that they are not more successful or more happy than other people.

Omarr is more than an astrologer, of course. He is possessed not only of a sixth sense but of a seventh and possibly an eighth. Which is what gives one an uncanny feeling in his presence sometimes. Add to this that he has a great sense of the dramatic, a Leo right to the bone.

He's especially impressive and dramatic when he invokes the aid of numbers, a technique he has elucidated in one of his books, *Thought Dial.* He frequently will ask a person to give three numbers quickly, without thinking. Whether the three numbers add up to 1,974,382 or just sixteen or twelve makes little difference: he reduces the sum to a single digit before you can say Boo. This number, according to his neo-Pythagorean system, gives a person's subconscious wish. Seven, for example, is a bad number; nine is the end of something, no dice, and so on. It's amazing what he can make the numbers do for him. At any rate, it's then that he assumes, unconsciously, the look of the seer, the blank, searching gaze of the mind reader. One has to remember that he was once a boxer; he still has the build of a light-heavyweight. The body is a boxer's, the face is that of a scholar, the look of pain and torture is Omarr's own: it goes with a certain genuine intensity of concentration. Seeing him on stage is, of course, another matter. There he looks quite at ease, ready for anything—in other words, the Master himself. Perhaps we also have to remember that not only was he once a boxer but a magician, a sleight-of-hand artist, as well. (When you get to know him personally you get the feeling sometimes that he is juggling you around.)

His courage and pertinacity are remarkable. Temporarily incapacitated as he now is (at this writing), he carries on quite as if everything were jake. Visiting him at the hospital where he was immobilized for several weeks, I had the impression of being at a cocktail party and not at the bedside of a man who had been stricken. Every night, he entertained his visitors, from bed, quite as if he were sailing in the morning for a trip around the world. He ate and drank his fill, smoked his usual big black cigars, joked and flirted with the nurses, stayed awake till all hours of the morning, dictated pages for his new book, and treated the doctors in attendance as simpletons whom he had to humor. (He inevitably made a few converts to astrology, particularly among the fair sex.)

The fair sex! That is his Achilles heel. When he falls in love he's just as helpless and ridiculous as any dumb cluck you can think of. (Maybe he's not so different from most of us in this respect.) In any case his charm, of which he has an abundance, deserts him; he becomes shy, boyish, says the wrong things, sometimes behaves like a downright idiot. Of course astrologers are natural prey for the fair sex. Women love to be told about themselves, be it good or bad. Besides, it is easier for them to admire an astrologer, to dote on him, than to follow the teachings or guidance of a guru. Intentionally or not, Omarr seems always to create about him the atmosphere of a dovecote. And these admirers of his are truly devoted, loving, sincere in their affection for him. Some have proposed marriage, even when he looked to be a goner. What more can one ask?

Whether it is so or not, to me it seems that he reads women better than men. I am thinking now of how he reacts, of his intuitive flashes, when he meets a woman for the first time. To be sure, women love attention; they are incurably vain and self-centered. And so, when a man like Omarr takes a woman's hand, studies the lines of her palm, palps the finger tips, turns the flashlight on it the better to examine the almost invisible lines, he has a woman at his mercy—or almost. These are not necessarily the women with whom he falls in love. What he likes is complications, trouble, trouble, trouble. The scrapes he has let himself in for would make startling reading. He would have been dead long ago had he not been something more than an astrologer.

I have often studied the expression on his face when he is studying a hand. (I forgot to say that he is just as adept at reading palms as he is in reading the stars.) His look of intense concentration makes one think of a blind man reading Braille for the first time. Sometimes he has the hoary look of the seer, the look of an aged Leonardo. The moment he relaxes and picks up his drink, his face broadens into an amiable smile and another story is on his lips. He has countless stories to relate, and they are all fascinating.

The big question is, does he know himself? Personally, I do not feel that this is so important. *It is enough that he knows us.* He knows us in the way an animal knows its prey. He knows without knowing. The way one walks, the gestures one makes or doesn't make, the way one wears his clothes, the way one smiles or frowns —by these and a thousand other details, many of them seemingly trifling, he knows us. Sometimes a look of pain comes over his face, as if he were examining an open wound. And what open wounds, what bleeding, screaming wounds most of us are! What ever makes us believe that we can deceive anyone? We are like open books, and our secrets are in vain.

There are many reasons why it is not an easy life, the life of an astrologer. Most of us, if we possessed the insight into people's lives that Omarr has, would be inclined to become pessimists. When one thinks that each year there are millions of readers who desperately gobble up what they can of the astrological forecast for the year, when one thinks that they are all hoping and praying for a break they will not get, that this year, last year, the coming year, all the years of their lives, will be full of hardships, misery, misfortune, probably loveless to boot, what is an astrologer to say to himself, how is he to regard humanity? It is true, of course, that if lived wisely life has much to offer—but who can, who knows how to live wisely? Even if one can read the stars like a book, even if he can read palms like a timetable, even if one has fortune on his side, there are still too many traps, too many pitfalls, too many hazards, too many impossible-to-foresee occurrences in life for one ever to be certain of anything.

Astrologers are aware of all this even more than psychologists, scientists, or philosophers, yet they seem on the whole to believe in life, to believe that life is worth living. They are especially aware of the element of chance. For them there is always that moment when the door swings wide open and all one has to do is to step through. But can one be awake and alert twenty-four hours of the day? Maybe the chance of a lifetime comes in the middle of the night, when it is no longer expected.

I for one would not want to see all that the astrologer sees when he does a horoscope. I would not want to know as much about myself as he obviously does. I would not want to depend on the wheel of fortune any more than I would on a savings bank, the verdict of a judge, or the diagnosis of a physician.

In putting the emphasis on success and happiness, as so many astrologers do, I feel that our real motive in living gets thoroughly distorted. I believe that a normal, healthy individual does not want to know his future, *he wants to make it.* I don't think he wants to be spared the blows of fate, either. The wiser he becomes the more he realizes that the root of evil lies in himself, that there is nothing out there to combat or to be afraid of or to protect himself against. He doesn't want to live on a dull, healthy plateau. There is enough of the animal in him to crave adventure, to take risks. He doesn't want insurance, he wants assurance, assurance that life at any price is worth the gamble.

Omarr himself is a good gambler. He takes plenty of risks. He does not want to live cooped up in an ivory tower. He lives with the stars and not by them. He is a very tenderhearted human being who takes his calling seriously but not himself. He is always more concerned about the other fellow than about himself. He is thoroughly aware that a new age is being ushered in, that we have one foot in it already but that the other foot is still mired in the mess called the past. He doesn't say, "Now a miracle must happen or we are lost"; he says, "We are living a miracle every moment of the day."

The Omarr-Browning Conjunction

Chapter 1

MERCURY GOES RETROGRADE
(How It All Began)

"The wise man controls his destiny—
Astrology points the way."
—SYDNEY OMARR

I was sitting in my study in Palm Springs, California, laboriously plodding through books on astrology, trying to figure out how to construct my own horoscope, when the telephone rang.

It was Sydney Omarr calling from Santa Monica, and there was an urgency in his voice.

"You must get started right now! Get something down on the typewriter, even if it's only a few lines or a paragraph," he said, "because Mercury goes retrograde tonight."

"What?"

"I said," he enunciated clearly and firmly, "Mercury is going retrograde tonight."

"What does that mean?"

"It means it's going backward as viewed from the earth, and when Mercury is retrograde all sorts of things go wrong. It's the fastest and smallest planet, the one closest to the sun. The adverse transits of Mercury indicate restless, irritating, harassing conditions and are very unfavorable for anything that has to do with communications and publishing. It's not a good time for starting or mailing manuscripts. Things get lost in the mail. Plane tickets get lost. It's a time of disruptions, red tape, errors in paper work, and so on.

"If you wait until Mercury is retrograde to start the book, it will only mean more delays and mishaps. So my advice is to at least get something written immediately before Mercury starts going retrograde."

I had listened attentively, making notes as he talked. He was terribly serious, as he always is, but I couldn't help letting loose a loud peal of laughter.

"You're just making all that up to get me started, and I'm not ready yet," I told him. "I haven't even learned how to do my own horoscope. I don't even know what my rising sign is. I can't figure out all those charts in the back of the books. How can I write a book about the world's greatest astrologer if I don't understand astrology?"

"You don't have to understand it. Do you understand how electricity works? Or how brain waves operate? Or why the swallows come back to Capistrano? If we waited to understand all these things, the world would be in a horrible mess. . . . Quick, give me three numbers," he said.

I reeled off three numbers fast—two, four, and five

"That's eleven. A higher octave of two. A master digit," Sydney intoned. "Eleven is associated with Uranus, the planet of astrology. The emphasis is on creativeness, intuition, teaching, and learning. Now is the time for expressing ideas, no matter how radical they are. Uranus rules the sign of Aquarius, and we're in Aquarius now. . . .

"You see," he added, "everything numerologically and astrologically says that this is the propitious time for you to start the book. With number eleven and Uranus in your favor you are in the very strong position of being both a teacher and a learner. That should be your approach to the book. Trust your intuition. Now I urge you to hurry up and get something down on paper before Mercury goes retrograde."

"How long will Mercury be retrograde?" I asked.

"Possibly a month or two. I'd have to consult my ephemeris for the exact time, and it's in the other room."

"What hour tonight does it start going retrograde?"

"I'd have to consult my ephemeris for that also. [An ephemeris is an astrological almanac indicating planetary motions.] But I know it's tonight, because Jeraldine called to remind me to get all my letters and bills and business details finished today, before Mercury goes retrograde."

Jeraldine is Sydney's ex-wife, also an astrologer. But with all their combined astrological expertise they couldn't make their marriage work. It lasted about six weeks, Sydney thinks. He isn't sure. As he says, "We both knew we shouldn't get married. Our aspects were all wrong. But we did anyway." They have remained friends, and Jeraldine still checks on him now and then—even to the extent of reminding him that Mercury was about to go retrograde, probably any minute now.

Apparently I hadn't a moment to waste.

I put down the phone, listened to my little alarm clock ticking away, then stepped out on my patio and looked up at the sky.

It had not been a typical Palm Springs day. It was one of those rare sunless, windy, and rainy days that come along only once or twice a year, usually just in time to put a damper on the "Bob Hope Desert Classic." Glowering clouds draped the San Jacinto Mountains, now a bare black outline of shadows. No planets were visible in the sky, even if I had known where to find them.

How does one take a sighting on a retrograding Mercury in a sky like that?

I returned to my desk, vaguely wishing that Sydney had taken the trouble to look up the exact time of the retrograde in his ephemeris. How much time did I have to the starting point? Perhaps until midnight? What if Mercury was already retrograde? But Sydney had said it would be tonight, and it was still today by my clock, or at least only late afternoon.

I jotted down more things to do in my special "Things to Do" astrology notebook: buy an ephemeris or some ephemerides (plural) to study. Buy a basic beginner's book on astronomy, one on the history and origin of mathematics, one on Greek mythology, and especially one on the *planets*.

Next I looked in my folder marked "Introduction" and found the transcript of one of our early tapes during which Sydney had told me the reason for previous delays on the book.

"You have Saturn on my moon in the ninth house," he had said. "Saturn restricts and slows down and coincides with delays. I knew this when we started. Remember, I said you can never meet the deadline with your Saturn on my moon, so we'll just have to be prepared for the delays and contend with them as best we can. Do you think your editor will understand?"

My Saturn on Sydney's moon in the ninth house?

Well . . . it was a rather esoteric way of missing a deadline.

Fortunately, an about-to-be-retrograding Mercury impelled me to apply the seat of the pants to the seat of the chair in front of the typewriter, and as I sat there pondering on the number eleven and Uranus, I had a strange compulsion to write something—anything—to circumvent the onus of Mercury in retrograde. Then I said to myself, you don't really believe all this superstition and nonsense. It's sheer madness, lunacy. (An astrological word, I'd discovered.) But somehow I couldn't bring myself to take any chances with planets going backward. . . .

How did I get myself involved with all this astrological mish-mash?

I remembered it clearly. I needed an astrologer to do a horoscope on Peter Hurkos, the Dutch psychic whose book I was writing. (*Peter Hurkos: I Have Many Lives*, Doubleday.) I had met many astrologers but knew none of them well—nor did I want to. By birth (Missouri), occupation, and inclination, I was a skeptic, particularly in matters pertaining to the occult.

I wasn't sure exactly where astrology stood in the occult arts and I didn't have time to find out. All I wanted was a horoscope for Peter Hurkos.

I had met Sydney Omarr only once, several years before, but in that brief meeting I had been impressed with his knowledge of a subject I knew nothing about, as well as his scholarly, soft-spoken way of discussing it. As a fellow journalist, I had followed his career and knew his reputation as a rather erudite, skillful, and sober protagonist of astrology—not the flamboyant Hollywood type. This was why I chose him to do Peter's horoscope, but I didn't get very far on that score.

When I called him, I introduced myself and asked if he remembered me.

"Of course," he said. "It was at the Shoreham Apartments. I remember it very well. I'm delighted to hear from you. How have you been? How do you like it here?" Chitchat.

"The reason I'm calling—" I began. But I didn't get to finish.

"Excuse me," he interrupted gently, "but what was your birth date again?"

"November 24. Why? I won't give you the year. That's an invasion of privacy. Besides, I didn't call you for my horoscope. I called to ask–"

"Give me three numbers quick," he interrupted again. "Don't think about them–just the first three numbers that come in your head."

"Two, three, four," I said impatiently. They were the first numbers that popped into my head. "What has that got to do with anything?"

"That's nine. Well, you've been going through a terrible emotional period, but this is going to change in October. You've been through a wringer, a tremendous upheaval, a terrible burden on your shoulders. This has been a horrific period for you. It has to do with contractural obligations and your marital situation."

He then proceeded to itemize specifically a number of problems I had been confronted with in recent months, and with such accuracy that I heard myself asking, "How do you know this?"

"Give me three more numbers again. Quick," he said.

This time I gave him four, six, and eight.

"That's nine again."

"Slower, please. How does that add up to nine?"

"Four plus six plus eight equals 18. You reduce that to one digit, and one plus eight equals nine."

"But why do I always come up with nine?"

"These numbers are buried deep in your subconscious," he explained, "and they are always symbolic of something. Numerology is an ancient science. Since remotest times, men have used numbers to express their thoughts. Number nine is associated with the planet Mars, the energy planet, and it represents the end of a cycle, the beginning of something new, but not right now, not this minute. You have to wait until October. But it will happen, just as you want it now.

"So just keep cool and don't blow your stack. [Exactly what I had been doing.] You remember that Mars in mythology was the god of war. And this combined with your sun sign, Sagittarius, could create problems. Sagittarians," he continued, "can be very blunt, sometimes to the point of rudeness, so just take it easy through these next few weeks. Don't be hasty. Don't do anything drastic."

He then added something about my moon in Saturn that was so

much gobbledygook to me. But I'll admit I was shaken. He couldn't have been more right about personal matters that concerned me—past, present, and future.

I felt quite uncomfortable. I didn't want to know any more about myself. I tried to change the subject and finally edged a word in about the purpose of my call. But he didn't seem much interested in doing a horoscope for Peter Hurkos.

"He's a Gemini . . . Did you know there are more twins born under Gemini, and more left-handed people, and more persons in jail born under Gemini than under any other sign?"

"That's very interesting and I'm willing to take your word for it," I said. "But I didn't call you for a lecture on astrology. I'm writing a book on Peter Hurkos and I need his horoscope."

"Why don't you do my book?" he asked.

"You're a writer. Why don't you write your own?"

"I haven't time."

"Neither have I."

He was too busy writing his books on astrology, he explained, and his agent was looking for someone to write a book about *him*, Sydney Omarr, the astrologer.

"I'm not the one to do it. I know nothing about astrology."

"You can learn," he said. "Anyone can learn to be an instant astrologer. Have you ever heard of Carl Jung's principle of synchronicity? [Yes, I had, but I was certainly no expert at it.] It's based on the simple theory that a relationship between such things as the positions of the planets and human events is non-causal, has nothing to do with cause and effect, but is the result of meaningful coincidence.

"So if you look at the sky and it's noon, you can predict that restaurants will be filled with people having lunch, and when the sun goes down, you can predict they'll be going home from work to dinner. Yet the fact that it's noon doesn't *cause* people to rush out to restaurants. Astrology doesn't *make* anybody act in a particular way; it merely provides information as to how a person is likely to act at a particular time, and whether it would be advantageous or disadvantageous to him.

"Now, do you know that if as a nation we had been astrology-minded, we would never have elected Lyndon B. Johnson as President, because he's a Virgo? No nation astrologically informed would have elected a Virgo president at that time, because Virgo, Pisces, Gemini, and Sagittarius, all those solar signs at that time, were under great pressure. . . ."

By now I was making notes, utterly fascinated.

"And you know, of course," Sydney went on non-stop, "that astrology was the first science, even before astronomy. It was astrology that created our first compass, our first guide to anywhere; our calendar and wristwatches are all derived from astrology. But because of academic prejudice some people still call astrology a superstition. The real superstition is not to use it, to ignore it."

So okay, forget the Peter Hurkos horoscope. Ten minutes after my first one-hour astrology lesson by telephone, Sydney's agent, Reece Halsey, called me, and without knowing Capricorn the goat from Cancer the crab, I was committed.

A lingering memory of a long-ago trip to India helped me make the decision. My husband and I were on a round-the-world research trip for a book (*The Other Side of the Mind*, with W. Clement Stone), during which we visited the famous Jai Singh's observatory in Jaipur, and while looking in awe at ancient, yellowed, time-worn charts and manuscripts on astrology, I remember saying, "Hmmm, I guess astrology once was considered a real science."

Many have asked me why I did not include astrology in that book or in other articles I have written on the occult arts, many of them exposés in that area. My answer has always been that I did not know enough about astrology to speak up pro or con. If you don't know it, don't knock it.

But that trip to Jaipur instilled in me a healthy respect for astrology, and my fascinating excursion into Sydney Omarr's world of astrology was to deepen this respect.

Now here I was with a retrograding Mercury flashing a celestial signal to get started, and a master digit, number eleven, in cahoots with Uranus, telling me now is the time for expressing ideas no matter how radical they are.

Sydney had told me to trust my intuition, that I was in the strong position of being both a teacher and a learner. But I must tell you right here in the beginning, dear students, that my qualifications as a teacher are limited. I would probably be categorized as a slow learner in the areas of transiting planets and Pythagorean theorems. However, I am willing to learn as I go along, and if any of my readers happen to be advanced students of astrology or numerology, kindly bear with me and take heart. At least I have made some progress. Up to now I had thought this was the Age of Aquarius, after seeing the rock musical *Hair*. But Sydney has assured me that we are still technically in the Age of Pisces, though the whys and wherefores are too complicated for slow learners. We'll just have to take his word for it.

I am inclined to agree with author Lawrence Durrell, a Pisces, in an opinion he expressed after first meeting Sydney Omarr. He said, "Either you are a great mind reader or there is a great deal to astrology."

Chapter 2

ASTROLOGY FOR BEGINNERS

"The answers are all in the skies."
—SYDNEY OMARR

It was inevitable, of course, that Sydney Omarr would wind up in Hollywood. He no doubt dialed number 22 on his Thought Dial and pointed himself in that direction.

Soon after he arrived he appeared on a now defunct radio-TV show with a "host" who specialized in scathing sarcasm. During the interview the "host" asked caustically, "And what do you predict is going to become of you, Mr. Omarr?"

Mr. Omarr calmly replied, "I'm going to become a household word."

His prediction was 100 per cent accurate, and why shouldn't it have been? After all, he had seen it written in the stars.

"The answers are all in the skies," he says. "All you need is the knowledge to find them, and then the wisdom and discipline to deal with them, to guide your life in accordance with the planets but without letting the planets control your destiny. Astrology is not fatalistic. You can still be the captain of your ship, the master of your fate, the architect of your own destiny. If everyone had a good, clear understanding of astrology, we would have a better world."

For example, astrology can guide you in just about everything, from when is the best time to have sex or a tonsillectomy, or plant your crops, to how to pick a mate, a pet, or the winning horses at a race track.

Astrology can guide you as to when is the best time to get married, divorced, sign important contracts, or have a tooth extracted. It can help you pick out the sex of your child. It can predict when you'll have emotional or physical problems and determine whether you have tendencies toward homosexuality, schizophrenia, or suicide.

Sydney emphasizes that astrology is a "scientific art" rather than an exact science.

"But medicine is not an exact science either," he is quick to point out. "Hippocrates, the father of medicine, said that any doctor who practices medicine without astrology is a fool. So that's why we have so many fools practicing medicine. Dr. Carl Jung, the late great psychiatrist, had the moral courage to admit his use of astrology. Now, if we could ever break down these prejudicial barriers, we could use astrology in many ways to benefit humanity not only in medicine but in other fields as well."

Sydney claims he can tell as much about a person from his astrological chart within half an hour as a trained psychologist can tell about a patient from several hours of consultation.

And it is not inconceivable, he adds, that astrology may one day be used to determine whether a person is predisposed to cancer. "Only, then they won't call it astrology. They'll have to change the name to make it seem more acceptable. Academic prejudice!"

In spite of academic prejudice, however, there are millions of believers in astrology, whose faith in the ancient concept that the celestial spheres affect human lives and global events remains unshakable. In the United States alone an estimated 32 million people, (according to a Gallup poll), are convinced that their future is written in the stars, and they spend an estimated $100 million annually on zodiac charts, astrology books and magazines, individual horoscopes, and consultations from some ten thousand professional astrologers.

It should be stated at the outset that the overwhelming number of practicing astrologers in this country have not the slightest understanding of the meaning of astrology or its historical background—nor do they care. It seems to make no difference to their clients.

But it does make a difference to Sydney Omarr, who chose not to go the easy route of rich and neurotic clients—though he has been sought by the wealthy and famous—but to dedicate his life to elevating the status of astrology in the scientific community and giving it credibility even among non-believers. He has the frail, somber look of a mystic or seer, but don't let that deceive you. College educated, a practicing journalist, and well grounded in subjects most astrologers can't even pronounce—from St. Thomas Aquinas' *Summa Theologica* to the Copernican theory, Pythagorean theorems, and Jung's synchronicity—he is known as the intellectual among contemporary astrologers.

He is the only one cerebrally equipped to do verbal combat on national television with some of the nation's leading astronomers (and that is a feat in itself!) and psychologists such as the irascible Dr. Joyce Brothers.

He has been an eloquent defender of his scientific art and certainly has done more to bring it out of disrepute and into a faint glimmer of academic recognition than any other astrologer.

As John Godwin said of him in his book *Occult America* (Doubleday, 1972), "Sydney Omarr is the youngster among astrology's Big Three [Righter, Zolar, Omarr], and cast in an entirely different mold. He is the intellectual of the trio, the 'highbrow astrologer' par excellence, skillfully battling to equate his art with modern scientific and psychological trends.

"He is also far and away the best writer in the entire field and perhaps the only one of his calling capable of engrossing nonbelieving readers. His popular fame stems from his astrology columns, which appear in 275 newspapers. But he carved a special niche for himself by producing a number of solidly cerebral books that earned him the acclaim of literary critics as well."

Sydney's *Thought Dial* (on numerology) has sold millions despite efforts of postal authorities to stop it. His annual *Astrological Guides* for each of the zodiacal signs sell into the millions. When *The National Tattler* once unwittingly dropped his weekly column, they were inundated with five thousand letters of protest within a week and the column was reinstated posthaste with profuse apologies to readers.

Yes, Sydney Omarr's name would become more than a household word. He soon overshadowed all his colleagues and became known as the most scholarly and highly respected in his field.

Author Henry Miller (*Tropic of Cancer*) is one of Sydney's most ardent admirers.

Actress Kim Novak has consulted Sydney on when to buy horses (she's an animal lover) and how to break a movie contract.

"She wanted to get out of doing a certain motion picture and asked me what she should do about it. I did her chart and told her that she should not break her contract, that the picture had badly aspected financing and something would happen so she would still not have to make that motion picture," Sydney recalled.

What happened was that Miss Novak fell off a horse, injured her back, and didn't have to make the movie or break her contract.

Arlene Dahl was so determined to have her last baby born with all the right astrological "aspects" that she rescheduled its Caesarean delivery several times, which did not endear her to her obstetrician.

Broadway producers have been known to delay their opening nights because the "aspects" were unfavorable, and there's even a famous hairdresser who insists that his clients have their horoscopes cast before he'll accept them.

When producer Alan Jay Lerner was filming the movie *On a Clear Day You Can See Forever,* he sent an aide to ask Sydney about doing horoscopes for the entire cast, including superstar Barbra Streisand. This would provide a promotional gimmick to fit in with the theme of the picture and it would also forecast the good and bad periods, the up and down cycles of the members of the cast. But the project was abandoned, paradoxically because of the cast's overwhelming enthusiasm for it and their apparent total acceptance of anything their horoscopes might tell them. Lerner is an avid astrology buff himself, but he didn't want to take a chance on his actors using their horoscope as an excuse not to show up on the set if, for example, their "aspects" were wrong on certain days.

"Of course, this is nonsense," says Sydney. "No legitimate astrologer tells you to just stay in bed if the planets indicate it's not a good day. They only warn you to use caution. It is the fool who allows astrology to rule his life; the intelligent individual lets it guide his life.

"Astrology is not fortunetelling. It isn't the same as saying this or that is definitely going to happen. An astrologer gives trends and cycles and accentuates potential. But it leaves free will. The choice is up to the individual. Astrology is like a traffic signal with a red and a green light. You can either stop at the red light or go against it. It's up to you. The horoscope is actually your road map of life, providing you with stop and go signals. But it is up to you to either follow them or ignore them.

"As Ralph Waldo Emerson said, astrology is astronomy brought down to earth and applied to the affairs of man."

Indeed, so permeating is astrology in the affairs of man today that there appears to be no end to the variety of uses made of this sometimes controversial scientific art, as Sydney calls it. Many major business decisions are based on charts of the heavens. Some companies use astrology in deciding which key people to hire, when is the proper time to sign contracts, whether a merger with another firm would be profitable, how executives would be likely to react to each other, at what time a new deal would be most likely to go through smoothly.

The Radio Corporation of America, the largest communications organization in the world, utilizes planetary positions to accurately forecast magnetic storms, which would interfere with message transmissions. John Henry Nelson, who is in charge of the program, freely admitted to Sydney that the forecasts are "astrological in nature," and though ridiculed by some astronomers, RCA reports 90 per cent accuracy.

Sydney is convinced that eventually astrology can be used successfully in predicting earthquakes. "But it must be done in conjunction with another discipline, geology," he says. "Once we define and understand what an earthquake really is, then, like all things, it will relate to astrological terms and we will be able to find the answer. But astrologers can't do this alone. [And he pooh-poohs the claims of those who say they can already predict earthquakes.] Working together, the geologist and the astrologer can arrive at some valid conclusions."

But already there are many practical uses of astrology, he emphasizes. For example, the effect of a full moon on animal, plant, and human behavior is a well-known fact.

"And so," Sydney says, "if I were a fisherman, I would fish during the full moon, because fish are more apt to bite then. If I were a law-enforcement official, I would have more men on duty during the full moon, because more crimes of violence occur at that time of the month. If I were a hospital administrator, I would have the maternity ward fully staffed during periods of the full moon, because more babies are born at that time, especially between 2 and 4 A.M.

"If I were a medical doctor, I would not perform tonsillectomies during the full moon, because there are more cases of postoperative hemorrhaging at this time.

"People become a little more agitated or emotional during the full moon. This can be verified in many police stations, fire departments, hospitals, and mental institutions, whose personnel are aware that erratic behavior is more likely to occur during this period."

A knowledge of astrology might even save your life, according to a report Sydney received from Roy Wilson, a fourteen-year veteran of the Charlotte, North Carolina, police department. A specialist in crime analysis, Wilson has noted that the astrological charts of all murder victims he has studied have shown clearly that trouble was on the horizon. "If these victims had been aware of the bad aspects in their horoscopes," says Sydney, "they might have taken extra precautions in their activities at that particular time. They might have been more careful about where they went or who they met, and it is possible that such precautions might have saved some lives."

Similarly, he believes the crime rate could be reduced by a careful study of the astrological charts of mental patients before they're released and prison inmates before they're paroled.

Charles Manson, who masterminded the Sharon Tate murders, for example, was a strong believer in astrology and often boasted of the fact that he was a Scorpio, the sign associated with the malevolent planet Pluto.

Sydney, who is an extremely kind man, wouldn't say anything really bad about any of the signs or their so-called ruling planets. (He prefers the term "associated with" rather than "ruling," which most astrologers use.) He is most generous when he says of Scorpio, "It is the most misunderstood sign in the zodiac."

During all my research I have found no one else, either in books or personal encounters, who is quite so benevolent toward Scorpio. Early in this astrological adventure a friend and I were comparing birth dates and discovered we were both Sagittarians. Her birthday is November 22, mine November 24. We're both "on the cusp," as they say, meaning close to another sign. Scorpios (scorpions) are born from October 23 to November 21.

"Aren't we lucky we just missed being Scorpios!" my friend said.

And it's true that all sorts of nasty characteristics are attributed to

Scorpio. For example, this one from the work of the noted French authority on astrology André Barbault: *Défense et illustration de l'astrologie* (*A Defense and an Illustration of Astrology*):

> "SCORPIO . . . Under the rule of Mars and Pluto: an instinctive nature, violent, passionate, undisciplined, rebellious, imperious, hard, aggressive, sometimes full of hatred, but also anguished, obsessive, morbid. . . . Obsessed by sex, suffering outbursts of passion. Politically, favors violence, is extremist, aggressive, fiercely militant, combative."

Can anyone think of a more perfect description to fit that demoniacal mass murderer Charles Manson?

He had spent the most part of his life in and out of correctional and penal institutions even before he was convicted for the Tate murders. If anyone had bothered to study his astrological chart and guide him accordingly, could it have altered the course of events? Would Sharon Tate and the others still be alive today? These are chilling questions, and viewed from the standpoint of history the answers would seem not so impossible.

It is a well-documented fact that Adolf Hitler, a great believer in astrology, employed several astrologers to advise him on the timing of his offensives—and this in turn led Winston Churchill to hire an astrologer of his own when World War II broke out. The man's duty was to try to determine, on the basis of Hitler's horoscope, the advice the Nazi leader might be getting from his astrologer, and what Hitler's moves were likely to be.

As Sydney says, "Astrology has been used throughout recorded history to study the affairs of nations. Kings, dictators, rulers, all had their own astrologers. Presidents and politicians have been believers in this scientific art, though some would not want to admit it."

Today virtually all scientists still reject astrology as an unfounded superstition. Yet it continues to appeal to the popular fancy—to such a degree, in fact, that nine out of ten people now know under which sign they were born.

Now that we have a nodding acquaintance with this "unfounded superstition" named astrology, we can advance to some of the specifics. The ancient sky watchers saw in the heavens twelve groups of stars—or constellations—that resembled animals or figures.

These were given names and became the signs of the zodiac: Capricorn (goat), Aquarius (water bearer), Pisces (fishes), Aries (ram), Taurus (bull), Gemini (twins), Cancer (crab), Leo (lion), Virgo (virgin), Libra (scales), Scorpio (scorpion), and Sagittarius (archer).

These signs are said to be ruled by—or associated with—the sun and the moon and eight planets: Mercury, Venus, Mars, Jupiter, Saturn, Uranus, Neptune, and Pluto.

To cast a horoscope, one must draw a circle and divide it into twelve equal wedges. Inside, the circle is divided into twelve so-called "houses," each of which depicts a different aspect of earthly life. On the outer rim the astrologer assigns the various zodical signs based on the time of the subject's birth. All that remains is for a given chart to be interpreted by the astrologer—and the interpretations may vary, the same as medical diagnosis may vary. But, based on empirical evidence, certain generalities will remain the same.

One of the first things I was impelled to do in beginning this book was to memorize all the signs, planets, and their corresponding symbols. Many readers will already know them, but those who don't can rapidly gain social status at cocktail parties by asking a person's birth date and then saying smugly, "Aha, Taurus! But you don't really look like a Taurus." You've made a friend.

NOTE TO READER: Refer to charts on the end papers of this book to find the signs, planets, and houses of astrology.

THE SYMBOLISM OF THE HOUSES

The meaning attributed to the twelve houses of astrology:

First House: The personality of the subject.

Second House: Money, fortune, goods, possessions.

Third House: The subject's social world, brothers and sisters, relations, neighbors, ideas, communications, short journeys.

Fourth House: Parents, hearth and home.

Fifth House: Pleasures, amusements, games, love, creativity, children.

Sixth House: Known as "the hospital of the zodiac." Chores and obligations, work, health. Small animals.

Seventh House: Marriage and partnership. Lifelong opponents, declared enemies.

Eighth House: Death; inheritance from others' deaths.

Ninth House: Religion, philosophy, higher education, long journeys. Large animals.

Tenth House: Profession, career, vocation, awards and honors.

Eleventh House: Friendships, other kinds of help and support.

Twelfth House: Called "the hell of the zodiac." Ordeals; secret enemies; snares and ambushes, illnesses, various misfortunes.

I must frankly admit that so far I haven't the remotest idea of how to conjugate these twelve houses of the zodiac. I am merely presenting (copying) them here for those who already know or want to learn how to play house in the celestial spheres.

Nor have I learned how yet to cast a horoscope, but I am including here instructions for beginners prepared by my able assistant, Dr. John LaCorte, who takes over when Sydney reaches the point of exasperation with a slow learner.

Personally, I am more intrigued with Sydney's interpretation of the zodiacal signs—such as that Virgo has an instinct for chastity, Taurus is the most amorous sign, Leos make lousy grandparents because they spoil their grandchildren, and there are more alcoholics born under the water signs (Pisces, Scorpio, and Cancer) than under any others.

Cancer, however, is one of Sydney's favorite signs, because there are more people in Who's Who in Commerce and Industry, more millionaires, born under Cancer than under any other sign. Also, Cancerians—or moon children—are good cooks and like to eat. "Food is equated to security. Their kitchens are always full. If I ever marry again, I'd like to marry a Cancerian, because she can cook. Also, Cancerians are very sentimental. They can always be counted on to cry at weddings."

Such were the small gleanings of astrological wisdom I was beginning to learn from Sydney. And there was more to come. He had accurately predicted the assassination of President John F. Kennedy. "We all knew this would happen. It was the Jupiter-Saturn conjunction." And he had forecast even before the presidential election of November 1972 what would happen to President Richard Nixon. Watergate probably wouldn't have happened if Nixon hadn't been born a Capricorn with Pluto in his tenth house.

The Malefics: How They Mess Up the World

Chapter 3

THE WINNER LOSES

(Watergate: Capricorn with Pluto in the Tenth)

> *"If he is removed, it will be*
> *because he removes himself.*
> *I don't think he will be impeached."*
>
> SYDNEY OMARR
> APRIL 10, 1974

Sydney is too star-struck to speak an unkind word about any of them. But some people consider Capricorn (December 22 to January 19) to be the worst sign of the zodiac, because it is ruled by the planet Saturn, generally associated with evil and selfishness. Saturn was named for Kronos, the deposed Greek ruler of gods, who was often likened to Satan.

Saturn is the second-largest planet, next to Jupiter. The word saturnine derives from the supposed influence of the planet Saturn and means sluggish, gloomy, grave, etc.

My *Coffee Table Book of Astrology*, in listing the twelve signs and their significance, notes: Capricorn, the goat. Ruler: Saturn. Earthy sign. Ambitious, persevering, tenacious, diplomatic, reserved, melancholy.

Do these descriptions fit anyone you know?

Richard Milhous Nixon was born January 9, 1913, at 9:14 P.M., at Yorba Linda, California. Sun sign Capricorn, moon in Aquarius, Virgo rising, and Pluto in the tenth house.

And that, in an astrological nutshell, is why we had Watergate, says Sydney.

More amazing is the fact that Sydney forecast with uncanny accuracy the scandals that toppled the Nixon administration—*even six weeks before Nixon's re-election in November 1972.*

In the November 12, 1972, issue of *The National Tattler* (on sale a week before the election), the Sydney Omarr astrological forecast, prepared six weeks in advance for syndication, read as follows: "It would be better for Nixon, in a personal sense, if his opponent won the election. The indications are that the winner loses, and if one must be precise, it is that McGovern emerges victorious even though defeated at the polls.

"Deciding factor (in the new administration) will be the economy, not the war. Questions, too, of who has the money and how the funds or contributions were obtained—these will figure prominently."

A significant part of the Watergate scandal, as it emerged in late April 1973, was the alleged allocation of campaign funds both to finance the break-in at Democratic headquarters and to hush up the crime afterward.

As for Sydney's emphasis on "the economy, not the war," it will be remembered that Nixon was plagued by a staggering economy as well as the high-level scandals in his second administration. Sydney's forecast was made well in advance of the 1973 slump in the stock market coupled with runaway inflation.

In the same column, Sydney wrote, "It is possible that the winner may not be able to serve his full term in office. . . . But the unusual chart that is Nixon's enables him to get what he wants—and he does not always want what is good for him. Thus, he probably wants the presidency and will get it. But my conclusion is—the winner loses.

"Saturn has returned to the area it occupied when Nixon was born. Only Franklin Roosevelt was able to get re-elected when this occurred. Lyndon Johnson was forced to retire.

"Nixon has Pluto at the top of his chart. Persons with this configuration seem to draw to themselves dictatorial attitudes or powers. Presidents with Pluto in the tenth [Nixon] have had unusual histories, serving one term or two separate terms, as in the case of Grover Cleveland. . . . My calculations show that in this next election week, the winner loses."

I repeat for emphasis: Sydney wrote this *six weeks* before the November 1972 election.

He had shown it to me when we first started our own tape-recording sessions for this book, early in April 1974. I didn't consider it especially significant at the time. But then, as Watergate and the Nixon tapes began unreeling, I became, somewhat guardedly, more intrigued with Sydney's prognostications. And, like Mr. Nixon, I kept the tapes.

"In view of recent developments, what would you now add to your 1972 forecast?" I asked one day during the full-blown Watergate bombshell on TV. "With all of Nixon's copious troubles, what do the stars say will happen to him now?"

"There is that tendency of Capricorn always to bounce back," said Sydney. "So you can't really count him out. Pluto in the tenth house attracts such dictatorial powers and such fanatical supporters that anybody else would have been gone by now. Just as Agnew went. With the kind of chart Nixon has, the more adversity he has, the more fanatical followers he attracts. He has one saving grace: he has this Gemini around him: Kissinger. He picked all his people wrong except Kissinger. He picked the right one there. Nixon, with Virgo rising and Kissinger's sun in his tenth house, might offset Pluto in the tenth. But with Saturn back in the same place it was at the time of his birth . . . well, ordinarily, I would have thought he should have had his demise by now. . . .

"But it still may be. He does have that kind of chart—you know, the winner loses. He shouldn't have run in the first place. But subconsciously he seems to want the adversity, and his followers thrive on it. Even if he remains in office, with Saturn being in Cancer opposing his sun, it will still be a period of crisis. It will be terrible for the nation. The planetary movements on Presidents also influence the course of history on nations."

I asked, "How could you predict all of this so accurately back in 1972, before the election?"

Sydney corrected me emphatically. "I don't predict. I make forecasts by astrological and numerological calculations. I think you get on the border of being a little cheap when you start making predictions," he said, "because anybody can do that, at least anybody who reads the newspapers."

"At the time, you wrote, 'It is possible that the winner may not be able to serve his full term in office.' What did you mean by that?" I asked.

"In astrology you can't take these separately," he explained. "The intuitive intellect puts together the whole, such as Pluto in the tenth and Saturn becoming activated in his house of health, the sixth house–meaning that people who depended on him, his underlings and the public in general, would become very much dissatisfied and put such pressure on him that emotionally and physically he might be distraught to the point of removing himself.

"You ask how I can foresee or forecast certain events. I have devoted most of my life to astrology. There are times when the so-called intuitive intellect comes flowing through, and this, combined with the numerological and planetary symbols, gives me the answers."

"What do you say now: will he be impeached, or remove himself, or what?" I asked.

"I say if he is removed, it will be because he removes himself. I don't think he will be impeached."

This was Sydney's summation of Watergate in April of 1974. It was four months later, August 8, 1974, that President Richard Milhous Nixon, a Capricorn with Pluto in the tenth, resigned in disgrace.

Sydney also accurately forecast other Watergate-related events, particularly in the earlier Nixon housecleaning of high-level confidants in the scandal that was surfacing. If the principals had read their horoscopes, they would have had a hint that something big and not too pleasant was brewing.

Former Attorney General Richard G. Kleindienst, a Leo, was warned to "review plans, especially those which involve travel. Messages could be garbled. Be sure your needs are understood and that you are being quoted correctly."

The forecast was a bit better for departing White House aides H. R. Haldeman and John D. Ehrlichman, whom President Nixon had praised generously in letting them go.

"Nothing is apt to come easy, but efforts will prove fruitful," was his forecast for Haldeman, a Scorpio. "Older individual displays confidence. Prestige rises as result."

For Ehrlichman, a Pisces, the word was: "You have plenty that is of value. No need to sell yourself short."

Most apropos was the horoscope for John Dean, a Libra: "Unorthodox procedures will best serve your purpose. Take course which rids you of unnecessary burdens. Create your own traditions.

Don't feel wedded to what others think or do. Be your own person—hear your own voice."

And that, as we all know, is just what John Dean did.

Earlier, Sydney also had forecast correctly the crisis over Senator George McGovern's running mate, vice-presidential candidate Thomas Eagleton. In his forecast for the week of July 23–29, 1972, he highlighted the twenty-fifth as the "most significant day" and wrote: "Political upsets are featured. Promises are the order of the day—and week. There will be power struggles. Deals are made, manipulations are featured. Battle of the wills takes place—there could be violence on the 25th."

Most significantly, he added, "It could be a day when promises are broken and hopes are shattered."

It was on Tuesday, July 25, that Senator Eagleton revealed he had been hospitalized three times between 1960 and 1966 for psychiatric treatment for nervous fatigue and depression—a confession that touched off a nationwide furor.

It will be recalled that McGovern at first denied there was any possibility that he would remove Senator Eagleton from the ticket, and then, less than a week later, urged him to withdraw from the vice-presidential race, thereby breaking his promise to the Missouri senator and to the people of the nation. Reports of Eagleton's alleged drunken-driving traffic offenses were later attributed to a political adversary and a "power struggle" for the Missouri senate seat. There were well-verified reports that McGovern was pressured to drop either Eagleton or his own key financial backers. Thus, manipulations did take place, deals were made, promises broken and hopes shattered, as Sydney had forecast.

What of former President Nixon's future? Would he make a comeback in public life, as some believed he would? I asked Sydney.

"He's already making a comeback through the back door," was his reply. "President Ford has been consulting him through intermediaries. This doesn't surprise me, as Gerry Ford is a Cancer sign, the opposite of Capricorn. Cancer and Capricorn are 180 degrees apart, and opposites attract each other. That's the yin-yang of the zodiac.

"Then you have to remember Nixon's resilience, with Pluto in the tenth and Saturn ruling. Capricorns tend to be tenacious and persevering and able to bounce back. With Pluto in the tenth their influence could be everlasting. With a chart like that, I don't think you could say he's finished.

"In my opinion as a student of astrology I would say that Nixon's resilience will keep him going, that he should never be counted out. He will always attract a hard core of long-suffering followers who are willing to suffer with him.

"Persons with Pluto in the tenth not only have a tendency toward dictatorial attitudes and ambitions, but they seem to attract to them people who encourage dictatorial powers.

"Hitler had Pluto in the tenth, you know."

No, I didn't know.

"Yes; that's why he gained such power and such an influential following. At that time, astrology was for the elite," he explained. "Astrology played a substantial part in the geopolitics of Germany and other countries during World War II. The British used astrology in an official manner: Captain Louis de Wohl, a fine novelist and astrologer, was assigned by British Intelligence to tell the British what Hitler's astrologers were telling him. It worked. De Wohl, after the war, was decorated for his services in this field.

"I have heard that our State Department, knowing full well that Hitler followed astrological advice (when it suited him), thought of finding their own Louis de Wohl, but there was so much pressure from astronomers that the project was dropped," Sydney said.

The dictatorial tendencies of Pluto in the tenth house do not always indicate evil intent, he explained. On a more personal level the dictatorial streak comes out even within families and among friends.

On a charitable note, which is typical of Sydney, he pointed out that many Plutos in the tenth really believe their dictatorial powers are used for the ultimate good. In other words, Nixon and his Watergate conspirators could have imagined that what they were doing was for the benefit of mankind.

"In some instances," he explained, "Pluto the tenth's dictatorial ambitions are regarded as being very benevolent. Like what's good for General Motors is good for the country."

On a Merv Griffin show early in 1975, Sydney startled the TV audience by stating that President Ford would not finish his term in office and that Vice-President Rockefeller would become President before the 1976 election.

Nothing seemed less unlikely at the time.

"Didn't you sort of stick your neck out on that one?" I asked the next time we met.

"Maybe so but that's what I said and I'm stuck with it," he said. "We can be wrong. And if we're wong, we're wrong. But I have a valid reason for my interpolation.

"Ford was sworn into office during the period when the moon was void of course. That means the moon was not making any aspects to other planets before it changed signs, and it has been found over the years that if you start something when the moon is void of course, it doesn't last. Those are really unstable periods of time.

"I was sure that Nixon, as a Capricorn, would appoint a Cancer as his successor, and I had thought that it would be Rockefeller, a Cancer. I was wrong about that," he admitted. "Instead, he appointed another Cancer, Gerry Ford, and Ford in turn appointed Rockefeller. But the important thing, astrologically, is that Ford was sworn in when the moon was void of course, which means that this isn't a situation very likely to be lasting for him. So, in interpolating we would assume that Rockefeller would take over. No one is ever 100 per cent right, of course. . . ."

Several months later, in September of 1975, newspaper headlines emblazoned the stories of two assassination attempts on President Ford in California—along with the sensational reports of the capture of fugitive newspaper heiress Patty Hearst, which, incidentally, Sydney had forecast a few weeks earlier.

As these lines were written, President Ford was still alive and well, and though somewhat shaken, still in office.

But I couldn't help thinking how close Sydney had come in his forecast, how close the two assassination attempts had come to his astrological calculation that President Ford's "situation" wasn't likely to be lasting for him and that Rockefeller would take over. At the rate the radicals are going, it could still happen before this is in print.

Unlike most self-anointed seers, prophets, and so-called astrologers, who actually know nothing about the basics of astrology, Sydney makes no pretentious claims for himself. He only claims to be knowledgeable in his field and to wish that others were more knowledgeable. His concern is genuine, frequently to the point of anguish.

"It makes me sad to have to sit here and read about these things and watch them on TV [assassination attempts]," he said, "and to know that many tragedies or near tragedies might have been avoided if more people only had a rudimentary knowledge of astrology. President Ford took his oath of office at a very bad time, when the moon was void of course. If people in official circles had known this and paid attention to it, they wouldn't have had him sworn in then in the first place. But since they did, they should have known enough to take better precautions—if they knew anything about astrology. Ronald Reagan knew better. He took his oath of office a few minutes after midnight, when the aspects were right for him."

With assassination fever at a high pitch, Sydney could safely have forecast that an assassin's bullet might yet shorten Ford's term in office.

"With all these lunatics loose," he said, "anything can happen. But astrologically it is not time yet for another assassination of a President. That—or the death of a President while in office—is supposed to happen in 1980, with the Jupiter and Saturn conjunction."

Chapter 4
JUPITER AND SATURN CONJUNCTION
(The Mysterious Death Cycle of Presidents)

"We all knew that Kennedy would be assassinated."
SYDNEY OMARR

The man who is elected President in 1980 should take extra precautions. This is the year of the Jupiter-Saturn conjunction.

Sydney was at his desk, in charge of the news bureau at radio station KNX (an affiliate of CBS in Los Angeles), when the word flashed that President Kennedy had been shot in Dallas.

Everyone knew that Sydney had forecast the possible tragedy to the President.

His recollection of the assassination is still painful to him.

"There I was in the middle of all the furor, taking Arthur Godfrey off the air and throwing special news bulletins in. I had a strange, errie feeling as I sat there writing the bulletins," he recalls. "I was two people, a news editor reporting one of the most tragic events in our history, and the astrologer who had forecast it. I remember looking at all the so-called tough newsmen around me and seeing tears streaming down their faces. And as I sat there knocking out the copy in the midst of all the sadness and turmoil, I couldn't help thinking, what in the world could Jupiter and Saturn have to do with this? And why, why, why?"

Sydney, of course, was not the only astrologer to forecast the assassination of President Kennedy. He is the first to admit that many astrologers around the world knew of the impending tragedy.

"We all knew that Kennedy would be assassinated," he says matter-of-factly. "But there is nothing miraculous about knowing that. It was the Jupiter-Saturn conjunction. It happens every twenty years, and no President elected under that aspect has lived out his term of office."

It is a matter of historic record, which has been noted by non-astrologers as well, that every President of the United States elected at twenty-year intervals since 1840 has died in office. In the total of thirty-eight Presidents (from Washington to Ford), only nine were elected at twenty-year intervals. Seven of those nine died in succession. They were:

PRESIDENT	YEAR ELECTED	SIGN	CAUSE OF DEATH
William Henry Harrison	1840	Aquarius	Pleurisy, pneumonia
Abraham Lincoln	1860	Aquarius	Assassinated
James Garfield	1880	Scorpio	Assassinated
William McKinley	1900	Aquarius	Assassinated
Warren Harding	1920	Scorpio	Pneumonia
Franklin D. Roosevelt	1940	Aquarius	Cerebral hemorrhage
John F. Kennedy	1960	Gemini	Assassinated

It is difficult to figure statistical probabilities on historical events, but as Sydney says, even conservative statistics would show these occurrences as significantly beyond coincidence.

Several theories have been advanced, ranging from an Indian curse on President Harrison (but why would this kill the other six?) to sociological-psychiatric speculations of assassination tendencies (but this would not account for the three of the seven Presidents who died of illness), and, of course, the astrological explanation of the Jupiter-Saturn conjunction. That is, when the two largest planets come close together.

To many this seems the most plausible of the theories so far advanced for the mysterious death cycle of Presidents, but to most bona fide astrologers there is nothing mysterious about it all. They know the Jupiter-Saturn conjunction to be the most important astrological conjunction. They know that it has occurred during the years when those doomed Presidents were elected—because they can check it out in the ephemeris. It's as plain and simple as that.

The mystery, of course, is *why* the twenty-year cycles coincide.

"If we knew all the answers to the riddles of the universe, we would be superbeings. We don't know *why* the cycles coincide, but they do coincide, and that's what Carl Jung meant by the term synchronicity," Sydney reminded me.

"Of course we were able to forecast that Franklin Roosevelt would win a fourth term and would die in office," he explained, "because he was elected in 1940, a year when Jupiter and Saturn were in conjunction. We knew the next Jupiter-Saturn conjunction would occur in 1960, the year when John Kennedy was elected. Of course, the circumstances were not quite the same, for he was young and in good health. But we knew that he was in danger because of the Jupiter-Saturn conjunction and that he probably would not finish his term in office."

Some astrologers were quite specific in their pronouncements. Eighteen months before Kennedy's assassination on November 22, 1963, Huter's Astrological Calendar, published in Germany, warned: "The horoscope of the United States President shows . . . the danger that a fanatic is preparing for his assassination."

In the October 1963 issue of *Astrology* magazine, Dal Lee wrote, "At this time we prefer to confine ourselves to a word of caution to the President. He should guard his health and safety. . . . We wish we could tell the President that November will be an easygoing month for him, but alas, the prospects forbid it." These words were written at least four months before the magazine hit the newsstands.

Astrologer Leslie McIntyre, in the November 1963 issue of *American Astrology*, warned of the coming aspects: "In the past, such configurations have coincided with personal danger to our head of state, all the more so in this case in view of the grievous attack by Saturn on Kennedy's natal trio of Mars, Mercury, and Jupiter, along with Uranus square his sun. November is obviously fraught with perils of several varieties."

The copy for this item was received by the magazine on June 3, 1963.

And in August of 1960 astrologer David Williams predicted that Kennedy would be elected President, would die in office, and would be succeeded by Lyndon Johnson. A number of astrologers went on record as saying that Kennedy's chart was "afflicted" or "heavy with death" and that Johnson's star was rising fast.

Sydney's friend Jess Stearn, in his book *A Time For Astrology*, quotes astrologer Franka Moore on the "assassination aspect" of both President Kennedy and his brother Robert Kennedy's charts: "John Kennedy had Uranus in the fourth house square Mars in the eighth, the classic assassination aspect. And his natal Uranus was square Mars, Mercury, and Jupiter in the eighth, and quincunx Saturn in his midheaven of career. All these afflictions were touched off by transiting Saturn in the fourth house opposing his career at the time he was murdered."

Robert Kennedy's "assassination aspect" was "Mercury in Sagittarius in the eighth house of death squaring Uranus in Pisces in the twelfth, the house of the secret enemy, the assassin."

This is pretty heavy stuff for a slow learner. In fact Sydney said we'd better skip it until I learn more about the "malefics." You need a different kind of dictionary when you're dealing with the science of the stars. Most astrology books provide one as an appendix, but Sydney doesn't include the word "malefics" in his Basic Dictionary of Terms—I suppose because he considers it so basic that everyone ought to know what it means. However, Jess Stearn's definition of the word is *Malefics—The bad guys in the zodiac—Mars, Saturn, and Uranus, which, like Pluto and Neptune, can also be good guys when well aspected or their challenge met by the individual.*

It is important to know this if we are to understand how a President's chart—or your own, for that matter—is "afflicted."

Affliction—An adverse aspect (usually a square or opposition, sometimes a conjunction) between planets, or between planets and house cusps.

It would appear that of all the "bad guys" in the zodiac, Saturn is the worst offender. It's the same satanic planet, remember, that rules Nixon's sign, Capricorn. Whether it's ruling Capricorn or conjuncting with Jupiter (one of the "good guys") or traipsing ("transiting") around the zodiac, Saturn seems to be usually up to no good. Uranus, Mars, and Pluto can be almost as bad, depending upon which of the zodiacal signs and houses they're in.

But even Sydney, who is loath to speak harshly of any of the planets, concedes sorrowfully, "As the chief instrument in the universe of all the ills that flesh is heir to, Saturn easily takes the prize for making trouble, and his aspects, as he slowly wends his way around the horoscope, are always productive of some form of discipline, sorrow, and affliction."

The late Grant Lewi, in his book *Astrology for the Millions*, has also noted the influence of Saturn on the lives of the Presidents of the United States not only in relation to the Jupiter-Saturn conjunction but in Saturn's transits around the zodiac. Of the seventeen Presidents from Lincoln to Franklin D. Roosevelt inclusive, according to Lewi, only one (Woodrow Wilson) has managed to serve out a term under Saturn's transit of his own place in the sun. Lewi also attributes the fall of the Kaiser and Napoleon to Saturn's transits and calls Saturn the "mainspring of the clock of destiny."

As for the Jupiter-Saturn conjunction, take another look at the signs of the seven Presidents who have died in office after having been elected at twenty-year intervals since 1840. Four were born under Aquarius (ruled by Uranus), and two were born under Scorpio (ruled jointly by Pluto and Mars). All "bad guy" planets, or malefics. Only one, John Kennedy, a Gemini, had a "good guy" ruling planet, Mercury (whose transits are not overimportant unless Mercury happens to become retrograde), but he had the Jupiter-Saturn conjunction when he was elected and that transiting Saturn in his fourth house when he was murdered!

John F. Kennedy knew about the "zero factor," as it is sometimes called, meaning the jinx on the year ending in a zero. But he was sure he would be able to break the jinx, according to Sydney. He didn't.

What will happen in 1980?

"If history is any indicator," said Sydney, "the man who wins in 1980 will probably suffer the same consequences of the Jupiter-Saturn conjunction. I have great concern for Senator Ted Kennedy. I have not studied his chart, but it would seem not unlikely that he could be persuaded to run in 1980 and win. If this should happen there would be the grave possibility of a third Kennedy assassination."

It doesn't take an astrologer to know that tragedies seem to run in the Kennedy family. All their charts generally must be afflicted.

And all the more reason, as Sydney says, that Ted Kennedy—or anyone else—shouldn't run that extra risk of the Jupiter-Saturn conjunction, which coincides with the mysterious death cycle of presidents.

As Sydney says, "Who would want to run for President in 1980?"

Some astrologers believe that the cycle may be nearing an end, because the conjunction goes into Libra, an air sign, in 1980, and previously it has occurred only in earth signs since 1840. (All the twelve signs of the zodiac are divided into four elements: fire, earth, air, and water.)[1] But the change-over into another sign takes time, and in Sydney's opinion the elements have nothing to do with it. The planetary conjunction will continue in whatever sign, and when or if the death cycle will end is pure conjecture.

"If I were the President elected in 1980," he said, "I certainly would take note of what has happened to every President since 1840 in that twenty-year cycle of Jupiter-Saturn conjunctions, and I certainly would take extra precautions. The man who is elected President in 1980, whether Republican or Democrat, should take extra precautions and have stronger security forces around him at all times, because the indications are that otherwise he would die in office. It could be because of illness or assassination, or perhaps he might resign. But historically and astrologically the cycle is associated with death. In any case, I would say that the man who is elected President in 1980 will not finish out his term in office."

"Are such deaths always fated if the charts are afflicted?" I asked Sydney.

[1] John LaCorte's note on the four elements of the zodiac: The concept of the four elements, fire, air, earth, and water, derives from the very early Greek cosmology, which is the earliest ancestor to our present sciences of chemistry and physics. For the Greeks there were only four elements—that is, ultimate substances from which everything else, the entire universe, is made. We now know of over a hundred and we keep finding more.

It is logical that a cosmological system such as astrology would incorporate these four elements, fire, air, earth, and water, into its own viewpoint of the universe. Each element is represented equally, but in a different way by each of the signs.

The grouping is as follows:

Fire signs:	Aries, Leo, Sagittarius.
Air signs:	Gemini, Libra, Aquarius.
Earth signs:	Taurus, Virgo, Capricorn.
Water signs:	Cancer, Scorpio, Pisces.

"No, definitely not," he replied emphatically. "There has always been this big controversy regarding fate versus free will among detractors of astrology. Most of them know nothing about the subject. They ridicule it because they think it implies that our fate, our destiny, is irrevocably written in the stars. This is utter hogwash, as any bona fide astrologer or serious student of astrology knows. The wise man controls his destiny; astrology points the way. Astrology provides the guidelines. What has happened before at a given time may happen again at the same time or at the same planetary positions. Synchronicity.

"We should learn what these guidelines are and observe them, be aware of their implications, and use the guidelines wisely in managing our own everyday affairs and controlling our destiny. The stars impel, they do not compel."

On the subject of assassination attempts Sydney pointed out that there have been only three eminent persons in recent times who were able to imprint their personalities on the masses and survived assassination attempts. They were Hitler, Franklin D. Roosevelt, and Governor George Wallace of Alabama, and all three had an astrologic "malefic" in common—Uranus in the first house.

According to my notebook on planets, Uranus was the first planet to be discovered by telescope, by Herschel in 1781. It is the planet of astrology, associated with genius and creativeness (don't ask me why), and is the ruler of the sign Aquarius (January 20–February 18), an air sign.

The first house means the first section of your horoscope, in which there are twelve sections just as there are twelve signs, but the signs must not be confused with the houses.

The houses are wedge-shaped divisions of the heavens as seen at any point of time at any place on earth, with 30 degrees to each section, adding up to a full circle of 360 degrees. Your rising sign, or "ascendant"—when you learn how to find it—begins in your first house.

Every department of human activity, I'm told, falls in one of these houses. The first house represents personality, action, personal appearance, disposition, and manner.

Thus, according to Sydney's interpretation of the aspects of the three men who have survived assassination attempts:

"Uranus in the first house represents one who attracts attention, publicity, and, on the negative side, notoriety. These people act quickly, sometimes carelessly. They seem prone to emotional and physical upsets. They can be vital, magnetic, attractive. But they must learn that attracting attention is only half the story; being able to fulfill promise and potential is the other, the more important half."

In other words, the malefic Uranus can play hob in your first house if you're not careful. . . .

John LaCorte, my assistant and interpreter of certain aspects of astrology, did some definitive research into the twenty-year cycle of presidential deaths in the United States and came up with a provocative question: Why doesn't it happen in other countries?

Since 1900, he found, the United States has picked its Presidents from a small and esoteric section of the population, specifically, one three-hundreth—1/300—of the total population. All have the sun and Saturn, and the moon and Mars, in similar relationship.

The characteristic earmark of American Presidents in the past forty years, he found, is *sun square Saturn, moon conjunct Mars.*

These aspects, he says, may have produced or aided in the production of a twenty-year cyclic pattern. With the Jupiter-Saturn conjunction occurring every twenty years, the position of Saturn in the individual's chart may have provided a combination of influences that resulted in death in office for several Presidents.

Sydney, of course, combines numerology with astrology in his interpretations. "And if you don't think astrology and numerology are related, read this," he said, flipping me a copy of an article by Bo Lozoff from the Oakland *Tribune* of February 2, 1973, entitled "The Mysterious Death Cycle of Presidents."

"Nobody seems to have a very sound answer to this riddle," Bo Lozoff begins, and then proceeds to relate some amazing "coincidences," or parallels, between two Presidents: Lincoln and Kennedy.

Both Lincoln and Kennedy were over six feet tall, both had seen military service, both took part in political debates, and both were remembered by their intense activity in civil rights legislation for black people. Both Lincoln and Kennedy were assassinated by

Southerners who were themselves killed while under guard, in the presence of their captors. Both Booth and Oswald were said by sophisticated observers to be parts of conspiracies rather than lone killers. Both Booth and Oswald died about two hours after being shot by a single bullet fired from a Colt-type revolver, by men who were known to be attention-hungry, emotionally unstable fanatics.

As the Bo Lozoff article also points out, the names of Lincoln and Kennedy comprise seven letters each, and the names of John Wilkes Booth and Lee Harvey Oswald comprise fifteen letters; the wife of each President lost a son while she was first lady; both Presidents were shot in the head from behind on a Friday while their wives were present.

Equally spooky are these vital statistics: Booth was born in 1839; Oswald was born in 1939. President Lincoln was elected to Congress in 1847, Kennedy in 1947. Lincoln was elected to the Presidency in 1860, Kennedy in 1960. Both men were succeeded by their Vice-Presidents, both Southerners named Johnson. Andrew Johnson was born in 1808 and Lyndon Johnson in 1908.

Perhaps the most ironic parallel of all, as Bo Lozoff says, is that President Lincoln's secretary, named Kennedy, told him not to go to the theater that night; while President Kennedy's secretary, named Lincoln, advised him not to go to Dallas.

"Does it ever make you feel that there's some aspect of life and destiny that we don't understand in the least? It should," Bo Lozoff concludes.

Sydney's belief is that it isn't vital to understand all the whys and wherefores of the universe in order to accept certain facts and put them to practical use.

"We may not understand how electricity works, but we know that it works. We may not understand how the human brain performs all of its infinite marvels, but it does. We cannot tell you why or how astrology works, but we do know from ancient times and empirical evidence that it does work, sometimes for good, sometimes for bad, and in ways we do not understand. When we accept this, even without understanding it, then we can utilize it for practical purposes in shaping our own destinies."

President Theodore Roosevelt was reported to be an avid believer in astrology and wasn't ashamed of it. He kept his horoscope mounted on a chess board in the White House and always told reporters, "I keep a weather eye out on Mars in my seventh house."

Franklin Delano Roosevelt's keen interest in astrology was well known. Wife Eleanor often wrote about it in her syndicated column "My Day." Indeed it would not be surprising if FDR's faith in the stars might have been responsible for Sydney's preferential treatment in the Army as an astrologer.

Incidentally, FDR was an Aquarian, and no Aquarian President has ever lived out his term in office, Sydney says.

Other political figures also have exhibited a keen interest in astrology.

Sydney's first job on the West Coast was as a reporter for United Press International, and he recalls that one of his first assignments was to interview Goodwin Knight, who was then Lieutenant Governor of California. When he called and introduced himself, "This is Sydney Omarr," Mr. Knight immediately recognized the name.

"Are you the Sydney Omarr I've been reading for years?" he asked. For years as a youngster Sydney had been writing for astrology magazines.

After some chitchat, Mr. Knight invited Sydney to come to his office. When he arrived, Knight first asked everyone else to leave the office for his conference with Sydney and then showed him his files of horoscopes which he had accumulated on every political person he had to deal with, Sydney said.

"He told me he got his start, his financial security, by using astrology to actually locate gold mines, to learn which mines contained gold and were worth mining. That's how we became good friends. But," Sydney added, "some politicians are sensitive about being regarded as astrology devotees."

Former Governor Ronald Reagan's mother is said to be an avid believer in astrology and very knowledgeable on the subject. It was presumably her influence that prompted Reagan to make the unusual move of choosing to be sworn in at the strange hour of ten minutes past midnight at the beginning of his first term, according to widely circulated reports at the time.

The planetary movements that affect Presidents and other heads of state also affect nations, Sydney explained, and frequently the two are intertwined. For example, former President Nixon's Pluto in the tenth ushered in the year 1975, a "Pluto 22" year that will be remembered as a period of recession equal to none since the Great Depression.

And Sydney had told me about it long before it happened!

Chapter 5

IT WAS A PLUTO 22 YEAR
(*And the Worst Is Yet to Come*)

"The solar system is like a poem; it unravels, gives you symbols to go by. . . ."

—SYDNEY OMARR

Cynics may find it hard to believe, but according to Sydney the food shortages, the oil crisis, the unemployment lines, the downward dip in the economy of the United States, the big recession of the year 1975—all were the result of a couple of malefic planets and the number twenty-two.

"And things are going to get worse before they get better," he warned me in the early months of 1974.

Incredibly, I have been watching it all happen almost exactly as he said it would, and Sydney Omarr is not a fortuneteller.

He is the modern counterpart of the ancient sky watchers who mapped out a meaning in the stars and applied them to the affairs of man. He is also an astute and skilled practitioner of the ancient art of numerology.

Drawing upon his rather awesome knowledge in both fields, he was able to forecast coming events with stunning accuracy.

Even as I write this, in the late summer of '75, his words taken verbatim from one of our tape-recording sessions in early 1974 still amaze me.

"We are in for a horrendous period which seems to be on the horizon now," he said. "And I can tell you now that 1975 will be the key year, because it's a Pluto 22 year.

"Whether Nixon is in or out his chart is still relevant to what is happening to the nation. With Saturn being in Cancer opposing his sun, it will still be a crisis period. It will be terrible for the nation also with Saturn being in Cancer, because Cancer is the birth sign of the United States—July 4.

"Of course we all know [meaning all competent astrologers] that 1975 is the year it's going to happen, because of the Pluto-Saturn aspects. We're in for a rough time, for hard times, a tremendous crash, a depression. The fact that the Pluto 22 year happens to coincide with the time that Saturn will be in Cancer makes it all the more definite that 1975 will be the year of great turbulence and crisis."

Saturn, as we have already learned, is that biggest troublemaker among planets, and Pluto is that same nasty number that toppled Nixon by transiting into his tenth house. Add to this the fact that Saturn, who is Nixon's Capricorn ruler, was moving in on Cancer, our country's national sun sign, which is ruled by the moon, and you can see what a sorry lot of messed-up afflictions this might bring.

"Saturn has just entered Cancer," Sydney went on, "so for two and a half years we will have a trial and testing period. There isn't much question about that. And then, with a Pluto 22 year coming up next, it is obvious that we are entering a very bad time. Astrologically, for the chart of the United States," he explained, "there will be three critical factors occurring in 1975, three critical transits.

"Saturn will be transiting the sun, Pluto will be squaring the sun, and Neptune will be in opposition to the ascendant. The solar system is like a poem; it unravels, give you symbols to go by. It's up to each individual to interpret." (i.e. the U.S. natal sun—where the sun was at the birth of the country, July 4, 1776)

"How do you interpret specifically the ways in which your poetic symbols are going to affect the United States?" I asked.

"There will be tremendous food shortages, an oil crisis, a stock-market crash, unemployment lines. Other persons will be growing their own food and moving further into the suburbs, away from the mobs. The dollar won't mean anything, because there's no gold to back it. Savings will be wiped out. The situation will be serious enough to force some banks to close. It will be desperate times, I can tell you that, a really Plutonian-type period. It was Pluto that ushered in sit-down strikes, gangsterism, Hitlerism. It is associated with the underworld, revolution, radicalism. A Pluto 22 year always ushers in turbulent times," he explained.

Why was 1975 a Pluto 22 year? What was the significance of the number twenty-two?

"The year 1975 adds up to twenty-two," he explained patiently. "One plus nine plus seven plus five equals twenty-two. And number twenty-two is associated with the Planet Pluto. There are only two numbers that can't be reduced to one digit: number eleven associated with Uranus, and number twenty-two, associated with Pluto. Both are master digits." (And both associated with those "bad guys" again!)

"Ancient civilizations were communicating by number symbols long before there was an alphabet, and guiding their lives by the stars long before astronomy became a science," he reminded me. "Greater and far wiser men than I were studying the stars, reading meaning into them, recording their movements, and interpreting them from the beginning of time. Man learned to measure the movements of the planets mathematically, and out of this ability came the birth of astronomy. Astronomers still deny it, but astronomy is a latter-day offspring of astrology and numerology.

"Such great scientists as Pythagoras, Ptolemy, Copernicus, Kepler, Newton, Galileo, and Tycho Brahe [he rattled the names off as nonchalantly as a child chanting his ABCs], all were involved with astrology and numerology. They have left us a legacy of a considerable body of authoritative knowledge. Who am I to question men like these? Who am I to dispute the Pythagorean theorem or Ptolemy's *Tetrabiblos?*"

Pythagoras was a Greek philosopher (c. 582–c. 507 B.C.) who believed that the essence of all things is numbers, that numbers are symbolic constructions, that all matter is essentially numerical, and that all relationships can be expressed numerically. He is considered the father of practical mathematics and is credited with inspiring the first part of Euclidean geometry and the theorem that bears his name. In music the Pythagoreans discovered that tones have numerical interrelations.

Ptolemy was the celebrated Greek astronomer and mathematician who was considered the great sage of the time (second century) and wrote a work entitled *Tetrabiblos*, or *Four Books on the Influence of the Stars*, a work that became the astrologers' bible in the ancient world.

Copernicus (1473–1543), the founder of modern astronomy, accepted the aid of an astrologer, Rheticus, in completing the treatise that immortalized him, a book entitled *De Revolutionibus Orbium Coelestium* (1543), which explained that the earth revolved around the sun instead of vice versa.

Tycho Brahe (1546–1601) was a Danish astronomer-astrologer who worked under the patronage of King Frederick II. He studied the tables prepared by Copernicus, did much to advance the study of the motions of the planets, and traced that of Mars to such an exactitude that Kepler, who was then one of his assistants, based his discovery of the three laws of universal gravitation on this research.

Johannes Kepler (1571–1630) designed a telescope with two convex lenses and crosswires in the focus for use as a pointer to fix the position of stars. In an address given at the University of Copenhagen he defended the practice of astrology, stating, "We cannot deny the influence of the stars without disbelieving in the wisdom of God. Man is made from the elements and absorbs them as much as food or drink, from which it follows that man must also, like the elements, be subject to the influence of the planets."

Some of Kepler's laws were incorporated into Newton's study of dynamics, and the great Galileo (1564–1642), who designed one of the first practical telescopes and through it discovered sunspots, craters of the moon, Jupiter's moons, and the rings of Saturn, also wrote about astrology. Two of his books contain horoscopes by him.

Johann Müller, also known as Regiomontanus (1436–76), was an eminent German astronomer and mathematician who also was the inventor of a new way of dividing the sky into the astrological houses still in use today. (According to John LaCorte, there are a number of house systems used today, but the most commonly used is that devised by Placidus, a Greek of the early Christian era.)

Sydney's knowledge of the historical roots of astrology, his familiarity with the works of great minds that have given it credence from ancient to modern times, and his appalling ability to quote from them by memory—or to reach in his bookshelves and find instantly the half-remembered reference he wants—are to my mind as awesome as being able to foretell the future by the celestial antics of Pluto and Saturn.

In one of our early lessons, he had begun to explain: "All nations are ruled by particular planets which influence their character and fate. This is a branch of astrology called mundane or judicial astrology. It deals with world events, war and peace, the fate of nations, cities and heads of governments, financial and economic conditions. There are specialists who do horoscopes of nations. Every nation, even every corporation, every building, has a horoscope. . . . The Burmese Government's constitution was based on astrology. The time was selected to coincide with the most favorable aspects of the planetary movements. That doesn't seem so radical to those who have studied astrology. Mundane astrology is a most ancient branch of astrology and a huge study in itself. . . ."

He broke off wearily, reached into one of his cavernous, crammed bookshelves, pulled out a small booklet and said, "Here; take this home and read it."

It was titled "The Basic Principles of Astrology . . . a modern View of an Ancient Science," a booklet published by the American Federation of Astrologers.

From it I learned that mundane astrology was in use, at a relatively primitive level, during the days of the Assyrian kings, around 700 B.C. The royal correspondence from their astrologer-astronomers contained such passages as: "Jupiter stands in the eclipse; it signifies peace for the king; his name will be honorable and unique."

In more modern times, the American astrologer Dr. L. D. Broughton predicted in his *Monthly Planet Reader* for January 1, 1861, that the secession of South Carolina would lead to civil war and that there would be no peace for the country until the summer of 1865. Broughton's predictions were based in large part on the pioneering work he did in associating the passage of the planet Uranus through the sign of Gemini with remarkable changes, unsettled conditions, and strife in the United States.[1] Later astrologers were able to foresee that America would be involved once more in a

[1] Ruth H. Oliver, "The Civil War Predictions of L. D. Broughton," *AFA Bulletin*, Vol. 24, No. 1, January 6, 1962.

major war with Uranus' next return to Gemini, which began in 1941–42.

As those with long memories will remember, this period marked America's entry into World War II.

Much has been written about the rise and fall of Hitler during World War II in relation to his own horoscope as well as the planning of his military offenses according to the advice of astrologers. Historians and astrologers may disagree on some details, but there is an abundance of well-documented evidence that during the war the Nazis formed a "monstrous alliance," as some called it, with astrology.

There are some who maintain that Hitler plunged the world into war on a particular date based on his faith in astrologers.

Nicholas Murray Butler, former president of Columbia University, claimed that Hitler was frequently in consultation with five astrologers, and that in 1939 these advisers told him that the month of September would be the high point of his career.

Hitler supposedly had his own private astrologer. His name was Karl Ernst Krafft (1900–45), a Swiss astrologer and the most famous astrologer of his time, in 1939. Krafft, according to Professor Hans Bender at the University of Freiburg, drew up Hitler's horoscope, in which it specifically stated that the Führer's climax would come in 1941–42 and that he would have to win the war by 1942 at the latest or else catastrophe would occur in 1945.

At least two of Hitler's henchmen, Propaganda Minister Goebbels and Rudolf Hess, were known to be strong advocates of astrology. Hess, who was Hitler's heir apparent and most trusted counselor, was the main patron of astrologers. But it was Goebbels who employed several astrologers to bring out a pro-German edition of *Centuries*, the prophecies of Nostradamus, as an instrument of propaganda.

There are many entries in the private journals of Goebbels that attest to his use—or misuse—of astrology in psychological-warfare techniques.

One entry, written in 1942, is as follows: "In the United States astrologers are at work and predict an untimely end for the Führer. We are familiar enough with this type of propaganda, for we have used it ourselves. Whenever we can, we will again exploit the possibilities which astrology has to offer. I anticipate important results from it, particularly in the U.S.A. and England. . . . We will recruit on our side all the specialists in prophecy of every type. Nostradamus must once again authorize us to quote from him."[2]

Nostradamus was the most renowned, the most celebrated and controversial figure in the world of astrology, and possibly the greatest of all seers. He was born Michel de Nostre-Dame in St. Rémy in 1503 and served as astrologer and physician to three French kings. The quatrains of Nostradamus are still consulted with the hope of finding the key to his chronology. Many of his predictions came true in his lifetime, and astrologers claim that others have come to pass since, such as the rise of Oliver Cromwell, the birth of Napoleon, and the exact date of the end of the Second World War. However, Nostradamus is reported to have said he was afraid that mankind as a whole was not ready to hear the whole truth and that predictions of the future would have harmful effects. Consequently he wrote down his predictions in obscure verse that were impossible for the layman to interpret.

But apparently astrologers could interpret them. There seems to be no question that during the war Hitler's court attached a great deal of importance to the prophecies of Nostradamus.

Consequently another famous astrologer, Louis de Wohl, was employed by the British Allied Headquarters to help in preparing a propaganda booklet based on the Nostradamus quatrains to be used against the Germans.

According to De Wohl, the Führer had been advised that (a) it is always opportune to attack a country when the two major "malefics," the planets Saturn and Uranus, are in the zodiacal sign that rules the nations against which war is to be waged; (b) Saturn and Uranus would be in Gemini, the "ruling" sign of the U.S.A. (according to some astrologers) until the late spring of 1942, and therefore a German attack should not be made before that time (Germany declared war on the U.S.A. on December 11, 1941); and (c) the war must be contrived on foreign soil.

De Wohl suggested that the Germans would probably use Brazil as a steppingstone for hostilities against the U.S.A. and produced astrological reasons to support his argument: "Brazil is ruled by Virgo and therefore she, too, will be under the hostile influences of

[2] Lochner, *The Goebbels Diary*, London, 1948.

Saturn and Uranus from the late spring of 1942 onwards. America has always been subject to grave events when Uranus transits Gemini."

It is important here to clear up two points of De Wohl's astrological interpretations:

1. His reference to the major "malefics," Saturn and Uranus. The third major malefic, Pluto, had only recently been discovered (in 1930 by Clyde Williams Tombaugh of the Percival Lowell Observatory in Arizona), and the effects of Pluto regarding the war could be known only in retrospect.

2. His reference to Gemini instead of Cancer as the ruling sign of the U.S.A. Most astrologers accept July 4, 1776 (the Declaration of Independence), as the birth date of the U.S.A., which makes it a Cancer sign. But some consider our nation's birth to begin with the opening of the Constitutional Convention in Philadelphia on May 25, and the historic events—the debates and actual drafting of the constitution—that took place in the following weeks, which would fall under the sign of Gemini (May 21–June 20).

Sydney doesn't like to quibble about such hairsplitting interpretations. In fact he doesn't even like to talk about Hitler's use of astrology, because "he used it for evil instead of good."

As for the planets, whether it's Uranus in Gemini or Saturn in Cancer, either one heralds grave afflictions for our country, he says.

The same, of course, applies to people.

"The major transits are the most important element in the science of predicting, and everything that can happen to the human being is determined, mainly, by these. The critical times in the period of transit," he explained, "will be those times when the sun and Mars or Pluto swing also into aspect with the superiors; as, for instance, when the transit of Mars or Pluto afflicts the body that is at the same time afflicted by Saturn and Uranus. These are very marked and very threatening.

"But it is very important that one never lose sight of the fact that most of the events of life are produced by *combinations of transits*, and that no one transit over a single place is ever productive of important events. It is always the combinations that are of consequence."

(For advanced students of astrology I recommend as must reading the section on "The Transits of the Planets" in Sydney's book

My World of Astrology. It is based on the work of Dr. Heber Smith of Boston, who was the teacher of America's first and foremost lady astrologer, Miss Evangeline Adams.)

Coming back to the year 1975 and the combination of Saturn in Cancer with Pluto 22, I asked Sydney, "What can we do about it?"

"I wish I knew," he said. "We can take certain precautions, but this is where astrology leaves off and you need experts in other fields to take over, to correlate. Astrology is good for telling us what is likely to happen, where the road will be rough, so to speak. But it cannot tell a person what to do.

"We need competent counsel from experts, preferably those who are also receptive to the idea that astrological warnings are valid. Some might tell us to stock up on dehydrated foods, to buy diamonds or precious metals or real estate. Where do you buy precious metals, and where do you store them? Is it wise to keep a huge savings account? How do you open a Swiss bank account? I am not an economist, so I do not know the answers to these questions. But, on the positive side, I think that anyone who has the foreknowledge of what is going to happen in the next few years will be better able to protect himself."

He stressed again the "radical" and "revolutionary" aspects of the "Plutonian period," its association with the underworld, the strikes, strife, "gangsterism," and Hitler-type tactics that were likely to occur.

All of this, I remind you, was from our tape-recorded sessions in the early months of 1974. In September of 1975, it will be recalled, most front-page news was devoted to nationwide teachers' strikes, anti-busing violence in Boston, and especially to the two assassination attempts on President Ford's life by avowed radicals (one, Lynette "Squeaky" Fromme, a disciple of Scorpio Charles Manson) and the capture of fugitive heiress Patricia Hearst, whose activities in the Symbionese Liberation Army underground were well publicized.

Page-one stories of the young "radicals" and "revolutionaries" were all over the place in the news media.

"How long will this Pluto 22 affliction last?" I asked Sydney.

"I think that once we get past 1977 the worst of it is over," he said. "We'll learn to build again. You see, we have to understand the symbolism of Pluto. (The planet's name is a euphemism for the Greek deity of the underworld, otherwise known as Hades). Pluto brings upheaval, often despair, because the old has been wiped out and a new concept has been born. It is often difficult to abandon the old and steer toward new, progressive roads. Pluto tells of the necessity for courage to try the new, to pull ourselves out of hopeless grooves. Pluto can be destructive, but unpleasant experiences often help us eventually to appreciate peace and tranquillity.

"The wreckage of Pluto is symbolic of the phoenix, a miraculous bird of Egyptian lore believed to live for five hundred years only to be consumed in fire by its own act. However, the phoenix rises again in youthful freshness from its own ashes and becomes an emblem of immortality. Pluto thus offers a lesson in hope. Pluto is the chance for a comeback. Pluto points out that often the old must be torn down for the new. Pluto is wreckage, often because we so desire, in order that we can start anew and rebuild. Pluto has been related to better conditions, in labor and other fields, but only after many heads were smashed and people attained a new dignity and a new unity."

"How long will it take us to recover from this Pluto 22 influence?" I asked.

"I think that now, with Neptune in Sagittarius," he said, "we will see a spiritual rebuilding from the destructive Pluto influence in the next eight or ten years. It may be very torturous. But it will be nothing compared to the next time."

The next time?

Yes, gentle readers, there's another Pluto 22 year coming up, and not too far away. It's 1984. One plus nine plus eight plus four adds up to 22.

"If I were forced to predict a year of the greatest conflagration of all," Sydney said, "it would be 1984, the next twenty-two year."

I keep asking myself, *How* does he know? *Why* should Uranus in Gemini or Saturn in Cancer or Pluto 22 have anything at all to do with what happens in our lives? How does Sydney Omarr get to be such a wise guy?

Who is Sydney Omarr

Chapter 6

PLUTO REVISITED: A BORN WINNER

"Omarr is more than an astrologer, of course. He is possessed not only of a sixth sense but of a seventh and possibly an eighth."

—HENRY MILLER

Sydney Omarr is not his real name, of course. Anyone could guess that. But by the time I finished trying to figure out why and how he changed his name to correspond with his "birth path," which is number twenty-two, I was ready to forget the whole thing.

I spent four hours hassling through two pages of transcript from our recording session on the origin of his name. I was certain at the time that I could do it faster than my hired transcriber, because, after all, I was there and she wasn't, and therefore I could understand it better and bat it out faster, right? Ho, ho!

I shall proceed slowly.

Sydney was born Sidney Kimmelman on August 5, 1926, in Philadelphia—a Leo, with the sun, Mercury, and Neptune all in Leo, and Libra on the ascendant. That was enough to shake me up, right there.

At a very early age—about three or four—Sidney Kimmelman caught onto the magic of numbers, and by the time he was fifteen he was wise enough in numerology to know that he had to change his name to correspond with his "birth path." By "birth path" he means his actual birth date, August 5, 1926.

"That's a twenty-two, one of the two master numbers. Remember, numbers eleven and twenty-two are the double numbers that are not reduced."

Yes, I remembered, even if I didn't understand.

He continued: "Numerologists claim that these two master numbers have such vibrations that if you can tie onto them, it would be like tying onto the tail of fate, so to speak, and you might have a very exciting life.

"You can't change the date of your birth, but you can juggle your name around to harmonize with your birth date. I was doing a magic show as a hobby and I thought that eventually I might turn professional. But my own name didn't seem to be right for the field. About this time I happened to see Victor Mature in a movie called *Shanghai Gesture* and his name was Omar. That appealed to me, but one *r* wouldn't do, so I added another *r* and changed the *i* in Sidney to a *y*. With two *r*'s and a *y* it became Sydney Omarr, or a twenty-two, which coincides with my birth path."

He had lost me.

"Why is twenty-two your birth path?"

"It's the total of my birth date—month, day, and year—August 5, 1926"

I slowly added 1926—one plus nine plus two plus six equals eighteen, plus five (for August 5)—equals twenty-three.

"That adds up to twenty-three," I said.

"No, it doesn't—" He almost broke up laughing. "Wouldn't it be funny after all these years if it added up to twenty-three. . . . But you're not counting right," he said "You see, August 5 is four and 1926 is nine—"

"Not so fast. Why is August 5 four?"

"August is the eighth month. Eight and five are thirteen, and you reduce them to one digit—one plus three—and it's four. You just add them, then reduce them, and they come out to twenty-two.

"You see," he continued patiently, "there are only nine numbers in the universe. Number eighteen, for example, isn't really a number, it's a combination of two numbers—one and eight. Once you finish with your fingers and toes, you start all over again. After nine, what is there? You're back to one, and then you have to count one and zero equals ten, then one and one equals eleven, one and two equals twelve, then one and three, one and four, one and five, thirteen, fourteen, fifteen, and so on. It's a startling concept, but there are no more numbers after nine. The others are just combinations or various octaves of those numbers. . . ."

I still can't figure out Sydney's numerology logic in arriving at his twenty-two birth-path number. I can understand that Aug (eighth month) plus five equals thirteen, which, reduced (one plus three), equals four, and that 1926 (birth year) totals eighteen. But Sydney adds the total eighteen to the four to come out to twenty-two. Why doesn't he reduce the 1926 (eighteen) to nine and add that nine to the four, which equals thirteen—or four when it's reduced?

Obviously he has his own illogical system for arriving at the magic number he wanted: twenty-two.

It is easier to figure out how he arrives at twenty-two with his name. As he explains, each letter of the alphabet relates to a number. Thus:

1	2	3	4	5	6	7	8	9
A	B	C	D	E	F	G	H	I
J	K	L	M	N	O	P	Q	R
S	T	U	V	W	X	Y	Z	

Thus SYDNEY becomes 1–7–4–5–5–7—or a total of twenty-nine, which, reduced, equals eleven.

And OMARR becomes 6–4–1–9–9—also a total of twenty-nine, which, reduced, equals eleven.

Then he adds eleven plus eleven, which equals twenty-two, the number he needed to coincide with his birth path.

"What really matters," he says, "is that you are comfortable with the system you are using."

He happens to be so comfortable with his own system that when reeling off multiplications, additions, subtractions, and reduced numbers on his frequent television appearances, the station's switchboards are jammed with people calling to tell him he's beating their own computers!

He astonished me by glibly reciting my own name in numbers:

N-5, O-9, R-9, M-4, A-1—equals twenty-five, reduces to seven. L-3, E-5, E-5—equals thirteen reduces to four. B-2, R-9, O-6, W-5, N-5, I-9, N-5, G-7—equals forty-eight, reduces to twelve, reduces again to one digit, which is three.

"Therefore, seven (Norma) plus four (Lee) plus three (Browning) equals fourteen, which is five."

He rattled it all off faster than I could even count the letters in my own name (but I caught it all on my tape recorder), and then said, "Your number is five. That means change and travel . . . the creative arts . . . communication of ideas. . . . The digit five is associated with the planet Mercury. . . ."

"But my sign is Sagittarius and my planet is Jupiter," I reminded him. At least I knew that much.

"Yes, I know you're Sagittarius," he said, in a tone that indicated he really didn't need to be told. With a slight grin he yanked a sheet of paper from his typewriter and said, "Here, I want to read you something. It's the lead for my column I'm writing today."

He read it to me:

> . . . When it comes to straightforward talk, it is difficult to top the Sagittarius woman. She usually means what she says and says what she means. Many are offended, taken aback, startled, while others find the lady refreshingly frank and a charming challenge. My Sagittarius women seem to flare up at me, only to later act as if nothing untoward had occurred.
>
> In all, I am kept off balance by Sagittarians, men and women.

We had a good laugh, but I also got the message.

There was one question, however, that I had to ask. "You've just been telling me about all the terrible things associated with Pluto and the chaos that can happen in a Pluto 22 year. Why did you want to change your name so it would add up to twenty-two when you knew the number was associated with Pluto? You've even written it in your own *Thought Dial*," I reminded him.

"I wasn't thinking of any planet when I changed my name. I was too young then. I hadn't created my Thought Dial yet. I hadn't yet combined the basics of astrology with numerology. That was to come later," he explained.

"Besides, I was only four years old when Pluto was discovered. It was several years before I became aware of the positive and negative aspects of the planets. Yes, twenty-two is associated with Pluto, but that doesn't necessarily always signify evil or negative aspects. There's a good side and a bad side to all signs and planets. A lot depends on other planetary positions.

"But in numerology number twenty-two as a master digit is a

symbol of success, with emphasis on building, creating, making master plans. I didn't even know that when I changed my name.

"All I knew was that it was important to have a name that would come out twenty-two, to correspond with my birth path. The letters in your name have certain numbers and the theory is that your name has a sound or vibration which reduces to a number. You can go in disharmony throughout your life if you don't respond to your name. That's why so many people change their names."

Singer Dionne Warwick(e), for example, added that extra *e* to her name in 1970 on the advice of a numerologist, who said that her life, both personal and professional, would take an upswing if she did. Dionne says it all came true.

Apparently, Pluto's negative aspects, if any, in Sydney's individual horoscope were more than offset by his lucky draw of number twenty-two, the symbol of success, to correspond with his birth path. The fact is he was having great success at picking the right numbers long before he changed his name.

He was still an infant in his mother's arms when he began picking the right numbers on the wheels of chance along the famous boardwalk in Atlantic City.

"I have no memory of it myself, of course. I wasn't old enough to walk yet; had to be carried. But I remember my parents and sisters later telling anecdotes about it, about how I was able to indicate what numbers to play by pointing, and they would follow my signs, put their chips on the numbers, and they would always win," he said.

"At first this was startling to them. They didn't know what to make of it. Then they began looking on it with great amusement, and finally it was just taken for granted that I could always pick the winners. I remember hearing a great deal of discussion among my relatives and my family about how and why I was able to do this. I guess they never figured it out. I haven't either. I don't know how I did it. Child's luck, I suppose. And I probably enjoyed the praise and attention I was getting."

When he was older and had learned to walk, his mother always took him along with her to visit the fortunetellers and palm readers.

"My mother was fascinated with fortunetellers," he recalled. "She used to take me from one to the other, and sometimes they would read my palm and tell me that when I grew up I was going to become a famous person in this field. My mother always found that very amusing."

All of Sydney's childhood summers were spent in Atlantic City with his mother and his sisters, Leah and Ruth. His father owned a grocery store in Philadelphia and stayed there to run it during the week, but he always spent weekends with his family at the summer resort city, commuting the sixty miles by train. Sydney was the baby of the family, a precocious child with platinum-blond hair and long curls. His older sisters adored him. They could hardly wait for their father to arrive so they could tell him all about baby brother's luck with the numbers on the boardwalk.

Sometimes Sydney's favorite cousin, Harry Korman, would join them. His earliest and fondest memories are of those wondrous sunny summers in Atlantic City with his family and relatives, his sisters and cousins, and the funny, new kind of people he was meeting on the boardwalk.

"There was always something exciting going on, a carnival atmosphere, and I was entranced by all these strange, colorful people and the way they talked and the things they did. It was a world of magic to an impressionable child. It made a deep impression on me. I can still remember it all vividly—at least from the time I could begin to remember anything," he said.

"When I was old enough to walk around by myself, I would haunt the fortunetellers. I remember, one was an old vaudeville star who went under the name of Willard, the Man Who Grows. He was very good to me. When he wasn't too busy, he would talk to me about many things, and he never seemed condescending to a small boy. Then he would give me a note, which usually said something like, 'Would you please talk to this boy?' and send me on to another palmist, or graphologist, or psychic, or astrologer. I didn't know what those words meant at the time, but I can remember listening spellbound by the hour as a man who called himself Professor Seward did a spiel about the stars and the planets and then sold something which he called horoscopes at a dollar each. I learned later that he was selling about a million a year."

Sydney admits, "I have no idea what drew me to these people, but I found them intriguing, and, looking back now, I suppose their collective impact must have had something to do with what I was to become, sort of an ingrained impression, so to speak, though at the time I had no concept of becoming seriously involved in anything of that nature in the future. I was much too young then to be thinking about my future."

But his early gift for picking the winning numbers developed with surprising rapidity. As soon as he could walk around by himself, he was putting his own chips on the Wheel of Fortune, the Wheel of Luck, the Wheel of Chance.

"I don't remember exactly what they were called, but they were something like roulette wheels," he explained. "Only, there wasn't legalized gambling in Atlantic City, so the wheels paid off in prizes, not in cash—something like cigarettes, toys, or a chocolate cake. All I know is that you would put your chip on a number, then spin the wheel, and I was always able to pick out the right number. I still don't know why."

From his boardwalk beginning, he progressed to the more sophisticated lottery numbers game in his home town of Philadelphia. He was still in his preschool years.

"I was too young to know what it was all about, but I can remember people coming into my dad's grocery store while I was there and asking me to pick out three numbers for them. My relatives and neighbors and friends of my parents were always calling on the phone to ask me to pick out three numbers.

"Apparently my average of hits was pretty high, because they always seemed happy about winning and kept right on asking me for numbers. It was some kind of a gambling game, maybe the policy racket, for all I know. To me it was just a game, a numbers game, and it was fun. But it was probably illegal," he added.

He also remembers picking the "Keno" numbers for his family and relatives.

"I didn't know what Keno was, either, but I sure heard the word enough. People were always asking me to give them the Keno numbers for tomorrow, and I would just pick some numbers out of the air. They must have won a sufficient number of times, because my parents made many new friends."

"Did the numbers come to you fast or slow?" I asked. "When you just pulled them out of the blue, did you have to think about them at all?"

"Oh, maybe twenty-five seconds, something like that," he said. "I never thought too much about it. Probably I would be fast or slow depending on how much attention I wanted. I was still only eight or nine years old at the time."

"Do you have any theories now as to why you were able to do this at such an early age? Were any of your grandparents or great-grandparents mathematicians? Or perhaps," I suggested, "you acquired this innate talent in some past incarnation?"

He didn't take to that suggestion. He choked back a small cough of laughter and responded with admirable restraint. "It is very difficult to speculate about a previous life. We have trouble enough trying to understand the present one. No, so far as I know, none of my grandparents or great-grandparents were mathematicians. I am sure now that what I was doing was Pythagorean numerology, but I didn't know that until I was a little older. The numbers were coming from the subconscious."

By the time Sydney was "a little older," age twelve and in the sixth grade, he was deep into "numberology" as he called it then, and reading everything he could find on the subject. By now he also had added some elementary astrology, palmistry, and magic tricks to his growing repertoire.

He was a voracious reader, bought all the books he could afford, and haunted the bookstores, especially Leary's, which was then a famous landmark in Philadelphia.

"I remember, the fourth floor had a big section completely devoted to astrology and numerology and what people call the occult arts. I used to spend hours there prowling through the books and reading. I remember a nice old clerk who was very kind to me. He would let me read the books right there even when I didn't buy any."

By the time Sydney was fifteen—shortly after he changed his name—he had written his first book, a short one titled *Sydney Omarr's Private Course in Numerology*. He had it mimeographed, and the nice old clerk at Leary's put it on sale for two dollars on the fourth floor.

It was about this same time, at age fifteen, that he also sold his first article—to a movie magazine. It was about the movie stars and their "number signs."

He then began writing articles for astrology magazines. One magazine, instead of paying him, let him place a two-inch ad free. He wrote, "Have You a Problem??? . . . Let Sydney Omarr Help You Solve It. . . ." He invited readers to send him their birth dates and two dollars and he would give them a "consultation" based on astrology and numerology. He promptly found himself in the consulting business.

"I was amazed at the response. People wrote to me from all over the country, as well as from Hawaii and Canada, about their most intimate problems. How brash I was! There I was, only fifteen years old, and giving advice on all sorts of things, some of which I had never heard of before. I blushed when I read some of the letters," he recalled. "Some were so embarrassing that there were times when I felt a sense of guilt, as though I were a mail-order Peeping Tom, and I seriously wondered whether this was a proper profession for a young man to pursue.

"My guilt feelings, however, were somewhat counterbalanced by my pleasure in the pursuit of more knowledge about astrology and numerology, and the gratification I felt at the overwhelming response from my mail-order clients, who seemed to be convinced that my advice had actually helped them!

"I got to the point where some very important people were writing to me."

There is one incident that stands out in his memory. He was reading the sports pages of the Philadelphia *Bulletin* one day during the time of the Kentucky Derby, and the name in the headlines was that of one of the jockeys who was riding in the Derby. Sydney thought the name had a familiar ring to it. He went to his file of mail-order letters and, sure enough, there was the name. The letter was from the jockey's wife. She had written that she was desperately in need of help and advice because her husband—this great racing hero—was beating her up and bringing other women home with him, then forcing her to watch while he had sexual intimacies with the other women.

"It was a very strange and startling experience for me, at that early age, barely in my teens, to be reading about a headline 'hero' on the sports page and at the same time knowing that in another area of his life he was no hero at all, but a rather shabby character," Sydney said.

"That jockey left an indelible mark on my impressionistic young mind. I later learned that this was to become a familiar pattern. People are not always what they appear to be on the outside. Once you gain their confidence and they begin to confide in you, a completely different kind of life begins to unravel."

He also learned something else from his mail-order venture.

"It proved to me that somehow what we now call the mantic[1] arts and sciences do work, for I never saw the persons who wrote to me, I never met them, they never came in for readings. It was all done by mail—and it all seemed to work."

It worked so well, in fact, that Sydney raised his price to five dollars for an astrological-numerological analysis of their problems, and if they wanted more advice, he would charge twenty-five dollars.

"In those days that was a lot of money."

He spent most of it on books and magic accouterments. He carried on his big mail-order practice, his magic acts, psychic readings, palmistry, and "numberizing" while still going to school.

The truth of the matter, he is quick to admit, is that he didn't do very well in school. He was always late for classes—when he bothered to go at all. He spent more time in Leary's Book Store and Kanter's magic shop than in most of his classes.

Some considered him a child prodigy, others considered him incorrigible. He was always in trouble, the Peck's bad boy of the school, but he usually managed to pull himself out of it with his magic acts and his amazing talent for "numberizing" people. Even in grammar school and then junior high he was "numberizing" people: Mae West; his school principal, teachers, and other disciplinarians; as well as his bewildered family.

In junior high his grades suffered so much that it was thought he might not graduate. But he did a magic show for an assembly program and all the teachers were so impressed that they raised his grades so he could graduate.

Edgar Bergen was always in trouble in junior high school too, he once admitted on a talk show, and finally graduated after doing a ventriloquism show at assembly.

Sydney's school principals and teachers approved of his magic

[1] Aldous Huxley introduced Sydney to the word *mantic*, derived from the Greek word *mantikos*, pertaining to divination. It is a synonym for the term "occult," which has negative connotations (secret, hidden, etc.). Sydney and other scholars prefer the term *mantic* arts and sciences to embrace such areas as astrology and numerology.

shows and his "numberizing"—or at least the "numerascopes" he did for them—but they did not approve of his interest in astrology and palmistry. They complained to his parents that they should make him stop "all this nonsense," because it wasn't "wholesome for a child."

There wasn't much his poor parents could do about it.

Sydney frequently spent all day long at Leary's or the magic shop. The school authorities would warn his parents again and sometimes suspend him, or call him in for another severe reprimand.

"I remember once when I was in very serious trouble and I was called in to the principal's office and he was going to expel me for missing school so often. I explained to him that I wasn't doing anything all that terrible; I was only reading books on astrology and numerology, and I said if he would give me his birth date I would do a numerascope for him.

"Well, he seemed intrigued. I guess he decided to test me. He gave me his birth date and I went home and typed out a five- or six-page numerascope and gave it to him. He was amazed at the things I told him. He showed it to his wife and then he told me, 'I agree with everything you said that was good and my wife agrees with everything you said that was bad. Maybe there's something to this.' Apparently he decided I wasn't so incorrigible after all. He became my friend," Sydney said, "and pretty soon all the teachers were asking me to do their numerascopes."

Paradoxically, the child prodigy in the numbers games flunked most of his math courses in school.

"I was never any good at arithmetic," he recalled. "I was always daydreaming in numbers. I mean, I would be numberizing Mae West, for example, and discovering that her personality number was three. This is the number that's supposed to describe the physical appearance, and it's usually a very curvaceous person. Like Mae West. That's what I was doing in school instead of arithmetic.

"I guess I probably flunked all my math courses. I don't remember. I think some of it had to do with the fact that I didn't know I needed glasses. I really couldn't see the lettering on the blackboard too well. But I would have flunked anyway." He shrugged philosophically. "The only thing I excelled in was English composition."

"Oh, I knew how to do simple arithmetic problems," he added.

"But not in any exceptional way. I knew about multiplying, division, adding, and subtraction. I could do them. But I didn't know anything about formal numbers—the Pythagorean theorem and geometry. What I was doing was Pythagorean numerology, and this is different, because it deals with the subconscious. I began to see from my reading that certain numbers are accentuated, giving an indication to universal meanings and answers. As Carl Jung said, man didn't invent numbers, he discovered them. It's kind of a cosmic knowledge."

Sydney drew heavily on this "cosmic knowledge" to get him through his state tests in arithmetic. Most of the tests, he explained, provided the pupil with a multiple choice of answers to a question, the choice to be marked in a square block beside it.

"I wouldn't pay any attention to the questions, only the numbers—the number of the question. If it was the thirty-fifth question, for example, I would check the second square, because thirty-five is eight (three plus five), and it attracts to it number two. So I would put my X in the number-two block.

"I instinctively knew that the numbers were subjective and the questions didn't mean a thing. The answer was the number that was attracted to the number of the question. If it was the fourth question, it would probably be the fourth block. Anything that adds up to eight or ten would be attracted to each other. If it was a six question, I would check either four or two. . . . So all I had to do was block them out according to my knowledge of numerology."

And so what if he did flunk a few math courses? The former Sidney Kimmelman, alias Number Twenty-two, the success symbol, feels certain that he scored as well or better on his state tests with Pythagorean numerology than if he had studied his textbooks.

Chapter 7
PECK'S BAD BOY IN THE MAGIC SHOP

"*Who is this zombie they call Omarr?*"
—FRITZIE ZIVIC

Sydney's fascination with magic and all the mystical arts was sparked by his adventures on the boardwalk in his early preschool years, but he didn't discover Kanter's magic shop until he was about twelve years old. He was always considered a rather strange child because of those peculiar and mysterious things he could do with numbers. He was regarded with awe and suspicion by most of his classmates and especially by the neighborhood bullies, who were always trying to pick fights with him.

He became interested in boxing, out of necessity, and became a pretty good boxer at a very early age. But he also had developed into something of a loner to avoid the bullies.

The Kimmelmans lived at the corner of Thirty-eighth and Spruce, in a house directly next door to Papa Kimmelman's grocery store, and at that time, Sydney recalled, it was a rather tough neighborhood. Most of the children were bullies, always getting into fights.

"There was really nobody I wanted to play with or be friends with, so I stayed pretty much to myself. I didn't have many friends. When I was home," he said, "I would spend most of my time hanging around my dad's grocery store."

The store was across the street from the University of Pennsylvania, and there was one student who came in often and would always take time to talk to the little Kimmelman boy.

"He knew I was kind of lonely, I guess, so one day he suggested, 'Why don't you go down to the magic shop and get yourself some tricks to play with?' I had never heard of a magic shop, but I looked it up in the phone book, the name he gave me—Kanter's magic shop. So I rode the trolley downtown by myself and I found it. I remember, there were two large signs that said KANTER'S, and between these two signs was another one, that intrigued me more. It said THE HOUSE OF MYSTERY. I knew the minute I walked into that HOUSE OF MYSTERY that I was hooked," he recalled. "From then on, Kanter's became *my* magic shop, as though I had a part interest in it. It changed my life, opened a whole new world for me. When I was in the magic shop, I really didn't care if I never went back to school again. As it turned out, I suppose I really wouldn't have been able to make it through school if it had not been for the things I learned from Mike Kanter. He is still known and revered as the father of all magicians," Sydney said, "and in those days he was a very busy man, with some very famous clients. But he took a fatherly interest in me, and he always took time to help me not only by showing me the secrets of the magic tricks and putting me in magic acts and contests but by just talking to me, listening to me, answering my questions, and giving me advice.

"All of this was very important to a twelve-year-old boy living in a world of daydreams that nobody seemed to understand. Mike Kanter left his influence on many lives, but he played a bigger role in my life than he probably ever realized."

Kanter's magic shop, on Walnut Street in Philadelphia, half a block from the John Wanamaker Department Store, was once known as the nation's foremost emporium of the occult and magic tricks of the trade.

And Mike Kanter—more formally, Mitchell Kanter, Prop.—once catered to the greatest, from Blackstone to Dunninger. His catalogues were considered the bible of magic. His client list was studded with celebrities: Edgar Bergen, Orson Welles, Walt Disney, James Stewart, Rita Hayworth, Jackie Gleason, Ted Lewis, the Duke of Windsor, Henry DuPont II, Johnny Carson, Dick Cavett, Veronica Lake, Warner Baxter, the Great Thurston, Fu Manchu, Galli-Galli, and Dante.

Mike is semi-retired now and caters only to a few special customers, but he still remembers with pride and affection the slender boy with big, brown, owlish eyes and a somber mien too old for his years who quietly attached himself to the magic shop.

"He was there so often he became a fixture," he told me. "My secretary hinted that he should take a job minding the store. At first I wondered why he was spending so much time at my place instead of in school.

"Then I discovered that he was a very serious and determined youngster, that he really wanted to get ahead and be important, and that he was willing to work hard at it and learn everything he could."

In an interview regarding his role and influence on Sydney's early life, Mike Kanter described how the rapport developed between them.

"He was always willing to listen and learn," he said. "He was very attentive when I gave him advice, and he always seemed so appreciative of any help I gave him. He was very unusual for a boy of that age. He must have been no more than eleven or twelve when he first started coming to my shop. Sometimes he took the trolley, but usually he walked all the way from his house, at Thirty-eighth and Spruce, to my place. He was so serious and so determined that I knew he would be successful in whatever he would undertake. I told many of my customers, 'There's a lad who's going to get somewhere. He's got the stuff it takes.' I'm glad I was right."

Mike soon was helping and advising him in his selection of magic tricks and was always patient with him no matter how much or how little money he spent.

"He was such an exceptionally fine type of youngster that I didn't mind giving him my time. In fact I couldn't help giving him all the advice that I thought would be helpful to him, because he always followed my advice and instructions, and I could watch him develop and improve.

"Naturally," Mike said, "I was beginning to feel very proud of him. He was very bright and brainy for his age, extremely talented and clever. But he also certainly did a lot of practicing with whatever he had, for, every time he came to my place, I could see the improvement. He became quite adept at working with billiard balls, coins, silks, and a few other effects.

"By the time he was fourteen, I entered him in a contest. At that time, one of the world's greatest and most famous magicians, Dante, was playing at one of Philadelphia's largest theaters. He was making a farewell tour of the country and looking for a successor to carry on his great show. In some of the larger cities he was sponsoring contests among young amateur magicians in order to pick out a winner and a possible successor for his show.

"I was in charge of finding the talent in Philadelphia, and I made sure that each and every one of them was an excellent performer, capable of giving a good account of himself. I chose Sydney as one of them; I knew he was that good. Dante and two others were the judges. I was not allowed to judge, because I selected the talent. If I were a judge, people could have said I used favoritism in picking the winner."

As it turned out, Mike still blames himself for entering another young magician, who won the contest. Sydney came in second.

"When it was over," Mike admitted, "I realized that I should not have permitted him [the winner] to enter, because he had entirely too much experience compared to the others. Actually, he was a professional, and well paid at many engagements. The way I looked at it at the time was that it would be a treat for our audience to see what a clever young performer could do. In my eyes he was just a youngster too, though older than Sydney and the others. Only afterwards did I realize that it wasn't really fair to the others for me to enter him in the contest, for he was really a professional.

"And if I hadn't entered him, Sydney would have won the contest. Instead he came in second, which, considering his age and the competition, was still pretty good, I would say."

Sydney's status as an amateur, however, didn't stay with him for long. When he turned sixteen, he told the American Guild of Variety Artists that he was eighteen and began performing as a professional.

One of Kanter's frequent customers was a magician who did a mind-reading act with his wife.

"It was a terrific act, and the man was a good friend of mine. He wanted Sydney to substitute for his wife while she was ill, and Sydney would have been good at it. But I advised him against it, and fortunately he followed my counsel, as he usually did.

"I like to feel that I saved Sydney from many pitfalls by advising him in certain matters. You see," Mike explained, "a man in my position, with so many years in the magic business and such close contacts with all these performers—well, I know too much about all of them, their good points and bad points and so on. Sydney was so young then, and I didn't want him to get mixed up with the wrong connections. I'm glad he followed my advice.

"He continued to follow up his interests in other areas—numerology, palmistry, astrology, spiritualism, and so on—and when I had the time I would discuss all these things with him also and try to advise and guide him in how to combine them in his acts. I was very proud of him. He looked and acted like a well-experienced professional. He had the talent. He stood tall and straight and was well-mannered. If he had to talk, he knew how to do so and what to say."

Sydney doesn't remember it exactly that way. When he first began performing in amateur nights at the Fay Theatre, for example, he found he wasn't fully prepared.

"In those days," he recalled, "all you had to do to enter an amateur show was to call up someone at the theater or send in a postcard and wait for them to call you. They were always in need of talent for their vaudeville stage acts. I had picked up magic rather quickly, but apparently I thought I was better than I actually was.

"I made a rash move and sent in a postcard, and the first thing I knew I got a call. I'll never forget it. When I heard my voice on the microphone for the first time, I got stage fright and pulled back, and no one could hear what I was saying. (He doesn't have that problem today!) It was a horrible performance, but I was more determined than ever to go out and try it again.

"Well, naturally, I developed what skills I had and kept at it until I started winning contests, third prize, then second, then first. You could only win three prizes; then you turned professional."

He first billed himself as Kimball the Great, a name he used only briefly, until he saw the Victor Mature movie *Shanghai Gesture*, with Mature playing Omar, which inspired him to "numberize" his name to Sydney Omarr.

His act was billed as a "mental magic" act and at first consisted mainly of magic tricks. Then he added a little astrology, numerology, palmistry, and spiritualistic tricks.

"I didn't believe in all that spiritualistic pretense," he explained. "My purpose was to expose the tricks that mediums do. I used to read everything I could get my hands on along that line. I bought quite a few books about exposing mediums. I spent all my lunch money on books (before his lucrative mail-order business), and I had quite a library."

He also spent his money on a personal investigation of mediums.

He remembers especially one lady medium he visited. He wrote his question on a slip of paper: "Will I be a good magician?"

"She read it wrong. She thought I asked, would I be a good musician instead of magician, but I knew she was reading it from one piece of paper while she was burning the other. This is an old trick, burning the paper you have the question written on. She wasn't very good at it, so I showed her how to switch the papers and do the burning. She was quite astounded," he recalled.

"Magic itself," he added, "is both an art and a trickery—but a real art as long as the audience knows that it is done by trickery. I never have believed that you should pass off spiritualistic or mediumistic tricks or so-called mind reading or telepathy as coming from some divine source. Telepathy, of course, is an authenticated genuine manifestation of psychic phenomena, and I guess so are some spiritualistic revelations, from what I have read. But in my opinion these do not belong in a magic act. I have great respect for the magician's craft. It takes skill and practice to learn those tricks, and for a while that was my main interest.

"But the more I learned about astrology and numerology, the more convinced I was that this was something on a far deeper and more serious level than magic. I knew that I had to make a choice. I couldn't go on combining the two. The magic acts were fun and they taught me a great deal. But the stars and the numbers weren't trickery. They were very real. I knew which direction I was going to take.

"I remember my feeling on some of those trolley rides in Philadelphia with my astrology books hidden under my coat," Sydney said. "I almost envisioned or knew that I would be doing this today. And that I would be famous. I didn't think too much about it at the time. I didn't worry about it or plan it. It just seemed so natural. I *knew* that this was what I was going to do. It was almost like precognition. I seemed to have a natural flair for picking the right answers from the skies and from numbers. I didn't know how it worked, but it worked. And I had experienced my first taste of meaningful success, an inner thrill at the thought of being able to help others. I knew then what I wanted to do, what I had to do."

It was all the more reason for his feeling of gratitude to Mike Kanter. Not that Mike specifically told him which way to go. But he helped him realize that his magic acts were only for fun and for money, and that he should separate the real from the fantasy and trickery.

More importantly at the time, Mike Kanter didn't ridicule or laugh at him. He wasn't bewildered, as his parents were, or scornful, like his teachers, or puzzled, awed, frightened, or resentful, like his classmates and neighborhood bullies. He had patience and perception, insight and understanding of a boy's quest for answers, and gave encouragement, friendship, and guidance at a time when he most needed it.

Kanter's magic shop became Sydney's own little world of retreat. And it wasn't so little, either. It was a two-story building with five rooms upstairs and three downstairs, all filled with marvelous "Magical Apparatus and Illusions," "Pocket, Parlor, Club, and Stage Tricks," books, catalogues, crystal balls, and psychic and spiritualistic props. Sydney never tired of browsing through the rooms, peeking into the books and catalogues, watching the customers come and go.

He was wide-eyed with wonder at the people he saw going in and out and at all the fascinating things he watched them do and saw them buy. He soon learned that Kanter's was a meeting place for famous magicians from everywhere, and sometimes they would pat him on the head and say, "Now, if you're a good boy, I'll show you a nice little trick." Then they would make cards and coins and eggs disappear, and pull beautifully colored silk scarves from their sleeves, and do wondrous, mysterious things with linking rings and magic slates that held him spellbound.

When he overcame his shyness long enough, he would ask how they did it.

"They usually just patted me on the head again, and they would say, 'That's the first thing you learn, boy, when you grow up to be a magician. Never, never tell anyone, even your best friends, how you perform your magic tricks.' This was a lesson I had ingrained in me from the beginning, and one that I was soon to learn would not stand me in very good stead with the neighborhood bullies."

"I could hold their attention for a while," he said, "but then there always came the time when they would demand to know how I did the tricks, and when I wouldn't tell them—well, sometimes it got pretty rough. That's when my boxing came in handy. I would say, 'Okay, let's box, according to the rules, open-handed.' They would usually go along with this or back off, because they knew I was good at it. At least it was better than having a gang of guys beating you up.

"I did take a beating now and then, because I preferred that to revealing how a magic trick is done. That's against the magician's code."

Thus, in a sense, and in addition to everything else he learned in Mike Kanter's magic shop, he was receiving early lessons in character building. He would later become as staunch a defender of the astrologer's code of ethics as he was of the magician's code.

Moreover, his magic tricks paid off significantly in extra dividends by improving his boxing skills, which in turn sparked his interest in professional boxing matches, and this in turn led him into another area of astrology: picking the winners by the stars. This was to bring him his first nationwide public recognition as an astrologer, and it happened in a most unusual way.

"You see," he explained, "I always loved boxing and had an interest in it, but I also had to use it for self-protection so much that I really became quite good at it. I probably could have become a professional. I fantasized about being out there in the boxing ring. At one point I even thought about giving up astrology for boxing. But it was pure fantasy."

It was Sydney's friend astrologer Carl Payne Tobey who told the story of how Sydney happened to start making his boxing predictions. Tobey got the story from Bill McGaw, former sports editor of the Philadelphia *Record:*

"When I was sports editor of the paper, this kid used to come in and bother me. He wore short pants. He was trying to sell me on astrology. He wanted to get some publicity for astrology. He told me what he could do with astrology, and I said, 'Okay, if you know so much about it, you start predicting the winners of the prize fights. And I'll print your predictions in my column. So he would come in with his predictions. Well, you know what? That kid predicted ten fights all together—and he was right on seven of them. Not a bad track record for a kid still in knee pants. He almost sold me on astrology."

That was only the beginning. On another occasion Sydney picked the winners in twenty-four out of twenty-six boxing bouts, a feat that put him in the big league of the publicity limelight. It was picked up by syndicated columnists such as Ed Sullivan and E. V. Durling, as well as sportswriters, of course.

Author Jess Stearn was sufficiently impressed with Sydney's uncanny ability to pick the winners in professional fights to write about it at length in his book *A Time for Astrology*.

"Philadelphia sportswriters joshed the teen-age astrologer but went along with his picks, and even the fighters were sufficiently impressed to be elated or deflated, as the prediction went. On one occasion lightweight champion Bob Montgomery, before a title bout with Beau Jack, cornered the stripling astrologer and demanded to know the outcome."

Fortunately for Sydney, perhaps, the stars smiled on Montgomery, as one journalist humorously reported: "Beau Jack's Aquarius will be rising, whatever that means, and Omarr says that ain't good. Montgomery will be ruled by Jupiter and the moon, and that is very copasetic. Mars also will rule Bob that night and that's the God of War, and with that gentleman on Montgomery's side; says Omarr, Beau Jack should have stood, instead of in the Garden ring, someplace else."

Later, Sydney picked Montgomery to beat top contender Fritzie Zivic of the fighting Pittsburgh Zivics. Zivic read about it in the papers and told a Philadelphia sportswriter:

"Who is this zombie they call Omarr who picks those fights by looking at the stars? They better lock that guy up. If I can find where he's sitting, I'll knock Montgomery right in his lap."

Sydney still smiles over the furor he created with his predictions and especially at Fritzie Zivic's indignant and disrespectful reference to the zodiacal houses.

"Imagine him saying I'm going to lose because I'm going into the fifth house. I don't have any fifth house, or even a fourth house. All I got is one house, and that one cost me thirty grand."

Anyway, Fritzie lost the fight, as Sydney had predicted he would.

Sydney's biggest attention getter was his forecast of the finish of Joe Louis in his bout with Joe Wolcott of December 5, 1947.

As a boxing buff, Sydney had been a Joe Louis fan since he was a kid in knee pants. In fact, he still insists that the first "serious" reading he ever did was a ten-cent paperback book on the life of Joe Louis. "It was one of those 'Big Little' books," he explained, a forerunner of paperbacks. When all the other little boys were reading *Donald Duck*, *Mickey Mouse*, *Terry Tunes*, and other cartoon books, he was reading the life of Joe Louis. So he was no stranger to the heavyweight champ's past, present, and future potential when the Louis-Wolcott fight came up.

He first analyzed Joe Louis's capabilities: "In his quiet, determined way, as shown by the sun-Mercury conjunction in Taurus in his solar chart, Joe has plodded on, meeting and overcoming obstacles. The Taurus emphasis can be seen in his thick neck and powerful shoulders. Joe takes a punch so well because of the development of his neck. Blows which would knock out an ordinary warrior resound off the Louis jaw, often failing even to jar him. His co-ordination and great willpower are emphasized by the sun-Mercury trine to his moon in Capricorn (the ruthless moon) in the eighth sector of his chart. Venus, his ruling planet, is in Gemini in conjunction with Saturn in the first house. It is trine Jupiter and Uranus in Aquarius in the ninth. Gemini has rule over the hands, and Joe's dynamite-laden fists were responsible for his sensational rise to the top of the boxing world."

Can't you picture sportswriters having a field day with all that?

With all these capabilities, Joe Louis was a ten-to-one favorite in the fight, but Sydney forecast that this would be the finish for Joe Louis because he was going to fight a second-rate fight.

"And he did," Sydney remembered. "I didn't predict that he would lose the fight, only that this was the finish of Joe Louis and that Wolcott would practically win the fight even though he might not get the decision. It happened as I had forecast. Wolcott knocked Joe Louis down—twice, I think it was—but Louis still got the decision. Everybody knew it was a second-rate fight, as I had said it would be. He even admitted it publicly. The headlines announced something like: JOE LOUIS ADMITS HE FOUGHT A SECOND-RATE FIGHT. Then *Horoscope* magazine published an article about me and how I had accurately forecast the outcome of the fight through astrology, and the syndicated columnists played it up and suddenly I had a lot of friends. I was the school celebrity."

He made no converts to astrology, though. People preferred to regard him as a "seer," a psychic, or a youngster unusually gifted with "second sight" about the stars as well as numbers.

He tried to explain that there was no mystery about it, that it was all based on the planets, the sun, and the moon—and the elementary principles of astrology. But no one listened to him—except Mike Kanter.

Actually he was then still in his infancy as an astrologer. He seldom had a fighter's correct hour of birth to go on, only his birth date, and hadn't yet been introduced to Carl Payne Tobey's concept of high and low lunar cycles. He would set up a solar chart based on the fighter's birth date and, lacking the hour of birth, his own complicated calculations of the degree of the ascendant, etc. The transiting planets for the day of the fight, which he learned from his ephemeris, were then placed in the zodiacal wheel. Although he took all the aspects into consideration, he interpreted the position of the transiting moon in the chart to be of paramount importance, as the moon relates to public contests.

"If the moon was going from the seventh house to the tenth," he explained, "then the fighter was in a strong position to win. If it was going from the first to the fourth, in the lower part of the chart, it seemed that he was not going to be utilizing the best of his abilities."

Later, as a professional astrologer, he subscribed to Tobey's concept of high and low lunar cycles, the high indicating a winner and the low a loser. But some of his boxing winners had been in low lunar cycles.

"The only way I can explain it as I look back," he said, "is that in public contests between boxers when the winner had a low lunar cycle, the moon was always in the seventh house of the public, which meant that he had the public favor.

"And as a youngster it seemed to mean that public acclaim was generally synonymous with a winner."

As a youngster, it would seem, Sydney's most remarkable feat—what with his magic tricks, boxing, "numberizing," and picking prize-fight winners—was that he ever got through school at all.

I asked his older sister, Leah Lederhandler, about this once when she was visiting Sydney in Santa Monica.

Her reply was, "He just had a marvelous mind. He never brought any books home from school, and he was always late—even when we lived across the street from his grammar school. But he was always reading. He bought books, all kinds of books, on those subjects that interested him. He taught himself everything from books.

"But he was playing the numbers when he was a child, practically a baby. How he figured it out I don't know. I remember those summers in Atlantic City when he first started doing it. We couldn't believe it, but then, I guess, we began taking it for granted. . . . He took up magic and began showing us his card and coin tricks in my father's grocery store. Then he started performing in different theaters and winning prizes. I remember, once, he brought home a chocolate cake.

"He had a very active mind and he liked sports, especially boxing. He became sort of a toughie with his boxing. He spent most of his time either boxing or doing magic tricks or playing the numbers and working on his astrology charts. He missed school a lot. Our mother was worried about him. She wanted him to be a lawyer or a doctor.

"Our family doctor would spend his time just talking to him, and he kept telling Mother, 'Don't worry, he's going to be all right.' I guess none of us understood him very well; he was always so quiet and strange until he came on with these magic tricks, and then he was like a different person," she said.

Leah remembered the consternation of her parents when her little brother, their only son, decided to change his name to Sydney Omarr "just so it would come out number twenty-two."

"But it must have been a lucky number," she said, "because right away he started to become better known, and when people came into the store to see Sydney Omarr they were always amazed that he was so young."

The Kimmelman family wasn't too impressed with all the "notoriety" their son was getting from his astrological predictions and writings. They still wanted to get him through school!

"My sister and I were in school and we didn't pay too much attention to him except like times on New Year's Eve," Leah recalled, "and then we would bring home all our friends so he could do his magic tricks for them. We liked to show him off because he was our little brother. Now we're very proud of him of course. We realize he's a famous astrologer even if we don't understand what he's talking about. But all our friends in Philadelphia," she added, "remember Sydney Omarr for his magic tricks."

P.S.: Sydney, the Voice of Astrology, and a typical Leo, had to get in the last word: "They don't have to understand it, but it so happens that more heavyweight champions have been born under Capricorn than any of the other zodiacal signs."

Chapter 8
JUPITER IN HIS FIFTH

"It was hopefully assumed that I would grow up to be something respectable. . . ."
—SYDNEY OMARR

I asked Sydney if he remembered when and where he first heard the word astrology. What I got was a dissertation.

"Certainly; I remember it clearly," he said. "How could I forget it? Actually, I must have heard the word during those summers on the boardwalk in Atlantic City but I wasn't old enough to know what it was so if I did hear it, the word itself left no impression on me.

"The first time I *remember* hearing it, in the sense that it made any impact, was when I was in grammar school in Philadelphia. I no longer remember the name of the teacher who mentioned the word. She was thin, pleasant enough, teaching science to youngsters—and her subject that day, so many years ago, was astronomy.

"My mind was wandering. It usually did. With the moon, Venus and Pluto in Cancer, in the ninth house of my horoscope, it was not always easy for me to remain down to earth. Ninth-house emphasis tends to make one live in the future; it makes for writers, publishers, poets—those who want to communicate, travel, express themselves. In the best sense, the ninth house provides vision. But the visions often are future ones, and the negative reaction is daydreaming. Sometimes those daydreams turn to realities.

"I suppose I was gazing out that school window while Miss What's-her-name continued to talk and explain. I remember she made some notes on the blackboard. Her writing was almost like printing. Years later, I was to learn from a book on graphology that people who 'write like printing' are interested in scientific subjects, often write about them or teach science classes. So Miss What's-her-name must have been suited for her profession, and probably had some ninth-house planets herself, with Virgo emphasis.

"She paid much attention to details and probably had some planets in the third sector of her chart too. I couldn't know at the time. She didn't think much of astrology. She said so. It was in the course of her discussion on astronomy that I heard—I think for the first time—the word astrology.

"Miss What's-her-name rushed over the word. Dismissed it. But I couldn't dismiss it from my mind. It was merely a *pseudo science*, she insisted. She did so without rancor, without knowledge, for she was a kindly woman. The classrooms were crowded. And there were many, like myself, who would rather have been out in the yard sparring or tossing a baseball around—many with planets in the ninth, restless, feeling the need for expression, recognition. Miss Science Teacher had said the word and gone on, discussing planets, the sun and moon, their distances from earth; their sizes and orbits. All part of the story of astronomy.

"She had probably forgotten she even mentioned that sidelight, that 'foolish sister' of astronomy: astrology. She had called it that: foolish. But my curiosity had been aroused. With Jupiter in the fifth house of my horoscope, my need for expression was to find unusual, perhaps foolish outlets. . . .

"I remembered Professor Seward, on the boardwalk, selling his horoscopes and talking about the signs of the zodiac. I had been fascinated by the mystical arts on the boardwalk: palmistry, numerology, mind-reading tricks. . . .

"But astrology was something else again. The word swam in my head. And the dedicated teacher was really innocent; she had no idea what she was starting when she said the word and quickly dismissed the subject.

"But I think I could perceive even then," Sydney said, "that astrology was to become a very familiar word to me. It was to change the direction of my life, to embark me on many trails—some happy and marked by reward, while others were full of ridicule, frustration, a desperate quest for knowledge, for more and more of it, until I was convinced the answer was up there, in the sky, in the heavenly patterns made by the planets as they journeyed around the sun. . . ."

"I am sure," he added, "that when I heard Miss What's-her-name in grade school ridicule astrology as a pseudo science and only a 'foolish sister' of astronomy, that only motivated me to learn more about it."

He undoubtedly also was motivated by the proper planetary positions, especially by having Jupiter in his fifth house, indicating a need for expression in unusual, "perhaps foolish" outlets, although of course at the time he was unaware of this. That wisdom was to come later, after he had embarked on his quest for knowledge about that "foolish sister" of astronomy.

All in all, in retrospect Sydney feels it couldn't have happened any other way. It was right there written in the stars, with Jupiter in his fifth house, that he would be deeply involved in what those around him referred to as "boyhood foolishness."

Motivated by both Miss What's-her-name and Jupiter, by the time Sydney finally reached his senior year in high school he had indeed acquired a rather impressive portfolio of knowledge about astrology—at least enough to impress one of his more avant-garde teachers, Dr. Alvin Bickel.

Dr. Bickel taught biology in the tenth and twelfth grades, and Sydney was one of his students.

The teacher happened to be a maverick within the educational framework of the day. He did not always adhere rigidly to the textbook of instructions on how his courses should be taught. Instead, he believed in encouraging his pupils to try their wings in other directions, and periodically he permitted them to do special reports on subjects of their own choice in the world of physical sciences.

Sydney's choice naturally was astrology, and his classmates, as well as Dr. Bickel, always looked forward to his special reports and listened to them spellbound even if they didn't know what he was talking about. By now he was the school celebrity for his boxing predictions and his magic acts, and this, of course, had elevated his peer status, if not his grades.

He was in the middle of his lecture on astrology one day when another teacher walked in, stopped dead in his tracks, and then, as Sydney recalls it, "All hell broke loose. The class was completely disrupted."

He recognized the man as the school's head physics instructor. He interrupted Sydney's lecture, shouting to Dr. Bickel, "This is disgraceful! What do you mean—permitting a student to discuss astrology in a biology class? It must be stopped immediately!"

Dr. Bickel wasn't about to be intimidated. Neither was Sydney. "I don't remember exactly all the words that were exchanged, but there was a rather noisy fracas," he recalled.

Some students began booing the physics teacher, others cheering Sydney and the biology teacher. The physics instructor, seeing that he was outnumbered, indignantly turned on his heel and walked out in a huff.

Order was restored in the classroom, and Sydney continued with his special report on astrology.

"I remember the whole thing vividly," Sydney said, "as clear as though it happened only yesterday."

And so does Dr. Bickel, who is still teaching—now physics instead of biology—in Philadelphia. When I contacted him, he not only confirmed the episode but he considerably upgraded Sydney's evaluation of himself as an inferior student.

"The lad was extremely sharp," he said. "To my way of thinking he had a very fine concept of his own study of astrology. He had read more widely than most of us and had a historical knowledge of astrology that I felt had some value and merit—certainly more than the rest of us had to offer on the subject, including the physics teacher.

"I clearly remember the day the gentleman came in and how upset he was to hear one of my students discussing the background of astrological charts and the way planetary movements could influence your life. It was offbeat, I know. But, then, there are still people who claim that I am quite offbeat—and bigoted. To me, education has never been exactly that which is in the prescribed folder which says this is the way we are to teach. Astrology then was very much in disrepute. And yet here was a student who had read more widely than most of us, who had a vast knowledge of a field we knew little about. When that gentleman came in and found this lad talking about astrology—well, he thought that capped the climax.

"Yes, indeed. I remember it very well. It happened in Room 226 in the West Philadelphia high school. The gentleman's name was Elwood Huff. He is now deceased."

"I have followed Sydney Omarr's career with tremendous interest," Dr. Bickel added. "So far as I was concerned, he was a good student and a real pleasure in my class. His real friends always had faith in him."

For the most part, though, astrology remained a forbidden word and a brand of "boyhood foolishness" that Sydney came to accept with equanimity. He recalls one incident that had a great effect on his family. His father had decided to invest in a new business, a big, fancy luncheonette in downtown Philadelphia.

"He had already made up his mind to do it," Sydney recalled. "Then he asked me whether he should go ahead with the transaction. I suppose this was only for his own amusement, trying to test his bright-boy son of fifteen. I'm sure he couldn't have been serious in wanting my advice. But I decided to give it to him anyway.

"I did what is called a horary chart for him—on whether he should invest. This is a chart set up for the 'birth' of a question. That is, the ascendant and houses and planetary positions are based on the time when the question is asked and then inserted into the person's birth planets in those houses. It is a fascinating branch of astrology, and I have had some remarkable results with it.

"My brand of horary astrology wasn't quite so sophisticated at the time. In fact, the horary chart I did for my father was the first one I ever did," he said.

"But it gave me a 100 per cent correct answer. It turned out that my father's planets were in a terrible position, indicating the most negative aspects for a financial investment of any kind at that time. I told him this. He merely smiled indulgently and went ahead with his own plans. The luncheonette went out of business in six months. He nearly lost everything he had."

Sydney would like to believe that his family's respect for his astrological skills went up after this, but he isn't sure.

"I think they accepted my talent as kind of unusual, but incomprehensible and not necessarily one to be encouraged. In a middle-class family such as ours, and with only one son, it was undoubtedly and hopefully assumed in the beginning that I would grow up to be something respectable," he said. "Like a doctor or lawyer." As his sister Leah also had told me.

Sydney remembers with deep gratitude the family doctor his sister had mentioned. "He became my great ally, and he succeeded to some extent in allaying my family's fears for my future. His name was Dr. Bloomfield. My family revered him, and to this day I feel deeply grateful for the encouragement he gave me and the gentle words of wisdom he gave my parents, especially my mother.

"When we went to his office, we sometimes had to wait a couple of hours for our appointment, but I didn't mind the wait. In retrospect it wouldn't surprise me if the doctor didn't plan this deliberately, because during the wait I always put on a show of various magic tricks and psychic demonstrations, much to the delight of the other waiting patients—but to the embarrassment of my poor mother. She was even more mortified when I upset the appointment schedule even further by putting on special demonstrations for the doctor and his nurse.

"But they always seemed to enjoy it. For a long time," he said, "I was puzzled about why we should have to pay the doctor instead of him paying me for my entertainment.

"I realize now that our family doctor was a man of astuteness and understanding. He not only encouraged me to develop my talents, such as they were then, but he also told my mother that this was something not to be feared or looked down on. He explained to her that when I grew older and decided on a career, whatever career it might be, these talents would be a definite asset. He talked to her about my skills, my enthusiasm, my personality; it was all very flattering," Sydney recalls. "But, more important, I know that it helped my mother to have a different outlook on something she had once considered merely boyhood foolishness."

On one occasion after Sydney had finished, a "psychic reading" the good doctor patted him on the head in amusement and gave him a most complimentary—and prophetic—warning.

"My boy," he said, "you are going to grow up to be a very attractive young man. You must be very careful when you give these readings to women. Always be sure there is another person present —for your own protection."

Sydney wasn't sure what he meant at the time, but he would find out soon enough.

No one has ever accused Sydney Omarr of being woman-shy. He adores women and the feeling is mutual. His personal as well as his professional life has been abundantly enhanced by female charms. He attracts women like a magnet. Much of this, as you might know, is because he's a Leo, the sign of strong, virile, magnetic, irresistible-and-all-those-other-adjectives sexual prowess. Also, Jupiter in his fifth house clearly indicates a great deal of experience with and attention from members of the opposite sex. Sydney is not about to shoo away all the ladies who swarm around him like honeybees.

"But it does sadden me a little to know they're interested mainly because I'm an astrologer. It certainly does my ego no good," he said, "to know it really wouldn't be the same if I had grown up to be just plain Sidney Kimmelman, a Philadelphia streetcar conductor."

Chapter 9
ARMY ASTROLOGER

"Instead of dropping bombs, we should have dropped astrological propaganda leaflets. . . ."

—SYDNEY OMARR

Sydney's number twenty-two didn't let him down. He managed to march up to the stage with his own graduating class to receive his high school diploma. His parents must have breathed a sigh of relief. It could even be said that he came through with flying colors if anyone wanted to count all those scarves and billiard balls that had flown out of his magician's sleeves and the multicolored bruises he had won in his boxing bouts.

The war was on (World War II), and he enlisted in the Army and went on active duty in August 1944, soon after he had passed his eighteenth birthday. He was assigned to the Air Force and became the only American soldier ever to be given full-time duty as an astrologer.

The way he got there was, as Sydney says—and to anyone knowing the obdurate ways of the Army—nothing short of miraculous.

"It is simply taken for granted that in the Army no one is ever assigned to a job he knows anything about. I just enlisted and they put me in the Air Force. I didn't really care where they put me," Sydney said. "But I was continuing to write my astrology articles, and I had become so accustomed to the typewriter that I couldn't write by hand any more. My handwriting was so bad that you couldn't read it.

"So one day I walked into the non-commissioned officers' quarters and asked if I could borrow a typewriter. This guy asked me what for, then gave me a strange look, and took me into headquarters to wait while he looked over my civilian record. I was amused at his reaction to my background in astrology. I could tell he was a complete skeptic. But he said, 'If you picked twenty-four out of twenty-six fights—not that there's anything to astrology—you must know something about boxing.' So he assigned me to the camp paper as a boxing writer. It was a tremendous break for me. I loved it. But I did think it was rather hilarious how it happened. If I had asked for it, I wouldn't have been given the assignment. I only got it because I asked to borrow a typewriter to write a piece about astrology and because of this guy's skepticism. He was a sergeant and sports editor of the paper. He knew nothing about astrology and didn't believe in it, would have no part of it. Yet he assigned me to special duty writing a boxing column because of my record of picking the winners in twenty-four out of twenty-six fights back in Philadelphia."

This happened during his basic training at Sheppard Field in Wichita Falls, Texas, and of course Sydney used his column to further the cause of astrology by continuing to predict the winners in fights.

He was soon transferred to the Ontario Air Force Base in California as a sportswriter for the Ontario *Wings*, and here he broadened his own base to include astrological predictions in other areas besides sports.

Among these was his pronouncement that the war would be over in mid-August of 1945, which is exactly when it ended, of course. His forecast, made some three months before V-J Day, brought him further national recognition.

Meanwhile he was continuing to write for astrology magazines, and, as might be expected, he had worked up a magic show for the GIs. By now, too, he had added a little hypnosis to his other esoteric skills—until it backfired on him.

"We were sitting around the PX having some beers, and as usual some joker started an argument. He didn't believe in astrology or hypnosis, any of those things. I was always being challenged to *prove* it, so I put this guy in a state of semihypnosis and made him think another GI had slugged him. Well, naturally he hit the other guy back and it turned into a big free-for-all."

Sydney wound up confined to quarters and assigned to mop up the PX.

But his lucky twenty-two was with him even there. It so happened that Rosemary De Camp, a beautiful movie starlet, was visiting the base at the time. She was interested in astrology, had heard about Sydney Omarr, and asked to see him.

She was taken into the PX while he was mopping the floor, and asked to speak with Private Omarr alone—just the two of them.

"All we talked about was astrology," said Sydney, "but my stock really went up. It isn't every soldier who gets to talk to a movie star while he's mopping up the PX."

Again he became an instant celebrity. It was not long after this that the commanding officer's wife asked him to give some readings for an Air Force charity. He was more than happy to oblige. His astrology, numerology, and palmistry readings raised a substantial amount of funds for the charity, as well as prestige for Sydney, who by now had become Sergeant Omarr. The Ontario *Wings* gave him a big spread of publicity, and the Army gave him a transfer to Okinawa, with his reputation as an astrologer preceding him, where he was assigned by the Armed Forces Radio Service to conduct an astrology program—the first of its kind.

His program, called "Sydney Omarr's Almanac," aired once a week. Soldiers, civilian personnel, and officers were invited to write to him with their problems. He would analyze their charts and give them advice based on astrology and numerology. The show received more mail than any other program.

Thus he became the first and only serviceman assigned to full-time duty as an astrologer.

He also did special tours with his magic show for GIs (eliminating the hypnosis bit), but his primary responsibility was his astrological radio broadcast—and private readings and consultations for high-ranking officers and their wives.

He was surprised at the number of high-ranking officers who would confide in him their most intimate problems.

A top colonel on Okinawa came to him one day in distress and asked for a reading. "I knew things were bad for him. I couldn't tell him everything, but I tried to give him some hope," Sydney said. "He would just sit there nodding his head. The next day, he committed suicide. I guess I wasn't very successful with that one. It made me realize the heavy responsibility I had on my shoulders and how I was getting into this thing deeper and deeper."

He was getting into it so deeply, in fact, that on one occasion he barely missed landing himself in serious trouble that could have put an end to his career. The incident occurred during one of those inevitable arguments over astrology.

"I remember we were all sitting around the tent one Sunday afternoon and this one guy began ridiculing astrology. So," Sydney said, "I just took out my gun and shot at him. Luckily, I just missed his head. I was kidding, of course, but the gun went off. Not a word was ever said about it later. I was lucky. The guys realized I had blanked out or something.

"But it really frightened me to realize that I could become so deeply involved subconsciously that I would do something like that. It taught me a good lesson. There have been many times since then, when I was engaged in debates with people over astrology, that I might have become angry and impulsive. But I always checked myself. I learned to use restraint. I have learned that this is a better weapon than a gun anytime."

Some thirty years later, Sydney was expressing himself rather vehemently on the use of war weapons in Vietnam. He had his own idea of how the war might be won—by using astrology instead of bullets and napalm.

"We should do what the British did during the Second World War, when they used an astrologer to anticipate the advice Hitler was getting from his astrologers. Since all East Asian countries are very much concerned with astrology," he said, "I think our intelligence people should have brought me and a number of other legitimate astrologers together. And instead of dropping bombs, we should have dropped astrological propaganda leaflets, since that would have had a tremendous psychological effect on the Vietnamese.

"We've been remiss in not doing this, and that's where academic prejudice against astrology has been so dangerous.

"We should have been using astrology in Vietnam, not to kill but to save the lives of Asians and Americans."

He is convinced that the war in Vietnam could have been ended sooner if America had dropped astrology bulletins instead of bombs. And who knows? He may have a point.

When he finished his stint in the Army, Sydney went back home to Philadelphia, a sergeant whose last official duty was *astrology!*

He was proud of that. He was twenty-one, and with that lucky twenty-two he already had "tied onto that tail of fate," so to speak, which he had envisioned when he changed his name.

By now he was in such demand as a writer for astrological journals that he had to adopt other pen names. He soon had his own astrological newsletter, called *Astrology News—The Trade Journal of Astrology*, and as editor and publisher he resumed his mail-order business with a quarter-page ad in each issue:

> HAVE YOU A PROBLEM?
> LET SYDNEY OMARR HELP YOU SOLVE IT!
>
> Omarr combines astrology, numerology and a psychological technique which reveals your character and the trend of your future. State your problem clearly, include your name and complete birth date. Your question will be answered personally by OMARR, whose articles and public forecasts have made him one of the nation's outstanding astrologers. $5.00.
>
> FREE: Booklet describing other Omarr services sent upon request. SYDNEY OMARR. . . . . Box 6391, Philadelphia 39, Penna.

Sydney wrote the ad himself, of course, and adorned it with signs of the zodiac as well as a most charming photograph of Sydney Omarr.

Chapter 10
THOUGHT DIAL

"If the Thought Dial *is unorthodox, then, to hell with orthodoxy. . . ."*

—CARL PAYNE TOBEY

I am not even going to try to explain Sydney's Thought Dial and how it works. That's *your* problem. But it works.

So far as I am concerned, it is totally irrational, but, then, a good many things in life are irrational.

All I know is that when Sydney says, "Give me three numbers—quick," and you give him three numbers—any numbers that pop into your head—he comes up with instant analysis. It apparently is a more sophisticated form of his early "numberizing."

Sydney says it's just a method of tapping your subconscious through numbers, something like "tuning in" to another world. He likes to remind you that Thomas Edison, before his death, was hard at work on a so-called "Telephone Between Worlds"—so he is in good company. "Wise men like Edison and Carl Jung have not been afraid to experiment with the abstract."

The Thought Dial is typically Omarr-unorthodox.

But as his good friend Carl Payne Tobey, the mathematician-numerologist-astrologer, says, "If the Thought Dial is unorthodox, then to hell with orthodoxy. We have been taught enough claptrap by orthodoxy. You can never be an intellectual until you toss orthodoxy and all of its superstitions out the window.

"Much that has been taught as science is pure superstition. A large part of astronomy is mere superstition. A large part of what has been taught as religion is superstition. We will meet the true science and the true religion as one and the same thing in the abstract, mathematical world. The Thought Dial deals with numbers. Frankly, I do not know whether it has anything to do with numbers and their actual characteristics as studied in [Fermat's] number theory or whether the numbers actually apply only as a part of some code between the conscious and the unconscious. I do know that numbers have characteristics and that no two numbers have exactly the same characteristics. Anyone who understands number theory knows that. Numbers are all a part of that great cosmic and abstract design, and everything that ever happens in the universe happens only in accord with the abstract design.

"Perhaps the Thought Dial is a means of contacting the abstract."

Whatever the Thought Dial contacts, it can be used for many practical purposes, I am told. Mr. Tobey once used it to find a friend's lost kitten in a linen closet, and on another occasion in locating some lost papers in Chicago.

It once was used to locate two bombs on a Mexico-bound luxury ship, the *Island Princess*. The ship was two hundred miles south of San Diego, California, when a tip was received that bombs were on board.

The cruise consultant, Jeraldine Saunders, was heading an astrology cruise from Los Angeles to Mexico when she became a heroine, according to a report in *The National Tattler* of July 29, 1973. The tip that a bomb was aboard came to Miss Saunders; Jim Brooks, cruise director; and Dean Kadera, sports director.

Miss Saunders, whose regular job was cruise consultant, was aboard the newest and most posh ship afloat (owned by Princess Cruises) this trip to lecture on astrology, numerology, and palmistry.

While trying to locate the bomb, cruise director Brooks suddenly remembered Sydney Omarr's book *Thought Dial*, which Miss Saunders had lectured on that morning.

"The book, which explains that the subconscious knows all the answers and tells the reader how to find them, shows how to make use of number symbols," the *Tattler* related.

Armed with three numbers from Brooks, Jeraldine looked into her Thought Dial and discovered the direction (northeast), but not the deck, where the bombs would be found.

Just as the book said, they were located.

While passengers danced, one bomb was found at 8:15 P.M., the second one at 8:57, and the news was dramatically announced by Brooks over the microphone to the 856 persons aboard.

Jeraldine, the astrologer, added, "Of course, I knew we were all safe, because I had chosen this particular cruise for my astrology cruise because the stars were in favorable aspects. I had checked my ephemeris long before I planned the cruise."

What the newspaper account neglected to mention was that Jeraldine had once been Sydney Omarr's wife—for six weeks, more or less.

It should be explained here to avoid further confusion that *Thought Dial* is a book (Wilshire Book Company, 1958 and New American Library, 1973), which comes complete with a separate "Thought Dial"—a cardboard telephone-type dial inserted in the book with instructions on how to use it. It has a movable arrow that can be pointed to numbers from zero to nine as well as to the two master numbers, eleven and twenty-two. Beside each number is the astrological sign for the planet associated with it. The Thought Dial (*Dial Your Thoughts!* Copyright 1959 by Sydney Omarr) looks like a fascinating parlor game—and probably is for a lot of people, though I am certain that Sydney and Mr. Tobey would shudder at the very thought of this.

The way Tobey explains it, "When you want to know the correct time, you can dial a number on your telephone and get the right answer, all automatically. In a way, the Thought Dial operates in somewhat the same manner.

"You may have a question on your mind. It may be a very serious question. Probably the more serious the better. You dial a number and zip comes the answer. To say the least, it is remarkable. It is almost as if you were telephoning some master of wisdom within yourself. He sees all and tells all. It would seem that Omarr has devised a means of bypassing the conscious and getting into the unconscious. I won't say the subconscious (as Sydney does), because I think it may involve the superconscious. I think the superconscious mind contains a super calculating device that makes all electronic calculators look like simplicity itself. Omarr appears to bypass the conscious in the same or a similar manner to that in which the conscious is bypassed in hypnotism. The function may not be too unlike the individual who prays for divine guidance and gets it. There are many people who do not believe this can be accomplished, never try it, and never get divine guidance. Perhaps the Thought Dial is a means of getting divine guidance. . . ."

Sydney is a man of flexibility and tolerance in matters pertaining to religion, but the concept of his Thought Dial was conceived without any thought of dialing a "divine guidance." It was strictly a matter of expediency for him when he got jammed up one time on his astrological readings.

He had been out of the Army only a few months when he was approached by two salesmen, one for the Doubleday publishing company, the other for a greeting-card company, who had read some of his work in *Horoscope* magazine and asked him to do a booklet on astrology. He did. He titled it *I've Got You by the Numbers*. It went over so well that the salesman persuaded him to go to Cleveland for a series of lectures on astrology in the May Company department store.

There was a promotional gimmick, of course. Those persons who bought a certain X number (in dollars and cents) of his book were to be given a private consultation by the great Sydney Omarr.

"I didn't know what I was getting into," he admits. "When I got there it turned out that everybody wanted private readings. I didn't have time to do their charts, with their birth dates and all the planets and so forth. There were too many people and I was too slow. I was there to sell books, and people were clamoring to buy books because what they really wanted was a private reading. I knew I couldn't keep up with them by using astrology. The numbers would be quicker. So I began asking each one of them just for three numbers, fast—and ultilizing my experience in numerology. Even so I had to work fast. I was surprised at my percentage of accuracy under such pressure. But I was able to come up with answers that usually seemed to be right.

"I remember there were people lined up all through the store waiting for a reading. I've never worked so hard or fast in all my life. I perspired so much that I had to change shirts three times a day, there were so many people. This went on for about six weeks, as I recall. But I guess it was worth it," he said. "I was told that we broke a five-year sales record in the book department of that store."

It was also worth it because those six weeks proved to him that his system of numerology, whatever it was that he was tuning into, really worked somehow—he didn't know how—with great masses of people.

"When I would ask for the three numbers, I would find, for example, that if they reduced to six the person was thinking of changing residence or was having a domestic adjustment. If the reduced total was one, it meant a new start; if nine, the finish of something; if seven, self-deception, and so on," he explained.

"Those six weeks really formed the basis of my numerology theorems, if you want to call it that. I had to test it right there on the firing line. This was different from having people write in with their problems and having all the time in the world to figure it out and mail back an analysis. Here were people who had just spent hard cash on books, and they were standing right there in front of me wanting answers.

"The numbers didn't let me down. I found that unfailingly they were a reflection of what an individual was secretly or subconsciously concerned with. I gave hundreds of readings in those six weeks, and then I went back home to Philadelphia, knowing that numbers held a far more symbolic meaning than I possibly could have realized when I was calling the shots right back there on the boardwalk or numberizing my way through school."

It would be several years yet before his *Thought Dial* would see the light of day in print. But it was his experience in Cleveland that really set him to thinking and trying to formulate some orderly pattern—or Omarr "number theorem"—that would have wide appeal. The more he thought about it, the more convinced he was that certain numbers must be associated with certain planets. This conviction was reinforced by his study of the writings of Carl Jung, for by now Sydney had become—and was to remain—an ardent disciple of Jung's.

He had discovered Jung's word "synchronicity," which Jung himself explains thus: ". . . simultaneous occurrence of a certain psychic state with one or more external events which appear as meaningful parallels to the momentary subjective state—and, in certain cases, vice versa."[1]

Jung also declared, "Since the remotest times, men have used numbers to express meaningful coincidences . . . those that can be interpreted." And he repeatedly emphasized that numbers are *not*, as is commonly supposed, invented by man but only discovered by

[1] *The Interpretation of Nature and the Psyche*, New York: Pantheon Books, 1955.

man; they are not inventions of the conscious mind but, rather, spontaneous productions of the unconscious; they were "pre-existent" to consciousness and a "predestined instrument for creating order, or for apprehending an already existing but still unknown regular arrangement"; they are perhaps the most primitive element of order in the human mind, an "archetype of order which has become conscious."

Jung's studies conclude that both numbers *and planets* (italics mine) can be used as a method of analyzing character, perceiving thoughts, and foretelling the future.

As soon as Sydney had properly digested all of this, he began matching numbers with planets, and this is what his Thought Dial is all about.

Basically he combined his knowledge of astrology and how zodiacal symbols are associated with various aspects of character, thought, and events, with the answers he was coming up with from his experimentation in numerology. The result is a compendium of number and planet symbols with typical Omarr embellishments. Briefly, here is Omarr's Number Theorem, or What the Numbers Symbolize:

Number ONE: This is the start, the beginning: it is birth and life, independence of both thought and action. It is a time for the new, for the launching of projects. This digit is associated with the sun.

Number TWO: This is a force that is emotional and negative rather than direct and positive. It is symbolic of diplomacy. It is a time for winning ways, for tact. This is a caution mark: wait and see. The number is associated with the moon.

Number THREE: This number represents a relief of pressure. It is symbolic of humor and versatility. It is a time for getting out of a rut. However, a scattering of forces must be avoided. The temptation is to try doing too much at one time. The number is associated with Jupiter.

Number FOUR: This is the square. It is routine and hard work and the handling of details. There is strength here but only if creative thought or imagination is brought into play. This is a time to slow down. The number is associated with Uranus.

Number FIVE: Change and travel, the creative arts, relations with members of the opposite sex, speculation—these are stressed. Communication of ideas becomes a necessity. Personal magnetism is heightened. The digit is associated with the planet Mercury.

Number SIX: Emphasis is on the home, change of residence, the rediscovering of loved ones. Diplomacy is a requirement here, just as with the number two, only in a larger sense. Stress definitely is on the home. The digit is associated with Venus.

Number SEVEN: The key word is self-deception: the tendency is to see persons and situations as they might ideally be instead of the way they actually exist. Not a time to enter into legal pacts. An aura of illusion dominates. The number is associated with the planet Neptune.

Number EIGHT: Power, strength, finances, reproduction, marriage, stress on business affairs—these represent the symbols of this number. It is a time for pushing ahead—hard. No time for a slowdown here. The number is associated with Saturn.

Number NINE: This is completion, the end of a cycle: a time to finish projects. Avoid new starts, be wary of new contacts at this period. Often indicates the bearing of another's responsibility. Universal appeal, wide publicity also shown. The number is associated with Mars.

Number ELEVEN: A higher octave of two. A master digit. Stress is on intuition, teaching. Hunches are to be trusted here. The influence is far-reaching; it is a time for expressing ideas, no matter how radical. The number is associated with Uranus.

Number TWENTY-TWO: A higher octave of four. A master digit. Emphasis is on building, creating, making master plans. Must not be bogged down with detail or influenced by persons with no vision. The number is associated with the planet Pluto.

As for the embellishments, one example will suffice: Number twenty-two. It may be significant to note that Sydney arrived at this interpretation for his Thought Dial several years after he had changed his name to match the number. In his words: "Number twenty-two is a symbol of success, a master symbol in that it is the

CREATIVE BUILDER. . . . The routine details must be left to others; the subject cannot afford to be bogged down with matters of minor importance. The message here is simple: Have vision, exercise intuitive intellect, don't try to do everything yourself. Number twenty-two is the master architect. . . . THIS IS THE TIME TO CARRY OUT IDEALS. . . . This is the time, shouts the subconscious, to turn dreams into realities. . . . The subject dialing this total must be the DREAMER OF PRACTICAL DREAMS. And that means he must MAKE his dreams COME TRUE. . . . The total of twenty-two as a subconscious symbol warns that movements, campaigns, plans, ideas, hopes, wishes must be on a GRAND SCALE. Anything small here seems doomed to failure. Even if the project is not a large one in a physical sense, it should be an IDEALISTIC one. . . . Ambition is keynoted. . . . Twenty-two longs for RECOGNITION. . . . There is power here; the goal is the highest, but it can be reached AND NO COMPROMISE SHOULD BE MADE. . . . Move upward and onward. . . ."

These words were just hot out of his typewriter when Carl Payne Tobey came into his life.

As Tobey tells it, "The first time I ever heard of Sydney Omarr was soon after he had started an astrology paper in Philadelphia (*The Astrology News*). In those days the most impossible thing in the world was an astrology trade paper. Sydney ran a story in his paper pointing out that the astronomical map on the cover of *American Astrology* did not conform to the astronomical map in *Astrological Guide*. The editors of both magazines were really mad. They got together and both of them lambasted the hell out of Sydney Omarr in their magazine editorials. I was intrigued. I wrote Sydney a letter and sent him a check for a subscription to his paper. I asked about him, found out he was practically a kid, in his early twenties [twenty-one], and I admired his spunk. I wanted to help him out, so I wrote him a letter of encouragement.

"Then, one day, he came in to my office in New York–I was writing a syndicated astrology column then–and I was amazed at how young he seemed, just a boy. I said to him, 'I'm not very alert today, so I guess this is as good a time as any to talk to you, because I've got something on my mind that's bothering me.' He said, 'Quick, give me three numbers.' So I gave him three numbers.

"He said, 'Now, you think this is the beginning of a new venture. It isn't. It's the end. This person you have in mind for your future—well, there isn't any future. You're already at the end of the relationship. It's all over.'

"Well, this sounded ridiculous to me because I was about to start in business with a woman—an astrologer who wanted to start a new astrology magazine if she could get a fifteen-thousand-dollar loan. I had talked to a friend of mine who had plenty of money and had agreed to give her a loan of fifteen thousand dollars. I was worried about the magazine and concerned about whether the girl could make a go of it—and this was precisely the moment when young Sydney Omarr walked into my office."

P.S. After Tobey got her the fifteen-thousand-dollar loan, she absconded. He never heard from her again.

"She was an Aries," he said, "and she wanted sole authority over everything. Anyway, what Sydney said turned out to be absolutely right: it wasn't the beginning of a new relationship, it was the end. [Tobey's three numbers must have been reduced to NINE, right? See, we're learning!] That prediction interested me, and I became more fascinated with Sydney Omarr. He told me about this idea he had for *Thought Dial*, how he would like to have it published so people could use it, and I felt that I wanted to help him. But then I moved to Arizona and he moved to California. . . ."

And eventually Sydney wound up publishing it himself (1958), with Tobey writing the introduction.

Besides their mutual interest in astrology, there was another reason that Carl Payne Tobey took an interest in young Sydney Omarr.

"I saw all the old-timers trying to bat this guy down because he was a kid," he said. "It took them a long time to get where they were and they resented a young person of that age coming into the limelight overnight. Well, that irritated me. And I thought about it from another point of view. I realized that there was only one month's difference between the birth date of Sydney and my daughter. They were the same age. I listened to this kid talk very intently, because I thought to myself, suppose this was my son going to a stranger, struggling to get ahead, and how would I want a stranger to treat him? I decided that was how I was going to treat Sydney Omarr.

"I tried to help him, and I sure never have regretted it. He never let me down. And I think, if anything, maybe I gained more out of the relationship than he did."

Sydney, of course, would be the first to deny this. He became as much a disciple of Carl Payne Tobey's as Carl Jung's. Almost. Tobey, now president of the Institute of Abstract Science, with headquarters in Tucson, Arizona, is blunt and outspoken in his beliefs, which, like Jung's, have had a strong influence on Sydney's philosophical approach to his chosen field.

"The greatest truths are abstract truths," he declares. "When we point to an object and say it is a tree, this does not involve any kind of truth. It has merely to do with man's idiotic habit of classifying everything into groups. The great abstract truths are mathematical truths, theorems, etc. . . . The only true science is mathematics. It is pure abstraction. Other, so-called sciences are largely hoaxes, for they are merely a matter of classifying things according to some predetermined arrangement. . . .

"I am convinced that actually *all knowledge* of any subject is within your own mind at all times, because it is there in the *abstract*. The problem is to bring it forth. There is an abstract world. You have contact with that world if you wish to exercise it. In the abstract world there is no time and no space. You can only have time when there is change. Nothing ever changes in the abstract world. Any mathematical theorem is the same today as it was in the time of Euclid, and Pythagoras in 500 B.C. The great mathematicians, who have been the greatest of all scientists, have been men who were able to contact the abstract world. . . . Even astrology is actually a study of the abstract and therefore is a form of mathematics.

"Our educators do not teach us to see into the abstract world. They merely teach us to memorize what others have recorded from that world or to know where to look it up in a book of formulas.

"The laws that govern the universe are abstract laws. . . . No astronomer can explain why all free bodies in space travel in ellipses rather than in circles. They just do. They obey a mathematical law. . . ."

This is essentially the same thought Jung expresses in such terms as "synchronicity," "meaningful coincidences," the "archetype of order" in the human mind and in the universe that comes from the abstract world of numbers.

The sooner we understand—if we can—that Sydney's philosophy

is a crystallized quintessence of Tobey and Jung, the sooner we will understand why he has often been called an astrologer *extraordinaire.*

Not that it is necessary to understand numbers and synchronicity and *how* or *why* they work. "They just do," as he has repeatedly emphasized. "It isn't important to *understand* these abstract truths or why they happen, but it is important to accept the fact that they do happen, and then we can progress from there.

"As Pythagoras said, 'Nature geometrizes!' We don't know why or how. The element of mystery has always been a common characteristic of numbers and planets and synchronicity."

There is a strong element of mystery in Sydney's own astrological interpretations which still baffles even his friend Tobey—himself an acknowledged expert in both astrology and numerology and also a student of Jung.

"To understand Sydney Omarr you have to read Carl Jung," he said. "He's really hooked on Jung's synchronicity. He's been a great student of Jung's over the years. Do you know that, out of eighteen volumes of Jung's collection, there are only five that don't have the word astrology in the index?

"But Sydney's brand of astrology is entirely different from mine. It's all mixed up with this Jungian background, and with the psychic and numerology. I know he is psychic as hell, though he won't admit it. He has his own particular way of making judgments, and it is very mysterious. His astrological interpretations aren't based on pure and simple astrology. They're a mixture of astute psychology, Jungian philosophy, his own number theorems, and a sixth sense—the psychic and all these mystical things. But the results are often phenomenal. So who can criticize that, even if it isn't pure astrology? After all, I certainly wouldn't consider myself or most astrologers as mystics, but I would say that Sydney Omarr is more than an astrologer; he's a mystic."

"And," he added, "he certainly is a personality that nobody forgets."

As for Sydney's Thought Dial, Tobey said he had used it several times and it worked for him "maybe four out of six times."

The book became a best seller and almost got Sydney in serious trouble with postal authorities. But that was to come later.

Personally, I am inclined to agree with Carl Payne Tobey, Henry Miller, and others who have called Sydney "psychic," or possessed of a sixth or seventh sense. He doesn't like the psychic label, cringes at the thought of being identified as a "psychic," which he considers far inferior to his status as a serious student of the scientific art of astrology. He will modestly concede that perhaps he developed a keener perception of human nature at a very early age through his practice of magic, "numberizing," and astrological consultations.

He has continued honing his "intuitive intellect," as he prefers to call it, until it is often mistaken for a psychic talent.

At least he seems to have something going for him besides his lucky twenty-two. I saw it manifested on many occasions throughout the preparation of this book.

Usually at the end of our tape-recording sessions, when I was about to leave, he would say good-by and then, "Quick, give me three numbers."

Any numbers I gave him nearly always reduced to nine. By now I was thoroughly familiar with what the numbers symbolized—at least the basics as laid out in his *Thought Dial.* Number nine: completion, end of a cycle, time to finish projects. Planet—Mars. I had it memorized, and so far as I was concerned it just meant the session was over, finished, end of two-hour cycle, time to go home.

But Sydney always came up with his mysterious and intriguing embellishments.

Once, he warned me and number nine, "You'd better be especially careful driving home this evening."

"Why?"

"Because Mars is on your moon. . . ." And something else was trine or sextile with Saturn or Scorpio, and my house of travel was badly aspected, and so on. I didn't get it all because my tape recorder was already unplugged and put away and I was ready to walk out the door. But I stood there quite stunned as I listened to his parrotlike recital of the planetary positions, houses, and numbers, all of which added up to an uncannily accurate description of my driving ability—or lack of it.

As any of my best friends (and a few traffic cops) will tell you, I do not function too well behind the wheel of a motor vehicle. I am what is known as a "nervous driver." Sydney has never set foot inside my car (neither does anyone else if he can help it), and we had never discussed the subject. It was, as he would call it, "mundane" trivia and significant for only one reason: He had no way of knowing this about me, but he knew.

On another occasion as I was leaving I remarked, "I have an important appointment. I don't want to be late."

"Quick, give me three numbers," he insisted.

"Two, three, four. Make it fast," I said.

"That's nine. You're going to see someone whose initials begin with an I or an R. This person is very independent, rather dominating. You will have to use flattery, diplomacy. The initials I or R—that could be a name like Ida or Rita. If you ask her birth date, I think you'll find she's Aquarius."

My appointment was with actress Ida Lupino. Her sister's name is Rita. When I asked Ida her birth date, she replied, "I'm Aquarius—February 4."

When I asked Sydney how he knew, he had his usual facile reply: "It's simply utilizing the Jungian principle of arriving at abstract truths through numbers and planets. And maybe a little intuitive intellect," he added.

I once asked him, "Why is it that my three numbers always reduce to nine? Is that number stuck in my subconscious?"

"It must be," he said, "but I'm not an expert in the Rorschach inkblot tests. I can't tell you *why* it's stuck there.

"Number nine is a very strange number. I guess mathematicians could explain it. But it seems that anything added to nine equals what is added to it, and if you multiply nine by anything it equals nine. When you add it, it loses all of its strength, and when you multiply it, it gains universal strength.

"Of course, you know that the zodiac is 360 degrees, which equals nine (three plus six)," he reminded me. "And love equals nine, the circle. That's L-3, O-6, V-4, E-5. It equals eighteen, and that equals nine. Anything that is complete is a nine; anything is incomplete without nine."

He peered at me solemnly and added, "Don't ask me why. I don't understand why."

Neither do I. We'll just have to take Sydney's word for it.

Astrologer to the Stars

Chapter 11
LEO IN LOTUSLAND

> *"Leo is by far the sexiest sign, followed by Scorpio. . . ."*
> —LINDA LOVELACE

Sydney's lucky twenty-two finally landed him in Hollywood, the fabled Lotusland of the film stars, and he became an instant celebrity.

But it would be remiss not to mention that somewhere along the way, and for some inexplicable reason, he acquired the strange notion that he would like to go back to school and continue the formal education that had held little, if any, fascination for him as a boy.

This was all the more peculiar, as he knew there was no school that offered courses in astrology.

"But I could go to college under the GI Bill, so I decided to take advantage of it," he said. And he decided to go into journalism. "After all, I had been writing most of my life: my astrology and numerology articles for magazines and my boxing column while I was in the Army. It seemed natural to go into journalism so I could combine it with astrology later."

That was his "intuitive intellect" at work. He enrolled first at Temple University in Philadelphia, later transferred to Mexico City College for courses in advanced journalism—and promptly became a protégé of the internationally famous hostess-entertainer Madame Bricktop.

"I had never heard of Madame Bricktop," he recalls with amusement, "but I sure learned fast."

He remembers vividly their first meeting. "I was in this place one night. It was called 'Madame Bricktop's.' I thought that was just the name of the nightclub. I saw this beautiful lady at the bar, about to go up on stage for her opening night. I didn't know who she was. I took her hand, looked at her palm, guessed her zodiacal sign, and gave her a quick reading. People were gathering around us. She had to go on with her act, but she told me to wait until she was finished, she wanted to see me. . . .

"Then she came back from her dressing room and we began talking. She told me about her big years in Paris, when people like Hemingway and Henry Miller—I didn't know him then—and the Duke and Duchess of Windsor and numerous other celebrities would come in to see her. She told me about one of the things she used to do to entertain them. She always kept a stack of astrology magazines in her dressing room. She would get a person's birth date, then run back to her dressing room and read up on it, and then come back and tell the person all about himself. She was fascinated with astrology and had never lost her interest in it. And so she was fascinated with what I was doing. . . ."

Sydney was living in students' quarters at the time. Madame Bricktop invited him to move into her luxurious apartment house to give readings there, as well as at her nightclub—for one hundred dollars per reading.

"She attracted people with a great deal of money," Sydney observed.

One of them was the colorful, controversial Mexican artist Diego Rivera, who inadvertently enhanced Sydney's reputation as a celebrity in Mexico by denouncing him in the press.

It came about in a curious manner. Rivera had been commissioned to do a painting for the Reforma Hotel in Mexico City, and when it was finished he signed it (in addition to his own name): "*Dios no existe*," which means God does not exist.

Since it is against the law in Mexico to deface or change any part of a work of art by someone as important as Rivera, his own embellishment stirred up quite a furor.

The painting was put in storage while a decision could be made as to what to do about it. "There was a tremendous controversy," Sydney recalls. "The big question was, would Diego Rivera remove that anti-God inscription or not? And if not, what was to be done with the painting? The Mexican press made a big thing of it and asked me as an astrologer to predict what was going to happen to the painting. I obtained Diego Rivera's birth date (December 8, 1886, Sagittarius) and did a chart on him, and I predicted that the painting eventually would be on display in a very unusual way, but that Diego Rivera would never erase those words."

As it turned out, that is exactly what happened. The painting was put on display, but the words "*Dios no existe*" were so cleverly concealed with something—Sydney doesn't know what—that no one could see them.

Of course the press played up the fact that Sydney Omarr had accurately forecast what would happen, thereby launching a public debate in the media. The painter denounced astrology in no uncertain terms. "I believe even less in astrology than I believe in *Dios*." And Sydney, with youthful brashness, responded, "This does not surprise me. It was to be expected, because his horoscope indicates traits of passion, stubbornness, and other characteristics that would cause him to do something of this sort."

It was a distinct plume in his well-feathered halo to have one of the world's most famous artists taking pot shots at him. It increased his status enormously, especially with his teachers of advanced journalism.

One of them, Rodney Voigt, promptly put Sydney's astrological skills to practical use in teaching his other journalism students how to be objective and open-minded. He would call on Sydney to give a talk and a demonstration on astrology, palmistry, and numerology. Then he would select one of the more boisterous skeptics to come to the front of the class for a reading by Sydney.

"Being young and somewhat lacking in compassion in those days, I was sometimes very blunt," he recalls. Sometimes the boisterous skeptics would blanch and their knees would buckle, as they listened in bug-eyed astonishment to what he told them.

Professor Voigt then would remind them that this was a good lesson for future journalists: They should not form an opinion on anything until they really looked into it.

It was this teacher of advanced journalism, Rodney Voigt, who was instrumental in getting Sydney his first job in Hollywood—as a CBS newscaster.

It didn't take long for the word to get around. Sydney Omarr was the new guru of the stars, astrologically speaking, a handsome young Lochinvar / father confessor who at one point early in his

Lotusland career was deftly dispatching fifty to sixty consultations a day.

"You'd be amazed," he said, "at the number of Hollywood people who pin their whole lives on astrology. Some of them won't even go to the bathroom without consulting an astrologer."

This may be a slight exaggeration, but not much.

Actor Robert Cummings, a Gemini, told me he consulted three astrologers and a numerologist before marrying his second wife, Gigi. "With my first wife all our signs were wrong—disaster.

"But I'm Gemini and Gigi is a moon child [July 4], and my moon is in Cancer and her rising sign is Gemini. I have Libra in mid-heaven and her moon is in Libra. So we have a perfect marriage." Astrologically speaking.

Tommy Smothers also times important events in his life by the stars. Before proposing to his future wife, Rochelle, he had their horoscopes compared so as to be sure of their happiness. They were later pronounced "man and wife" at exactly 11:58 P.M., the time according to the stars to be the most propitious for their marriage.

Sydney told Tommy Smothers that his TV show would be canceled—and he told Muhammad Ali that his draft-resistance fight would turn out all right.

Among his early clients were such star-conscious stars as Kim Novak, Jennifer Jones, Mae West, Gypsy Rose Lee, Arlene Dahl, Jayne Mansfield. . . . The list could go on and on, but, as Sydney says, an astrologer's role is like that of a psychiatrist. A client's file is confidential. The nature of a specific personal problem cannot be revealed (as, for example, a big-name movie star who was consulting him before her well-publicized attempt at suicide).

But there are some whose so-called "secrets" are an open book, others who have no aversion to being publicized as case histories—and those whose charts Sydney can read and analyze without having met them.

Of *Marilyn Monroe*, a Gemini, he says: "She had a tremendous need for self-expression. Her horoscope shows that she was far different from the 'dumb blonde' sex symbol that was her public image. She had the talent to be a fine and versatile actress, but she was locked into the sex-symbol image that she hated."

Paul Newman and Robert Redford: "Good friends in real life. . . . Their horoscopes showed that a combined effort would be very rewarding for both of them. The success and acclaim of *Butch Cassidy and the Sundance Kid* proved that, and so did *The Sting*. However, the movement of Robert Redford's planets and the timing of the making of the movie *The Great Gatsby* were in conflict. As a result, the movie did not have the acceptance and profit that was expected of it."

Telly Savalas: "The horoscope of Telly Savalas reveals that success, fame, and sex appeal are related to his head. After he shaved his head for a movie role, his career began to ascend. His 'Kojak' show became one of the most popular on television, and his personal popularity is astounding."

We wouldn't need an astrologer to know that!

Sydney soon gave up his extracurricular consultations for film stars to spend his time studying and writing about astrology and appearing on radio and TV shows—not to entertain audiences (though he usually does) but to inform them.

"I decided I didn't want to be known as just another astrologer," he said. "I wanted to devote my life, my time, to those things which would give astrology more credibility."

Certainly no one has contributed more in the pursuit of this credibility than Sydney.

Chapter 12

LATCHING ONTO THE STARS CELESTIAL AND CINEMATIC

"Sydney Omarr couldn't have known these things about me. . . ."

—BETTE DAVIS

♈

ARIES

(March 21–April 19)

Sydney had no problem latching onto the top stars and the top shows. He and Bette Davis, and Aries (April 5, 1908), once appeared together on a Johnny Carson show. As Sydney recalls it, "Aries-like, she practically took over the Carson program during the discussion of astrology. As it turned out, this brilliant actress was knowledgeable, so much so that she defended it and demonstrated its techniques. She made her points in a definite, sincere manner, and she was gracious enough to declare, over a nationwide hookup, that my analysis of her horoscope was amazingly accurate."

Before the show he had been provided with Miss Davis' birth data. From this he prepared the following notes, which he read on the show: "First thing—this woman's chart, combined with mine, reveals she could be physically attracted to me. I'm flattered.

"What Bette Davis needs is someone she can approve of, look up to. She pushes, tests, probes—like a princess seeking someone who will turn out to be Prince Charming. Fantasy, you see, is a very real part of her makeup. I would say to her: you want to approve, to respect, to find someone who is daring, has initiative, can lead. Your heart is open, but you want to be sure. So you test by appearing to be bossy. You test by appearing to be critical. And all the time you are hoping that the other person will put his foot down. You want a man in the real and best sense. But, according to your chart, you very often find men who, for their part, are looking for mothers.

"Miss Davis' chart shows she is interested in borderline subjects like astrology, is an actress to the marrow of her bones, and has only recently emerged from a cycle that could be described as challenging, depressing. She learned many lessons from this cycle, chief of which was not to brood about what might have been, about the past, but to look forward to the future and to new opportunities. She is impulsive, headstrong—a bright light, one might say, who attracts numerous moths, people who take advantage of her and who might be described as 'psychic vampires.' They draw from her, sap her energy, deplete her emotionally. This is fascinating. One does not like to condense such a chart in this manner. I'll conclude by stating that between 1942 and '44—probably 1943—she had one of the most trying mental-emotional periods of her life. She can be grateful that the dark era is finished."

The above was based on more than Miss Davis' sun sign, Sydney explained. He had access to her complete solar horoscope, month, date, and year. But much of the chart symbolized Aries, and Miss Davis was forthright "in an Aries manner" when she expressed frank amazement at what she termed the astounding accuracy of the reading, brief as it was.

"Sydney Omarr couldn't have known these things about me unless he knew my life story," she declared.

Syndey says, "I had not read the Bette Davis story then, and to this day I have not read it—except as I 'read' it in her available birth data."

Miss Davis' chart shows that Aries is independent but seeks warmth, is domineering but seeks one who can dominate, and, Sydney adds for all others who are Aries: "You, who are born under this zodiacal sign, surprise and contradict. You do so, to a great extent, because you want to test us by catching us off guard. You want to bare us, to rip off our emotional armor. You want to see us stripped of pretense. To do so, you often surprise and, at times, infuriate us."

"If born under this sign, your solar ruling planet is Mars, and the element of your zodiacal significator is fire. You are, thus, fiery, as opposed to being tranquil. You are attractive, dynamic, and delightfully surprising. The memory of you lingers, because it is next to impossible to forget you.

"You are a natural pioneer and are often engaged in projects considered ahead of your time. Your aim is high, and it isn't easy, Aries, for you to find people who pass your tests.

"But listen, Aries, it is necessary for you to make sweeping changes, to strive for the new, to look to the future rather than hanging on to the past."

Furthermore, if you are an Aries, Sydney can tell you what other signs are favorable—or unfavorable—for you in your future.

Those born under the signs of Taurus and Scorpio are especially fortunate for you where personal possessions, material gain, and money are concerned.

Your sign is favorable in relation to Aquarius, Gemini, Leo, and Sagittarius.

But, Aries, you must exercise caution in dealing with Libra, Cancer, and Capricorn.

You are neutral in relation to Taurus, Virgo, Scorpio, and Pisces.

With another Aries the relationship may be physically tiring but spiritually rewarding.

Leos attract you physically. They help bring out your creative resources. But you burn up energy in association with them, because both you and Leo are fire signs, and when together you are not likely to stand still. Leo is in your fifth solar house and gives you get-up-and-go. He can be a spark plug for Aries; he challenges you, encourages you to express your natural warmth and kindles the flame that could burn into romance.

You also are physically attracted to Taureans. Taurus is associated with Venus, while your ruling planet is Mars. Mars and Venus represent physical attraction. Taurus falls in your second house, which is concerned with income potential, material possessions, and your ability to collect facts. Thus you will find that Taureans are financially good for you.

But listen, Aries, the Taurus person may be a bit slow-moving for your taste. You tend to be aggressive and want immediate action, and you become impatient with one who procrastinates. Taurus ponders, analyzes, and deduces before taking action In some ways,

Taurus is good for you; he sets an example of patience. In business dealings with Taurus, try not to force your view. Taurus can be determined, and this determination, at times, becomes obstinacy.

This and the following interpretations for each sign are taken from Sydney's book *Astrology and You* (Pyramid).

♉

TAURUS

(April 20–May 20)

Sydney describes the classic Taurean as big, stubborn, and easygoing. But he can be roused into action bordering on the violent. He cites Joe Louis and Charles "Sonny" Liston as examples of pugilistic Taureans.

On another level, actor James Mason is an example of the creative Taurus: a distinct style, a personality not easy to penetrate.

Taurus (the second sign of the zodiac) is associated with the planet Venus and is of the earth element. Taureans, on the whole, tend to be earthy and sensuous. The pleasures of life have great appeal. At times, so much so that you tend to get into a rut, says Sydney. You find a comfortable spot and hibernate. It's often necessary to shake, challenge, and goad you into action. Born under a fixed sign, you tend to be immobile, even when you have problems to face. Unfortunately, in this life we more often have to face them.

It is necessary, Taurus, for you to become more flexible; you tend to fix your mind on one goal and to aim toward it without considering anything else. You don't want to be distracted, especially where money is concerned. You are sensitive when it comes to finances and material possessions. You can become obstinate; and this obstinacy is caused by a fear of change, of new circumstances. Because you are so concerned with your possessions, it is not easy for you to give of yourself.

Be versatile without scattering your forces; be determined without being stubborn; appreciate gain and profit without becoming avaricious.

As to your favorable and unfavorable signs: Gemini individuals are likely to be fortunate for you where money is concerned, and Capricorn persons prove beneficial when it comes to investment counsel.

Your sign is favorably aspected to Pisces, Cancer, Virgo, and Capricorn. Your sign is not favorably aspected to Leo, Aquarius, or Scorpio. In relation to Libra, Sagittarius, and Aries you are neutral. In association with another Taurean there is much social activity and a struggle to get down to practical affairs.

Although Pisces is favorably aspected to Taurus, you must not expect miracles, Sydney warns. Avoid placing Pisces on a pedestal.

♊

GEMINI

(May 21–June 20)

Gemini, an air sign, is associated with the planet Mercury, and it most certainly is mercurial, Sydney says. There is a restlessness that stands out as your trademark. You have a distinct push in the direction of a confusion that can be orderly or can deteriorate into chaos, but your sense of humor is a great asset. You are intellectual, restless, mobile, usually in the thick of things.

Bob Hope is a Gemini and a good example of a person who exemplifies the quick wit and travel associated with this sign.

Your sign can be exasperating, Gemini, because you are subject to changes, variations; your opinions are not fixed. Rather, you are versatile, flexible. You tend to become involved in rumors. People tell anecdotes about you. Your hands are apt to be tapered as opposed to square; they are apt to appear delicate as opposed to solid. You touch people; you need people.

You can love more than one person at a time, and you do fall in and out of love. You are exuberant; activity is essential to your well-being. You are restless, going here and there, planning more than one project at a time. . . . I have always found Gemini attractive, but extremely difficult to pin down. . . . Marilyn Monroe and Judy Garland were born under Gemini.

You are a complicated, complex individual, Gemini. You often are not sure of what you want or need. You become involved with people destined to hurt you. The double nature of Gemini (the twins) is something to marvel at—or draw back from in fear. It all depends on who does the looking, and for what purpose. The double nature, Gemini, means that you can look one way and go the other. You can go in one direction but be headed elsewhere. You can be with one individual and be thinking about someone else.

Favorable signs are Cancer, Capricorn, Aries, Leo, Libra, and Aquarius; not favorable are Pisces, Virgo, Sagittarius. Gemini is neutral with Taurus and Scorpio.

♋

CANCER

(*June 21–July 22*)

Cancerians are protective of family and home; they have a sharply honed sense of security. Born under this sign, you are aware of the good life, particularly food. Many great chefs were born under this sign. Men sometimes annoy their wives by getting in the way in the kitchen. That's Cancer, building the nest, accumulating wealth, stocking staples, being concerned with the home and homemaking.

Cancer women know their men; they attract men who take care of them. During a family emergency, however, the Cancer woman can be counted on to come up with reserve cash or other assets—and always a good larder. I have often said that if I should marry again, it should be a Cancer woman—because I love to eat!

Cancer is of the water element, a cardinal sign, giving natives the drive necessary to accumulate material goods. On the negative side, being associated with the moon, people of Cancer can be moody and ultrasensitive. You tend to be so concerned with that proverbial rainy day that you forget to enjoy life this minute, right now.

Cancer people have oval-shaped or "moon faces." The Cancer person is also called moon child.

Milton Berle, Nelson Rockefeller, Bill Cosby, and Art Linkletter were all born under Cancer.

Money is important to Cancer, more so than to the average person. Statistically, more persons listed in Who's Who in Commerce and Industry were born under your sign than any other, so there is a proclivity here for attracting money.

Cancer is favorably aspected to Taurus, Virgo, Scorpio, and Pisces, unfavorably aspected to Aries, Libra, and Capricorn, neutral in relation to Sagittarius, Gemini, Leo, and Aquarius—although the two latter signs play very significant roles where your finances are concerned.

With Gemini, you tend to be confused. Gemini affects that part of your chart concerned with the unexpected and hidden matters, subtle influences, behind-the-scenes activity.

Listen, Cancer: with Gemini you will have to be prepared for a lot of maybes—maybe today, maybe tomorrow. . . .

With Sagittarius there are also problems to overcome. The two signs are not well aspected. Sagittarius makes you aware of your health, is apt to get you on a diet and physical-fitness program. You could rebel, because Sagittarius prods you in the direction of routine, basic duties, and resolutions. You tend to have some ideas of your own in this direction. So, Cancer, be ready for some disputes with Sagittarius. . . .

Your intuitive intellect is sparked by Pisces. Trust your hunches when Pisces is around. Pisces and Cancer are favorably aspected, and the potential is a great one. With your moon and Pisces' Neptune there should be no limit to your horizons. I would encourage such a relationship, you could use some Pisces in your life!

♌

LEO
(July 23–August 22)

There is a personal magnetism surrounding Leo that creates showmen, successful entertainers. Leo is vitality and creativity. Leo attracts but can also repel, because envy rises in the minds of many who resent the bright sunlight that Leo symbolizes. I am not saying that Leo is perfect and that those who find fault are merely victims of jealousy. I am saying that Leo, associated with the sun, is a bright light that can also be harsh. But the light tends to endure rather than sputter.

Mae West is a good example of Leo on the distaff side, while Mike Douglas is a good example of a television personality whose Leo attributes have taken him from obscurity to nationwide prominence. I know both of these Leos. And both exemplify a kind of charm, attraction, an aura of sexuality that is the hallmark of the sign.

Those born under Leo are obstinate, determined, colorful, exaggerators, at times boastful, but usually reserve the latter for challenges. You were born under a fixed sign and the fire element. You live for love; without it, the greatest success imaginable could be nothing. That's a key: love, affection, appreciation, applause, encouragement, the knowledge that someone who cares is in your corner. You are gregarious; you can plan, even plot, train, and prepare alone, but for the "performance" you need someone by your side. You get along better without food than without love.

That's part of being born under the natural fifth zodiacal sign; it is a characteristic peculiar to Leo; it applies more, with greater intensity, than it does to the rest of the signs.

Because of your need for love, you are vulnerable and you can be hurt. You have a way of making the wrong choices; at times, you choose someone who is attractive but lacks depth. You have a tendency to lose your perspective when it comes to placing your affection. Review your life, Leo. I think you will find that you meet the right person at the wrong time. You are generous, even extravagant; you are a romantic lover, but you could waste your energies and emotions on an undeserving person. The key is better timing and judgment. Overcome your impulsiveness; otherwise you will constantly meet the right individual under the wrong circumstances, and the cycle, much to your ultimate sorrow, will continue. Of course, it doesn't have to be that way. But to correct it and bring love into the focus of personal happiness, self-discipline is a requisite. And disciplining yourself, Leo, is not exactly your cup of tea. If mature, you learn this lesson. Otherwise, you repeat mistakes. One leading astrologer, who specializes in love, claims that you seem intent on misplacing your affection—and that your problems in this field can be laid to "unwise and impetuous love-making."

(NLB'S NOTE: *If all of this isn't Sydney Omarr talking to himself, a Leo, I'll eat my typewriter ribbon.*)

Favorably aspected signs for Leo are Gemini, Libra, Aries, and Sagittarius; not favorably aspected are Taurus, Scorpio, and Aquarius; neutral in relation to Cancer, Capricorn, Pisces, and Virgo, although the latter promotes financial gain.

Sydney's favorite female Leo is Mae West, who was so impressed with the horoscope he did for her that she asked him to come up and see her sometime. He did.

"I walked into her living room," he said, "and there was a chimpanzee—a real, live chimpanzee—very studiously working out on the parallel bars, just as though he were a person. A curious sight."

♍

VIRGO

(*August 23–September 22*)

Virgo has a way of sizing people up; it is a sign associated with Mercury, and it is analytical, mercurial. Virgo is Arthur Godfrey and that quizzical look. It can be delightful and, at times, foreboding. Virgo can be a shell, beautiful and expressive, yet withdrawn, like Greta Garbo. Virgo can be quiet charm or it can be exuberance; it is service and work. Virgo wants to be in the thick of the action but is not always desirous of being affected and touched by happenings.

Born under this earth sign, you can be extremely practical. Born under the natural sixth sign, you can be health-conscious to the point of being fanatical about fads, vitamins, devices, exercises, and diets. Born with Mercury your solar significator, you can flit from one subject or person to the next. Your intellectual curiosity is such that you would choose trouble over boredom. You take a serious view of life and are concerned with the philosophies of great persons. But, of all philosophies, your own is most important; you develop, nurture, and are very serious about your own philosophy. . . . Perhaps, Virgo, you should be concerned, beyond a superficial level, about your own actions, responses, fantasies, and ambitions. . . .

A fascinating facet of your character is that you have an affinity for contradiction. You tend to criticize what you desire; you are a labyrinth of feeling and emotion. You want to be involved, yet you pull away. You want to be outgoing, but you are basically shy. You want to be of service, but you could shirk duty under the cover of indifference. It should be obvious by now, Virgo, that you do not exactly make life easy for yourself. . . .

It is important for you to replace self-doubt with a greater sense of self-appreciation. Otherwise you will brood and become an emotional basket case. . . .

You are almost fanatical where security is concerned. Bills must be paid, the books balanced, the job finished. . . .

Virgo is favorably aspected to Cancer, Scorpio, Taurus, and Capricorn. It is adverse to Gemini, Sagittarius, and Pisces, and neutral in relation to Leo, Aries, and Libra, although there is a financial connection with Aries and Libra.

Virgo and Gemini both have the same ruling planet–Mercury–and getting together could spark ideas. I would be the last one to discourage this association. But, Virgo, you'd better put in an order for additional vitamins, because Gemini is going to keep you on the go!

Sophia Loren is a Virgo, born September 20, 1934. She has an analytical mind, loves to match wits with others. "It doesn't surprise me at all to hear that she's an excellent poker player," says Sydney. "She is often attracted to men intellectually at first, and then physically. It should have surprised no one that she married an older man."

♎

LIBRA
(September 23–October 22)

Librans emanate a kind of beauty and balance, a gentle trait that belies the fact that they also are natural fighters for justice. Of course, Libra, your idea of justice may not always coincide with the beliefs of others. That matters not, because you prefer to do battle for the underdog, for unpopular causes. This reveals a contradiction: you want peace, but are ready to fight when in your opinion the cause is just.

Among famous Librans was former President Dwight D. Eisenhower, who had the typical Libra characteristics. He gave the impression of wanting peace and quiet, yet his great fame was based on his exploits as a military man.

The ancient symbol for Libra is a balance scale, denoting that the classic Libran has a natural instinct for fair play, justice, and harmony. The sign is associated with the planet Venus, the planet of beauty and love.

If you are a Libra, your emotional or love nature is out of the ordinary. Your emotions often betray you and mingle with logic. The two–emotion and logic–often take a stance against each other. This leaves you in the middle, striving to balance those Libra scales.

Brigitte Bardot was born under Libra (September 28, 1935), and she has the typical Libra-like quality of always trying to balance one thing against the other, but, woman-like, not being able to make decisions. She has admitted publicly, "I'm a Libra and I simply loathe making any decisions. All decisions are hard for Librans. I try to arrange my life to go around or bypass decisions, to avoid them if possible. Sometimes you can travel faster on the ring roads of life, no?"

Love is as important as food for the Libra lady, and she is worth winning. But you must expect evasive action—and never push too hard for direct answers. There is no black and white with her; there are shades of good and bad, and you may as well get used to that idea.

If you are a Libra, you have much in common with Leo, especially where flattery is concerned. You both love it! As a matter of fact, the two signs are sympathetic and well aspected to each other. Obviously, Libra, you must learn to judge people in a more realistic manner: judge by actions, not mere words. . . . Your sign is considered favorable in relation to Leo, Sagittarius, Aquarius, and Gemini, not well aspected to Cancer, Capricorn, and Aries, and neutral in relation to Virgo, Pisces, Scorpio, and Taurus.

♏

SCORPIO

(October 23–November 21)

More astrologers regard your zodiacal sign with awe than any other. This is because Scorpio can be secretive and forceful, mysterious and direct; Scorpio is the organizer, tearing down in order to rebuild, magnetic, sensuous, with the demeanor of one who is guarding a treasure.

Scorpio is the natural eighth sign, is associated with the planet Pluto, is of the water element, is fixed, and has much to do with what is hidden and with the handling of other people's money. Johnny Carson, a Libra, is often mistaken for a Scorpio.

Among luminaries born under Scorpio are Rock Hudson, Katherine Hepburn, Richard Burton, Petula Clark, Walter Cronkite, Grace Kelly, and Billy Graham.

You can be forceful and resourceful, Scorpio. You are creative; individuality is your hallmark. . . . You are a natural detective and reporter; you may be part of a crowd, but you never surrender your individuality. You so appreciate power that many feel you are overly ambitious and sometimes overbearing. Some simply can't take you, while others seemingly cannot do without you. Obviously, Scorpio, you represent a dilemma; your magnetism draws, your insistence upon getting to the heart of matters tends to repel.

Pomposity is your natural target, but whether or not you choose correctly, whether or not your aim is accurate, is open to question. Sometimes you appear to be most harsh to your friends and kindest to strangers. Your curiosity is easily aroused; you tend to engage in numerous affairs of the heart.

Obviously, Scorpio, you can be abrasive. You never quite get a smooth edge. A roughness persists, despite polishing. You abound in intrigue. You delight in behind-the-scenes planning and maneuvering. Your memory is such that you cannot forget a slight, but you also reward loyalty. . . . You break rules, but make your own. You play the game to win, not to draw. You are a driving force for others and for yourself. . . . You seldom waste time with trivial things or people. . . . You are seldom, if ever, a bore. People may disagree with you but they can't ignore your views, policies, or declarations.

Your sign is favorably aspected to Virgo, Capricorn, Cancer, and Pisces; you have problems with Aquarius, Leo, and Taurus. Sagittarius gets you going financially; your sign is considered neutral in relation to Libra, Aries, and Gemini.

I would say that Scorpio and Pisces, these two water signs, are admirably suited for each other. There is excitement, attraction, the adventure of sharing knowledge. There is a spark here. . . . But listen, Scorpio, avoid bullying tactics. Pisces is stronger than you might imagine. And Pisces is capable of retaliating. . . . But the uniting of Scorpio and Pisces is a very exciting prospect. (What better example than Burton and Taylor? Elizabeth Taylor is a Pisces.)

♐

SAGITTARIUS

(November 22–December 21)

Sagittarians sometimes irritate me because of their tendency to procrastinate. They have so much ability that, perhaps unfairly, I want to see them use it to advantage and immediately. But many born under this sign have lofty ideals that sometimes immobilize them: they fear that their techniques are not perfected, that their methods are too rough, that there is yet so much to learn. True, I admire idealism and perfection, but I would rather see a "rough" effort than a void. That, Sagittarius, is what I wish you would learn. Do it. Talk about it later. Perform it. Present theories later—not the other way around.

Your principles are at times too high for you to settle for anything less than the best. You are Sagittarius the archer, but your aim is so high that you throw up your hands if your arrow misses the target. And then you retreat into a world of procrastination. That's what I oppose: the fact that one with your great potential does not always utilize it. But once a Sagittarian makes up his mind to do something, it does get done, despite often overwhelming odds.

Such famous persons as Irene Dunne, Mary Martin, Margaret Mead, Julie Harris, Noel Coward, Frank Sinatra, J. Paul Getty, Beethoven, Winston Churchill, and Walt Disney were born under the sign of Sagittarius.

Sagittarius is associated with Jupiter, the largest planet and a harbinger of good. Sagittarius is a fire sign; you are intense, idealistic, warm, passionate. Your drives are varied, scanning the spectrum from theater to education, from art to politics. It isn't always easy to pin you down; you wonder and wander. Long journeys are almost second nature, a definite part of your makeup. For you, the open road leads to an open mind. And that is one of your many aspirations. . . .

You are versatile, artistic; your ability to express yourself could lead you to a career in acting, art, designing. You are fascinated with the idea of communicating to others and thus would be attracted to the fields of writing, publishing, advertising, motion pictures, and television. You are a fine storyteller. For you, Sagittarius, literature and journalism and the teaching of philosophy or religion are the most congenial occupations of all.

Sagittarius is favorably aspected to Libra, Aquarius, Leo, and Aries, not favorable in relation to Pisces, Virgo, and Gemini, and neutral to Scorpio, Capricorn, Taurus, and Cancer.

♑

CAPRICORN

(December 22–January 19)

I have been impressed with Capricorn's ability to work with time. You have an affinity with time; you understand it, you can wait and win; you can cope and bide your time.

Obviously, Capricorn, you are *not* what you might appear to be on the surface! (There's Richard Nixon again!)

You were born under the tenth zodiacal sign; your ruling planet is Saturn. You either protect yourself in the clinches or you are wide open. There does not seem to be a compromise. Very few really know you, but you make a display of being frank. Open and closed, frank and obscure, that's you, Capricorn.

Among famous Capricorns are Ava Gardner, Marlene Dietrich, Steve Allen, Cary Grant, Danny Kaye, Ethel Merman, Jane Wyman, Loretta Young, Albert Schweitzer, and that great writer Henry Miller. Henry is my close friend, but he keeps a secret side to himself—secret and sacred, as he might put it.

Capricorn is an earth sign; it is strong and at times overly formal. You have a keen sense of drama, always living life to the hilt. Your sense of timing becomes an invaluable ally. Nothing can stop you but yourself. . . .

Obviously you are a controversial figure, apt to be ahead of your time. You are appreciated yet reviled, loved yet feared. Your touch can be cold but your heart is warm. That's you, the classical Capricorn.

Capricorn is favorably aspected to Scorpio, Pisces, Taurus, and Virgo. Aquarius could activate the money sector of your chart, while Leo also appears connected with your money, particularly in the area of investment or legacy. Capricorn is not favorably aspected to Aries, Libra, or Cancer. Your sign is neutral where Sagittarius and Gemini are concerned. In relation to another Capricorn, the combination could be difficult, because each Capricorn attempts to explain, analyze, and take over the operation. It is not easy for two Capricorns to blend!

♒

AQUARIUS

(January 20–February 18)

It is said that more famous people were born under Aquarius than any other sign; it also happens to be true that more people are born from January 20 to February 18 than during any other period of the year. Aquarius is a fixed sign, of the air element; it is a sign that depicts the unusual, the unique, and, on occasion, the eccentric. It is out of the ordinary, and the Aquarian is, at times, recognizable by a kind of "horsey" look, an elongated face. When I appeared on national television with Aquarian Joey Bishop, I noticed this emphasis; he has the moon in Scorpio, which, combined with the Aquarius sun, gives the impression of a subtle secret. I did his horoscope and read it during the broadcast. It was particularly well received because people tend to be fascinated with Aquarians. The classical Aquarian does seem to be carrying a secret, to be listening to his own, private tune. This is exemplified by another Aquarian, actress Kim Novak. Her interest in Uranian subjects stamps her as unusual, unorthodox, which are key words as far as Aquarius is concerned. Jack Lemmon, Lana Turner, Carol Channing, and Victor Mature are other examples that typify this dynamic, challenging zodiacal sign.

Uranus is the planet associated with your sign, and it is also considered the planet of astrology, aviation, electricity; it is the unusual, the sudden, the eccentric, and at times the outlandish, but always the dynamic and surprising.

These factors symbolize you, Aquarius. You are sophisticated, yet retain enough childlike wonder to be fascinated by the new and the strange. Many people find you enchanting because your curiosity enchants those not accustomed to seeing, perceiving, appreciating. You are, in a very real sense, a seeker of knowledge—and your methods are unorthodox. Your sense of adventure is highly developed. While others may be contemplating a move, you take action. While others consider, you discover. There is a crackling, electric excitement about you. . . .

Aquarius is favorably aspected to Sagittarius, Aries, Gemini, and Libra. Your sign is not well aspected to Taurus, Scorpio, and Leo.

Aquarius is neutral in relation to Capricorn and Cancer, and to Pisces and Virgo, except that the latter two signs do activate Aquarius concerning finances.

NLB'S NOTE: As a Sagittarian married to an Aquarian, I naturally have more than a passing interest in anything Sydney says or has written about both signs. And I must admit that most of it is remarkably "right on"! Even to his physical description of my husband's elongated face and kind of "horsey" look—(Sydney's word, dear, not mine), his childlike fascination with the new and the strange, his unorthodox methods, and his sense of adventure. All of these interpretations were written long before Sydney and I met, and to this day he has never set eyes on my husband. But those who know us would certainly recognize us in Sydney's astrological word painting:

You, Aquarius, are attracted to those born under Sagittarius. On the positive side, the Sagittarian helps fulfill your hopes, wishes, desires. On the negative side, there is a tendency to be a pleasure-seeker, to be extravagant, to nourish pipe dreams.

The Jupiter of Sagittarius combined with your Uranus significator adds up to the excitement of expansion, of dreams, of faraway goals. But you must, with Sagittarius, overcome a tendency to take things for granted. You must put thoughts on paper, outline goals, take definite steps rather than being satisfied with mere dreams.

You are an individual who looks to the future, who goes to the brink, who seeks the excitement of discovery. With Sagittarius you are encouraged along these lines. The combination is especially good for communication, writing, journalism. [My husband was a newspaper photographer.] The association with Sagittarius appears to be quite favorable. It should be encouraged. The Sagittarian brightens your life [Aha] and helps you to attain significant goals. . . . Your Uranus and the Jupiter of Sagittarius combine to promote imagination, daring, and romance. With Sagittarius life will not be dull.

I could rewrite that last line to read: With Aquarius, life will not be dull! It was Aquarius, not Sagittarius, who dragged us off on those long-ago pipe-dream Odysseys: the South Seas on banana and copra boats and our sojourn up the Niger to Timbuktu. . . . No matter what your sign is, if you want excitement in your life, marry

Aquarius! Take it from one who's been there. Unless Sydney blue-pencils this one out!

♓

PISCES

(February 19–March 20)

Pisceans can be secretive and seductive. They are poetic and delicate but practical enough to complain about aching feet. Authoress Anaïs Nin is my idea of the classical Piscean. She once told me that my knowledge of Pisces was "miraculous." That's because, in my analysis of your sign, I do emphasize the symbolism of Neptune. That's the planet associated with this, the twelfth zodiacal sign. It is illusion; it can be deceptive but is real enough; the presence is there, just as in a cloud. Yet solidity appears to be lacking. A kind of subterranean, clandestine aura surrounds Pisces; the women can lift their eyebrows and cause hearts to palpitate. The men can be funny, secretive; they can appear soft, but they make formidable adversaries. Jackie Gleason is a Piscean; his interest in psychic phenomena typifies the Piscean desire to know beyond the immediate, to delve into the unknown. Elizabeth Taylor symbolizes the Piscean who uses eyes, as well as more obvious physical assets, to attract, to create an aura of sex, romance, who is a part of the theater, which is what the twelfth house signifies, among other things. . . .

These Pisceans can make addicts of us before we even are aware that indeed we are unknowing targets!

Pisces is a water sign; your emotions often dominate logic. You are impressionable, intuitive, sensitive, emotional, capable of capturing and delineating moods. Listen, you born under Pisces, you can be quiet while a storm rages inside. You never tell all you know, and secrets are second nature.

Obviously, this water sign intrigues me. There is a delicate touch about you, a projection of the gentle but firm, the giving but solid, the dainty but capable. Actress Jennifer Jones seems to me to typify many of these qualities.

Pisces has a willingness to delve into mystery, to create mystery, to breathe romance, to highlight intrigue. There is sensuousness here: the promise is ever present, a labyrinth leading closer to fulfillment.

I firmly believe, despite declarations by some standard texts, that your sign is more reserved than weak; your apparently mild, retiring manner is a way of holding back, of sinking into deep water of thought, of analyzing, of playing a key role behind the scenes. If nothing else, you are the actor, the drive behind the production, the organization. You make the scenes play; you perform magic before our very eyes.

Other famous people born under the sun in Pisces include Dinah Shore, Harry Belafonte, Rex Harrison, John Steinbeck, Albert Einstein, George Washington, Victor Hugo, Chopin, Handel, and Michelangelo.

There is a paradoxical quality about you Pisceans: you can deceive and be deceived. You love beauty but can become involved in ugly situations. . . . You are strong in the face of adversity, but you maintain an aura of gentleness. . . . You are charming and sexy but give the illusion of being aloof and unworldly. . . . You may be wispy, but you can produce bursts of energy. . . . You are artistic, musical, and moody. Fantasy is part of your everyday world. . . .

At times, you see people and situations as you wish they could be. The key is to see people and groups as they actually exist. It is fine to be idealistic. It is quite something else to leave reality, to take off in flights of Neptunian fancy. . . . It is necessary for you to avoid excess, especially where drugs are concerned. Pisces persons are ultrasensitive to drugs, both alcohol and the other kind. In fact, all three water signs, Pisces, Cancer, and Scorpio, tend to be more addicted to alcohol and drugs than all other signs. So watch it, Pisces!

Your sign is favorably aspected to Capricorn, Taurus, Cancer, and Scorpio; but you have problems with Gemini, Sagittarius, and Libra. But where Aries and Libra are concerned, money activity is indicated. . . .

These are Sydney's capsule nuggets of wisdom from his world of astrology. By unlocking the secrets of your personal sun signs, he says, you can control your destiny. Never forget:

The wise man controls his destiny. . . . Astrology points the way.

Chapter 13
THE KENNEDYS

"*Caroline is in a dream-fantasy world. . . .*"
—SYDNEY OMARR

Some of Sydney's most dramatic astrological-numerological readings have been done not by private consultation but in public print, like the following three excerpts from *The National Tattler* on members of the Kennedy family:

JACQUELINE KENNEDY ONASSIS

On July 28, 1929, a child was born who was destined to be far from an ordinary individual, and today she is perhaps the most famous woman alive! Jacqueline Kennedy Onassis—manysided: sensitive, energetic, positive, enthusiastic, sincere, reserved. She loves her children, has a reverence for the past, is capable of holding her own under great difficulties, and, as many Leonians are, is suited to a kingly or queenly, well-cushioned throne.

Upon examining her natal chart I find it shows that fame and wealth could be her only possible fate.

Cancer, a water sign, is in the cusp of her eighth house and indicates that Jacqueline would marry a man with strong affinities for water. Both of her late husbands had a connection with water: President Kennedy was a PT-boat captain in World War II and was also very fond of sailing, and Aristotle Onassis was a superwealthy shipping magnate.

Sagittarius as her rising sign shows her love of travel, foreign countries, and foreign people: Onassis was Greek; and Jacqueline is known to suddenly appear in any country in the world without a moment's notice.

A final indication of Jacqueline's unusual destiny lies in the fact that Jupiter and Venus, known as the "greater fortune" and the "lesser fortune" of the ancients, fall in her seventh house, the house of marriage, partnerships, and associations. John F. Kennedy and Aristotle Onassis were both extremely wealthy.

CAROLINE KENNEDY

Caroline Kennedy (November 27, 1957, Sagittarius): She has a voice and it will be heard. There is precociousness here—also genuine talent. This lady could even pull a Margaret Truman on us.

If I could talk directly to her, I would say: Caroline, please develop and use your voice. Your chart indicates artistic ability, a desire for self-expression so strong that, unless you find a constructive outlet, you will rebel, get involved in what many will consider highly unorthodox activities.

"You could move (change address) in 1975. You'll be busy with drama, music, possibly a combination of both." [NOTE: In late summer of 1975, her mother took her to London and enrolled her in a special art seminar at Sotheby's.]

"Your uncle Ted will have his political ambitions revived, and despite second thoughts on the part of your elders, you might become involved."

Yes, Involvement is the key to this chart. The sun in Sagittarius, the moon in Aquarius, a six birth path: this Caroline will be heard from; she will fall in love and there will be shouts of approval, and condemnation.

Some years ago, for the *Tattler*, I forecast that her mother would "marry a foreigner." She did, and that is on record, and let me tell you, Caroline is not going to be in any person's shadow—mother, father, or any other member of the family.

In 1975 she "separates" from the family, cuts the umbilical cord, wants to keep her own place and to have her own place and will not be kept in her place.

Caroline can be pushed only so far. She has a temper and it

flares. She also is a basic humanitarian, is drawn to the underdog, is a sucker for a sob story, is better at helping or understanding others than supporting her own best emotional interests.

She wants to travel, to be knowledgeable about comparative religions, customs of people: she wants to be involved in the world, not a make-believe situation based on what others think she should be or might be or could be.

Mars in Scorpio and Venus in Capricorn, and this young lady can tell us all where to get off if we insist on it.

Caroline smolders. She has a memory that would rival a senior elephant. She does not forget easily, and she falls hard.

Caroline is in a dream-fantasy world. She suffers quietly, and she does not approve of many things that mama Jacqueline thinks are just divine.

The cycle here is on the upswing. Caroline has been through emotional Hades—and, yes, there has been damage. Mama and the rest of the clan have—not through any purposeful pattern—worsened the situation.

Caroline has bruises, scars of the emotional variety, and they have not been detected—prior to this time.

A sun-Saturn conjunction is a "mark" of one whose parents were separated by divorce or circumstance—and it leaves an indelible mark. Our Caroline, with Uranus dancing in Leo and retrograde in motion, is a sticking pin in her mother's conventional side.

That is to say that the Leo sun of Jacqueline is pricked by the Uranus (smasher of conventions) Leo of daughter Caroline. Caroline's Uranus conjuncts her mother's sun and then some—and a rift between the two is as predictable as the sun rising and setting. And Caroline, please know it and accept it and stop, repeat stop, cutting into yourself and ripping yourself apart. Please!

Your future? You already have fallen in love with more than one person—simultaneously. That may be part of your pattern: a deep, abiding, sincere love. But you are too big, too universal to be confined to one nation, one concept, one person—you love and love and give, and you simply are not going to be caged.

You also eat too many sweets, and low blood sugar is your adversary. Know it and do something about it!

Is Caroline our poor little rich girl? No, she is no simpering do-gooder lollipop early Shirley Temple. She is human, will know what she is doing and do it anyway and break up her home when it becomes evident that she has outgrown her lover or husband. That is the way it is—and much more, too.

Caroline will travel, study, dramatize, ask embarrassing questions, especially about religion. Her mother is fascinated by her, may even dote on her. But Caroline feels distant, wants to spread her own wings, and although she "feels" for mama, cannot always reach her. It is John F. who remains her ideal, and she is intelligent enough to know that, had he lived, she might have rebelled against papa, too!

JOAN KENNEDY

This is a person of opposites, beginning with her birth (September 5) at the full moon when the sun (Virgo) and moon (Pisces) were opposite each other. These, "the lights," are the pivotal points, the driving forces of a horoscope—the sun and the moon—and they are pulling and pushing at each other, and that is not the finish of this "opposition signature."

Saturn is with the Moon in Pisces and is in opposition to Neptune in Virgo with the sun. This is a delicate mechanism. It is the sensitive balance of her mind planet, Mercury, in the sign of the scales, Libra. This chart tips over, and the scales, the balances, the mechanisms, swing precariously between balance and collapse.

This lady Joan has a quality that is a saving grace; . . . it is a sense of humor. While she cries inwardly, wrenched and tortured within, there is a quiet, mocking voice that chides in a humorous manner.

It saves lady Joan, this ability to scoff at her own foibles. The same quality can be negative in that it also indicates a scattering of forces, being here, there, and everywhere—until the wind whirls and whishes and an emotional hurricane gets wound up and smashes down—and then not even the laughing voice within can calm the storm. It must run its course.

This is the horoscope of one who lives with confining adversity, one who can handle it and be its companion and suffer with it and encourage recovery. Truly, Joan Kennedy is better at aiding others than coping with her own storm warnings.

The numerical pattern tells me of an individual who is haunted by a fear of not being able to live up to her self-image, her responsibility. She can be pierced with the terrible fear of a panic that swooshes down and engulfs and can be chased only by the laughing voice within. The voice at this time is whispering, You must transform your life style—get the pattern changed even if it does mean separation, temporary or otherwise.

You can change your life—you are more sensitive to the balance-pull than most—and, for now, you have to (at least temporarily) get away from the suffocating of it.

You will, too. And you will do so in your private way.

This horoscope is desperately candid. It reveals problems in co-operative efforts, including partnerships and marriage, much more so than faced by the average individual.

As her ideal dreams are shattered, she pulls in the reins of her own happiness until the bit chokes. The drama is here, as Mars in Leo would attest. It is a theater of violence, Mars being in her solar twelfth house.

Here is what I know: Whenever Joan Kennedy digs deep into a situation or person, she usually comes up not with pay dirt but with glitter that crumbles. She has now reached a point where she anticipates disillusionment if not defeat.

If I were talking to her and not to myself, I would insist that she "get away from it all" for a while. If this she would do, she would save herself and aid tremendously a delicate balance within the family circle.

Chapter 14
RESIDENT ASTROLOGER ON TV

"But nobody knows this about me."
SHELLEY WINTERS

Despite certain restrictions by the NAB code, Sydney's fame and popularity spread until he was in constant demand on national television shows. In recent years he has become a semiregular or—to use a highbrow term more befitting his prestige—resident astrologer on the highly rated Merv Griffin Show.

Many of Merv's shows, as his millions of viewers know, have been devoted entirely to one theme, and his astrology shows have been among the most popular. Sydney frequently has enlivened the show with his horoscopic readings of celebrity "mystery guests" known to the audience but not to him.

He is given only the date, time, and place of birth of the person an hour or two before show time—just long enough to prepare his notes and read them back to the producer. His contract includes a clause that any written material he reads on the show must first be approved by the producer. The mystery-guest theme almost didn't get off the ground, because Sydney was too accurate in his readings of two of the earliest mystery guests, Jackie Vernon and Vincent Price. The producers decided nobody would believe him. Certainly the audience would conclude that he had known beforehand who the mystery guests were, and even the producers themselves were suspicious that someone had tipped him off. They decided to sack the whole idea.

Sydney was infuriated.

To cancel the mystery guests because of his accuracy was to accuse him of dishonesty, he fumed, and also a bigger fraud for the audience than if he did know their identity. Even while the battle of wits raged, Sydney still had no idea, in spite of his beleaguered horoscopic accuracy, who the mystery guests were.

He won the bout with his TV producers, and the astrological mystery-guest theme became an immediate hit.

One of the most memorable of his mystery guests appeared with him on a Merv Griffin show that aired June 22, 1972. It was a show devoted to Cancer, the moon child. The mystery guest was a Cancerian, as were the other guests on the show, and also many in the audience.

Merv, as was his custom, opened the show with some generalities on Cancerians (he's a Cancer himself, birth date July 6), interspersed with specifics from Sydney.

Herewith is the condensed transcript, part paraphrased but most of it verbatim, from the Merv Griffin Show on Cancerians—and may you have fun guessing who the Cancer mystery guest was. . . .

MERV: Today we are devoting our whole show to astrology, because a new sun sign is upon us and these shows are very revealing. The sun sign is Cancer—the moon child. . . . On each horoscope show, I usually give some of the characteristics of a particular sign. . . . As you probably know, the symbol of the Cancer sign is the crab. (He holds up a copy of *Sydney Omarr's Astrological Revelations* on Cancer the crab.) There are two basic Cancer types. The first has a handsome, round face, soft skin, a wide, grinning mouth, almost circular eyes, rather a baby-face look. . . . Think of the man in the moon and that's a perfect image. That's me. I am a Cancer.

The second type is more common, naturally. The unmistakable look of the crab is immediately noticeable in the face. That is not me! [Laughter] You will see a fairly large skull and overhanging brow and high cheekbones. The brows seem to knot together in sort of a permanent frown.

Most Cancerians are a little top-heavy, and they waddle slightly when they walk fast, whether the body is plump or wiry. The women usually wear a sweater size considerably larger than the skirt size—or they will be absolutely flat-chested. Gina Lollobrigida is a Cancerian. So is Phyllis Diller.

Food somehow represents security to Cancerians. Whether he actually eats it or not, the crab feels safer when the larder is full and overflowing. Just talking about food brings a rosy glow to his expressive face. Henry the VIII and Charles Laughton were Cancers. . . .

He then introduced his other Cancer guests: movie star Jane Russell ("who was brought to fame by none other than Howard Hughes"), songstress Della Reese, and football star O. J. Simpson.

"And of course our mystery celebrity is hiding backstage somewhere. If we can find him it's going to be very exciting."

He then introduced "the most widely respected and widely read astrologer in the word": Sydney Omarr, a Leo.

SYDNEY: You mentioned Cancer and food, Merv. And it's true—food is very important to Cancer people. I teamed up with a well-known chef, Mike Roy, and we wrote a book called *Cooking with Astrology*. And, you know, most of the people who buy that book are born under Cancer. Food is equated with security for Cancer natives [Sydney's word for subjects]. Many of them have weight and diet problems. . . . But whenever I meet a lovely lady, I always hope she was born under Cancer, because then I know she will also be able to cook.

MERV: Who do Cancerians usually marry?

SYDNEY: Very often they marry Capricorn persons—but they have affairs with Scorpios. [Laughter] . . . It's not wise to underestimate Cancer. These persons are shrewd, discerning, ultimately practical—wonderful to have around during times of crisis or emergency. And they can almost always be counted on to cry at weddings and other solemn ceremonies. They are very sentimental. So, when presenting a gift to Cancer, be sure it has sentimental value. The classical native of this zodiacal sign wants to feel there's a reason, a bond, some special thought behind the gift.

MERV: Old money would do!

SYDNEY: Yes! Cancer persons like money. They are able to accumulate great wealth. In some instances they just accumulate strings and bags, but in most cases it's money. There are more persons born under Cancer who become millionaires than under any other zodiacal sign. Nelson Rockefeller is a Cancer. . . . There have been only two Presidents so far born under Cancer: John Quincy Adams and Calvin Coolidge, and Coolidge was the only President to be born on the nation's birthday, which is July 4.

MERV: So America is Cancer.

SYDNEY: Yes; well, it was born July 4. And as a nation we are very food-conscious, you know. Cities have birthdays, too, the date they were incorporated. New York City was born under Cancer, and there are more restaurants in New York than any other city in the world. . . . Also, you know, each sign is associated with a certain part of the body. And Cancer is associated with the upper torso, especially the breasts. If you want to be psychological about astrology, perhaps that explains why this country always has been so aware of food and breasts.

MERV: Well, Jane Russell I can understand! But how do you explain someone like Phyllis Diller?

SYDNEY: [Ignoring the question] That lady out there in the second row, who's nodding her head—now, give me three numbers quick, spontaneously.

LADY: Nine, twelve, eighteen.

SYDNEY: That's three . . . There's a great deal of movement involved, and traveling. . . . You'll have to skip your usual routine for a while. . . . But you will find that by October the greater freedom you are looking for will come about. Right now you feel that you are closed in by a wall.

LADY: [In a shriek] I'm going to have a baby in September! [Lots of Audience Laughter]

MERV: That's very good, Sydney! You sure can't see it from here. [Meaning her tummy] . . . Are you contemplating any kind of traveling?

LADY: Not like this.

MERV: Where are you from?

LADY: Originally I'm from England.

SYDNEY: Well, that's a little traveling to get here, I'd say—unless you swam.

MERV: Very interesting. He sure can pick them—not only personal characteristics, but when they're about to deliver! . . . Now, our mystery guest is standing backstage. The studio audience will see on their monitors exactly who it is, as you, Sydney, read whatever you've charted about this person. . . .

Herewith is a copy of the original notes Sydney typed to himself dated 6/15/72. (This was the date the show was taped for airing 6/22/72.)

NOTES TO MYSELF FOR MERV GRIFFIN MYSTERY GUEST . . .
Birth date—7/7/1912 . . . 6 A.M. . . . *Canada*

Short notice here. . . . What is Merv trying to do to me? . . . This guest is a mystery not only to me but to many persons. . . . Individual is known to many because of UNIVERSAL APPEAL. . . . Looks calm on outside . . . but factors in chart show that he, or she, has drive [lots of applause here on tape], gains power, draws persons and challenges, is a pioneer and capable of accumulating wealth. . . .

BUT I MUST SAY . . . as I am now saying to myself . . . that the intriguing aspect here is an outgoing manner, but this was achieved after a CHILDHOOD STRUGGLE WHICH FEATURED REJECTION [caps are Sydney's].

This individual is introspective, a perfectionist. . . . Engages in a demanding sport for recreation and is as happy at winning in this area as when it comes to putting across a business transaction.

Nothing halfway here—all or nothing. Venus in prominent spot would give full or moon face, combined with a great appeal to women. Uses this in commercial sense . . . gaining money through success with women as audience, or potential customers for products.

Merv has come up with a tough one here. Approximately ten

years ago suffered personal tragedy . . . no matter how long or short a time ago . . . and I am pressed now for time . . . event colored native's life, actions, and reactions, and served as catalyst for a kind of crusade.

Native inwardly feels a mission is part of his being, a necessity, a REASON for his life.

He says: I WAS REJECTED. . . . DID I MAKE THE SAME MISTAKE? . . . DID I DO TOO MUCH ASSERTING AND NOT ENOUGH LISTENING? No matter the outward appearance of confidence . . . native is plagued with self-doubt. Yet there is a debonair, attractive appearance, smiling to the world and concealing a hurt which goes back to those early, early days when literally native searched for home, for parents . . . a search for security and love.

I don't want to make Merv cry, because his chart shows that he—Merv—is a sentimental devil.

LISTEN: There is no need to cry. This subject, this mystery guest, has overcome obstacles . . . is charming and is winning the most important struggle of all . . . that of self-identity . . . and that of fulfillment.

NEXT TWO YEARS VERY SIGNIFICANT. . . . Mission will be accomplished . . . message will be universal . . . and this much-traveled individual is getting ready to pull up stakes . . . to make a mark in yet another land.

ONE MORE NOTE: This individual can look at you warmly and at the same time be sizing you up for your usefulness. So, Merv, wipe away those tears—there is no need to cry for your mystery guest. The only person who will be crying will be me . . . if I'm way off base.

MERV: I don't think you are. Will our mystery guest come in, please.

[Considering that Sydney wrote his notes before the show and not knowing who the mystery guest was or how his reading would affect the studio audience, it is even more amazing that he had mentioned the tears and "no need to cry," for when he read his notes on the mystery guest's personal tragedy and his "crusade" and "mission," Merv, the mystery guest, and many in the audience were close to tears.]

The mystery guest came out on stage, visibly moved. He shook hands with Sydney and said, "That's pretty good!"

"That *is* good!" echoed Merv, and to the studio audience, wildly applauding, "And a tough one, too!"

The mystery guest was Art Linkletter.

LINKLETTER: I'd say he was about 75 per cent correct. Everybody knows of my personal tragedy (the suicide of his daughter). Everyone knows of my crusade against drug abuse.

. . . About being rejected as a child—it's true that I was an orphan and I was rejected by my own parents. But I was adopted by very loving people, and I never felt rejected through my childhood. Although they were poor, nevertheless it was good to be the adopted son of an itinerant Baptist evangelist, because when the depression arrived in 1929, I didn't notice it. [laughter] That was just money—it wasn't love and care. I wasn't rejected that way. . . . The original rejection didn't bother me at all except when I was quite young and I found out that I was an adopted orphan. I was about eleven or twelve, and I went through the usual, I suppose, psychological reaction. . . . I was really left by a very rich, powerful family who apparently wanted me to live with the ordinary poor people before I came into my kingdom. And I'd look out the door each morning for the Rolls Royce to arrive, and it never arrived, so I finally went out and got it myself. . . . But I wouldn't say that I really felt rejected. It's a strange thing when you're adopted. . . . It depends on how you feel. I'd say to myself, my real parents are the ones who brought me up and loved me—not the ones who happened to biologically reproduce me. I think parenthood is earned and not an accident of birth. . . .

As for the "demanding sport," well, I have always been an ardent sportsman and for years I was a nationally ranked handball player. Now I'm an ardent skier and surfer. . . .

MERV: I wonder, Art, do you follow astrology?

LINKLETTER: No, I don't. I admit that astrology mystifies me, and there are some things about it that stagger me from time to time. But I reject it simply because my sense tells me that the stars really don't have anything to do with us. . . . I refuse to believe it. I just won't believe it. In the first place, I am religious and I believe in my religion. Secondly, I'm scientific, and I believe that genetics direct us. In the third place, I think astrology is great for people who want to believe it, but I think that most of the things it says are just good and general.

SYDNEY: May I say something, please?

LINKLETTER: Sure.

SYDNEY: I respect your views, Art, and I know you do mine, too. In the first place, astrology of course has nothing to do with being anti-religious. As a matter of fact, as I often point out, the so-called wise men of biblical times were astrologers and—

LINKLETTER [Interrupting]: Astronomers!

SYDNEY: No, they weren't! The newest translation of the New Testament makes it very clear that they were astrologers. Now, to get to your point about science: five of the greatest scientists to walk across the stage of world history were first and foremost astrologers. Kepler, Copernicus, Ptolemy, Isaac Newton, Galileo. Now, some people have tampered with our history books and have called them astronomers, but actually any fair scientist or historian will readily admit that astrology has been a fountainhead of knowledge, out of which have come astronomy, mathematics, medicine, and many, many other subjects.

LINKLETTER: But not recognized as a science.

SYDNEY: It is recognized as a scientific art. Now, the only thing that is recognized as a science would be pure mathematics. Medicine is not recognized as a science; it is a scientific art, also.

LINKLETTER: Astronomy is a science.

SYDNEY: Well, only because you're dealing strictly with measurement, mathematics. Ralph Waldo Emerson said, "Astronomy is the most useless science. Astrology is astronomy brought down to earth and applied to the affairs of man." You see, astronomers were the early apprentices of astrologers. They did the calculations, and the astrologers made the interpretations. Johannes Kepler, for example, made many of his astronomical discoveries merely to sharpen his horoscopic predictions. . . .

LINKLETTER: Well, I would never engage in a debate with you about something which you know four hundred times more about than I do. . . .

SYDNEY: Of course, I respect astronomy, just as intelligent astronomers respect astrology. In fact, I frequently debate with astronomers, and one very renowned astronomer has actually become a good friend of mine. Since I got him interested in astrology, he now has the nerve to call me to find out the correct time for him to launch his next attack on astrology.

LINKLETTER: Well, it seems that everything I read in the astrology columns is mostly generalities. Like today is a good day not to get leprosy. And I agree. Or don't walk across the street without looking both ways. . . .

SYDNEY: Art, may I point out that I would challenge any psychologist who had interviewed you for, say, two or three hours, to come up with any better findings than I did—in the same amount of space—and with only your birth date to go on. I'll bet every small dollar I have that I would be more accurate—not only with you, but with everyone.

LINKLETTER: You were very accurate.

SYDNEY: You know that I'm not a genius. I just know my astrology. Carl Jung and other great scientists leaned on astrology, and if more great men would become really interested in astrology, it would be a boon to humanity. I think it's a crime to ignore any scientific art that might benefit mankind. Academic prejudice is a virus and a disease, just as deadly as other kinds of prejudices. And when academic prejudice causes us to stay away from a subject just because we're afraid of its name, I think that's pretty dangerous.

LINKLETTER: I don't think you should stay away from it—

DELLA REESE: You mentioned that you're very religious and therefore you don't believe in it. Well, I am religious too, and I feel there is a certain amount of credibility in astrology because God put it here as a function. I cannot believe that everything else has a function and the stars are just supposed to twinkle. It's just out of character. . . .

MERV: And of course religious people do believe in miracles, and they're kind of hard to explain, too. . . . I promised Art to get him out of the door this minute. You have an engagement tonight, Art.

LINKLETTER: Yes, I do have another engagement—with a gypsy fortuneteller!

[He thanks the audience and turns to leave.]

MERV: Hey, that's a wall, Art!

[And Art Linkletter walked right into the wall. He was that shaken by his confrontation with Sydney.]

Later, Mr. Linkletter confirmed to me in an interview that he was indeed "frankly aghast and surprised" that Sydney had "hit it on the head" with him on the Merv Griffin Show.

"Even though I don't believe in astrology," he emphasized. "I don't think it's a science, and it is against my religious beliefs. I do not believe in fortunetelling per se, or the power to divine people's destiny. I think it's entertaining, amusing, and fun to speculate, but I personally consider it [astrology] in the same genre as an entertaining parlor game. However, I would be the last to say that Sydney Omarr isn't an extremely conscientious and well-versed man in his field, as astrologers go."

Such jibes do not offend Sydney. They only sadden him, because, as he says, men of Art Linkletter's caliber should keep an open mind.

Shelley Winters was the mystery guest on the Leo show. She is not only a Leo but she has Gemini rising, and your rising sign plays a prominent role in your horoscope. This and other factors, Sydney said, indicated to him that Miss Winters was ambidextrous. When he told her this, she gasped in astonishment. "But nobody knows this about me!" She was ready to believe that someone had tipped him off regarding everything else he told her so accurately—or that he had had time to do research on her. But how could he have known that she was ambidextrous when no one else knew it?

"It's because Gemini is so prominent in her horoscope," Sydney said with a shrug, as if anyone should know.

"I have found over the years," he explained, "that more ambidextrous and left-handed persons are born under Gemini than any other sign of the zodiac. Also, there are more twins born between May 21 and June 20 under the zodiacal sign of Gemini than under any other sign. The Dionne quintuplets were born under Gemini, and the attending physician had Gemini rising."

"Also," he added casually, "there are more people in jail born under Gemini than any other sign."

Kim Novak once told Sydney, "No one knows me like you do." And Gypsy Rose Lee, who appeared with Sydney on a Mike Douglas Show, admitted shakily in front of the whole television world, "I feel uncomfortable around Sydney Omarr, because he seems to know what I am going to say and do before I say it or do it."

On a nationally syndicated show hosted by Regis Philbin and called "The Unknown," Sydney gave a "blind" reading of a mystery personality who turned out to be Mr. Blackwell (he never uses a first name), the noted fashion designer with the barbed tongue who has made Hollywood history with his annual "Ten Worst Dressed Women" of the year.

Mr. Blackwell's reaction: "Well, I thought only I knew me like that! It's unbelievable, almost frightening. I had no idea you could see all that in *that* [indicating the horoscope Sydney held in his hands]. If I wanted the world to know about me, I could have talked to someone for five years and not have it done any better."

He later confirmed this to me when I interviewed him on the subject, although, having known Mr. Blackwell for years and having spent many amusing hours with him on previous interviews and at press conferences when he announced his "Ten Worst Dressed Women" at his posh mansion in the exclusive Hancock Park area of Los Angeles, I really didn't need his confirmation. Even I was more than a little incredulous at some of the facts revealed in Sydney's "Notes to Myself," based only on the mystery subject's birth date: 8/29/1922, 1:30 A.M., Brooklyn, New York.

Here are excerpts:

> . . . What a series of contradictions! Tough and gentle, loving beauty, yet a figure of controversy. The subject, I perceive, would appreciate this kind of audacity . . . because he, himself, jumps the boundary of convention. He speaks his mind in such a manner that his words very often make headlines.
>
> He has much to do with women but is conventional while also being autocratic, domineering, an arbiter of morals or fashions.
>
> What is Regis trying to do to me? The subject or native rebelled at early surroundings, has traveled extensively, is surrounded by members of opposite sex but doesn't often have much to do with women on a personal level. [All true.]
>
> Now, listen—I am telling myself—Regis really picked a puzzler. This guy, the subject, came out of a Dead End environment [True—he was one of the original Dead End Kids in the movies.] and now probably lives in a palatial residence. [And how!] He is loyal, faithful to one individual, but that person is not necessarily of the opposite sex. [Correct. His manservant, confidant, and live-in "secretary" and business associate is male.] Yet women do play a paramount role in this person's life. He makes his way by advising them, selling them . . . especially along lines which involve manners or fashion. [Is Sydney using astrology or a phychic X-ray machine?]
>
> This man, the subject [How does he know he's a man?], has a public image which is completely different from what he is in private. To the outsider, he is unconventional, flouting the rules, breaking them, daring the powers that be. [Right on!]
>
> In private, he abhors sloppiness, ridicules those who dress and act differently; he rails against women who act like men. . . . But he, himself, gravitates toward the unorthodox.
>
> I feel he has been deeply affected by early environment, more so than the average individual. Did his parents tell him the exact truth? Did one parent have an overwhelming influence? Did he court the disfavor of parent or parents to such a degree

that he scratched and clawed on his own? These are questions I must ask him, because I feel the answers are *yes.* [Yes!]

Now, Regis has picked me a subject who is more likely to scratch you than to punch you. I don't want him to do either to me. This man can accumulate a fortune. He is fastidious. Listen—at times this joker is so concerned with cleanliness that he puts paper under the cuckoo clock! [Well, that is stretching it a little, but not much.]

He wants to be surrounded by beauty, is sensuous, has much to do with women—but this is likely to be strictly professional.

SECRET TO MYSELF WHICH I WILL READ ANYWAY: He could have been a gigolo because he gets his money through women. *But I feel he probably sells products to women . . . products having to do with fashion, comfort, or luxury*—probably all three.

What a hell of an early childhood! Whatever his is, whoever he is, he deserves credit for merely being there, or having survived. That is the name of the game for him: *survival.*

Subject was born under Virgo. He can be brutally frank, especially when such frankness serves his own purposes . . . such as gaining wide publicity by criticizing *sacred cows.* He, incidentally, is likely to call them *crows.* [He has called them much worse than that.]

This man will get international attention and recognition. . . . Whatever else he is, he is basically truthful, stands tall for principles and will say: *Sydney Omarr is something. I'm sure he is the best in what he does, but who the hell knows what he's doing?* [Almost precisely what Mr. Blackwell said to me.]

That's our subject. . . . Tough but truthful, rough but sentimental, touched by the truths I have hit home. . . .

That's enough, Regis. What more do you want at these prices?

If I didn't know Sydney by now and trust him, I would swear for sure that he had cheated on this one. But forget it. Nothing ruffles his benign, becalmed, professorial feathers more than even the gentlest question: Didn't he have a hint of whose birth date he was reading!

To this day, Sydney has never met Mr. Blackwell and didn't even know that he lives in a mansion in Hancock Park until I told him.

As for Regis Philbin himself, he also was jolted by a couple of candid Omarr readings on his own, now-defunct syndicated TV show called "That Regis Philbin Show." Sydney informed him before the entire listening audience that his show was going to be canceled. It was. The amiable Regis is not only willing and ready to supply the details but he has become one of Sydney's biggest boosters—along with a few million others. Mention Sydney Omarr's name to him and he goes off in a tailspin of superlatives. "He is terrific! He is the best there is," he proclaimed before I even had a chance to ask.

"Let me tell you what happened. I had Sydney as a guest on my very first 'That Regis Philbin Show.' That was back in 1964. I asked him to do a horoscope for me and tell me how the show was going to do, whether it would be a success. He said, 'I'm sorry to tell you this, but you are going to have problems. I don't think you'll make it; the show won't last.' Well, we did have problems, so five months later I brought Sydney back as a guest a second time and asked him, 'What is your prognosis now?' He was extremely gentle and kind. He said, 'I hate to be the bearer of bad tidings but I think you'll get the news within forty-eight hours that the show is going to be canceled.' I got the news in thirty-six hours that my show was being canceled in two weeks.

"Then, about a year ago [1974], I had an offer to go to St. Louis and host a TV show. I asked Sydney's advice. He urged me to stick it out in Hollywood, because my chart showed that I would soon have other offers in national television.

"And all of a sudden here I am with four shows going, two of them on a national network, ABC, and two in Los Angeles." (The L.A. shows: "Almost Anything Goes" and "Ninety Minutes A.M." On ABC-TV: "The Neighbors," a game show, and Regis Philbin movie reviews.)

No wonder Regis Philbin has become one of Sydney's strongest supporters and admirers.

The same can be said of another ABC-TV personality, Hollywood's Rona Barrett, who consulted Sydney during a minor crisis in her career and asked him which direction she should go. She followed his advice and, in her own words, "It was the beginning of a brand-new cycle in my life. I got my 'Good Morning, America' show and in the month he said I would. Practically everything he said was 100 per cent correct. And he didn't even do a big, full-blown chart on me. He told me how things were aspected for a three-month period. But Sydney Omarr is an expert in his field, one of the best. He knows astrology, he knows what he's doing, and he doesn't need your full chart to find the answers to specific problems. It's like a great surgeon who usually knows how to apply his science properly in any given area of his wide scope of knowledge."

Quite a testimonial from a lady not given to lavish praise of most people.

Maxine Cheshire, a syndicated columnist with the Washington *Post* who takes a dim view of astrology—she once wrote a series of articles highly unfavorable to that high priestess of prophecy, Washington seer Jeane Dixon—told me about an experience she had with Sydney.

"I was trying to check out whether it's true that Ronald Reagan utilizes astrology," she said, "so I called the American Federation of Astrologers and they referred me to Sydney Omarr. He surprised me by asking my birth date, and then he began reeling off all these things about myself that amazed me. My first reaction was that someone from our newspaper syndicate had told him about me, that it was a gag and they were putting me on. Then I realized that no one at my paper knew I was going to call Sydney Omarr and he was telling me things about my personal life that no one else could have known anyway.

"He was so absolutely accurate that I just sat there on the phone listening in stunned silence. It really spooked me.

"You know, basically I don't believe in this astrology garbage," she added, "and being a reporter, I intend to do some investigating and find out how this man, whom I've never met, knows so much about my personal affairs."

I wished her luck and asked her to give me a report on the results of her investigation.

"I'll be happy to," she said. I thought I detected a tone of anticipation in her voice.

It would be a real feather in anybody's cap to come up with evidence that Sydney was tipped off in advance.

I told her to call me back collect as soon as she found out anything. She promised to do so.

I'm still waiting.

A friend once remarked to me, "Sydney Omarr must have a good press agent." He doesn't have a press agent. Period. He doesn't need one. Not with Rona, Regis, Maxine, Merv Griffin, and all the other Omarr addicts who have been mesmerized by him.

I queried Merv Griffin and his talent co-ordinator, Paul Solomon, about Sydney's role with their mystery guests.

Was it possible for Sydney to get a tip-off, to know who the mystery guest would be, to look up the birth dates and research his subject ahead of show time?

Paul Solomon replied rather indignantly, "Sydney doesn't operate that way. He is too honest, too much aboveboard to stoop to anything like that. I'm convinced that he doesn't look up anything. Also, I know it from the time factor involved. I am the one who feeds him the information on the birth dates, and he says, 'Okay, I'll call you back.' But he'll say, 'You're putting a lot of pressure on me. This is terrible. I don't have time to do this. It's very bad that you do this to me at the last minute, Paul. You know I don't approve of this.' Then he'll call back in ten minutes with a rundown that is so accurate you can't believe it. In those ten minutes, he would not have had time even to look up the birth date. Of course, a lot of it comes from his being psychic."

Merv added, "Obviously he's not looking up the dates. He's extraordinary, that's all. None of us at first believed this mystery-guest thing. We used to say, 'Come on, Paul, you told him who it was.' We all said this. Paul would give him the mystery guest's birth date and then come back to us with Sydney's reading, and it was so right on target that we would say to him, 'For God's sake, Paul, you gave him the guy's name.' But he didn't, of course. We couldn't stay in business running a show that way and deceiving our audience. . . ."

How are the mystery guests chosen?

Paul Solomon answered: "What we do is have three, four, or five celebrities for each of the shows. Then it's up to the producer to decide which one of these will be our mystery guest. They are all booked in advance and instructed not to tell anyone that they're going to be on the show. Our mystery guest would give us his birth date and then we would give this to Sydney only an hour or two before show time. . . ."

Merv added, "Sydney is psychic, you know. Sometimes he just

skips over the astrological side of it and heads right into this psychic business. He can get a very funny feeling about you."

As I have mentioned, everyone insists that Sydney is psychic. He hotly maintains he is *not*—that his readings are based purely on astrological and numerological calculations and interpretations.

Why does Merv have Sydney on his show so often?

He is very frank in his reply: "Astrology has started more fights on my show than any subject we've ever tackled. Art Linkletter practically called Sydney a charlatan right to his face. In essence what he said was, you're all a bunch of phonies. This has happened on many of our astrology shows and we couldn't figure out why. We thought that astrology would be one of our most agreeable themes. But it hasn't been. It always turns into a fight. There are avid believers and disbelievers. Many are very vocal about it.

"We have had other astrologers on the show, but Sydney is the best. I think his ability is remarkable. He's very accurate. Of course this [astrology] is a science. He's not really predicting. He's just applying his knowledge of astrology. Because of the NAB code we have to make a statement somewhere on the show that not everybody believes in astrology. We can't come out and endorse it.

"But Sydney Omarr can really almost make you believe in it. He has a sense of show business, and he presents himself so well that the rest of them, well, they're just astrologers, not performers. Sydney also has something else going for him. He is extremely knowledgeable in his subject. He has all the answers in his head. He is quick. He's a very good showman, an excellent showman. He had a knack for antagonizing people, and this always starts a fight. The fighting is good for the show.

"The worst kind of show is when everyone sits around and is compatible. That can get the show bogged down. But Sydney really gets people stirred up. There is something about his personality that just infuriates some people, and sometimes our mystery guests and other guests would just attack him. He is so absolutely positive about everything he says. He comes on and reads these pages about people, and there's nothing that turns off a TV audience faster than somebody sitting there reading something. But Sydney does it with class—and authority. His attitude is, How dare you question me? This really seems to antagonize professionals in other fields—for example, psychologists like Joyce Brothers. What he said about her—

well, how much more on the nose can you get? But she was incensed. She was our Libra guest. We really had a good fight on that show."

One of the best, in fact.

Sydney doesn't really like to talk about the televised tiff he had with the famous lady psychologist, but here are his notes, dated 10/26/72.

MERV GRIFFIN MYSTERY GUEST

Oct. 20, 1928, N.Y., 6:21 P.M. [*birth date*]

Notes to myself on Merv's mystery guest: This one is intriguing, challenging. If someone said to me, "Omarr, put it in two words," I would have to reply *musical psychologist.*

Here is why: This person, the native, deals with moods, interprets, analyzes them, stylizes them. Here is an individual who may appear soft on the outside but is plenty tough down the stretch, is capable of overcoming odds, can come up with the right answers at the right time. But native is not always sure about own personal answers.

In 1955, native's life changed in decided manner. Next year also will see changes of major nature which include travel, and native is already having taste of this. . . .

Here is a person who knows the meaning of adversity, of suffering. Family situation was important and still is. . . . And where finances and emotional commitments enter picture, this person is very much involved, especially in connection with family obligations, memories. Individual is regal, plenty of pride, can wait, knew early what amibitions were and endures much to fulfill them.

Health perhaps has left something to be desired of late. Hypertension is no stranger here. . . . Voice plays outstanding part in makeup of this person. . . . Must be wary of kidney problems and should be ready for change of residence by 1974. Recent travel is but a preliminary. Much of past is being erased, and if native looks back to 1970, around August, there is recall of how it feels to have the world seem to come crumbling down, to have relationships severed and to have it appear that no one understands—and more—that everyone seems to be totally lacking in desire to comprehend.

Yes, hard lessons are no stranger here. Our subject, however, has survived, and it will soon be evident that happy days are here again for this sensitive, aware, basically fine human being.

One more thing: Native draws persons born under Cancer and Capricorn. . . . These persons play important roles. And when we hear native's voice, it will be a pleasant experience—throaty and direct, which is also the native's manner—forthright, analytical, and honest.

I am not personally acquainted with Dr. Joyce Brothers. Therefore, I cannot verify Sydney's percentage of accuracy in his horoscopic analysis.

But it isn't too difficult to draw your own conclusions from the fact that Dr. Brothers went into a "seething rage," as some described it, and uttered a number of very defensive statements and accusations against Sydney, strongly implying that he could have gone to the county records, looked up the births for the day, and found out what celebrity was born on that day."

This, however, would have required some rather fast footwork, as Sydney had only forty-five minutes between the time that he was given her birth information and the time that he had to call in what he was going to say on the air.

Sydney clearly established her as a psychologist, which was a feat in itself.

One person who viewed the program was Dr. John LaCorte, a young professor of philosophy at California State College, Dominguez Hills, who later was to become my assistant on this book. He told me: "This was a case, par excellence, in which professional prejudice was blocking any type of rational comprehension of what was really occurring in Sydney's analysis. His description of this [to him] unknown celebrity was uncanny in its accuracy. I am not familiar with the personal aspects of Dr. Brothers' life. However, any doubts that I might have had about Sydney's accuracy were quickly dispelled by observing the face-to-face encounter between Sydney and Dr. Brothers that ensued.

"The fact of Sydney's accuracy seemed to me to be more than established simply by the way in which Dr. Brothers attempted to maintain her intellectual superiority, shall we say. We have here a typical case in which a member of the scientific-academic community will attempt at all costs to undermine the evidence, even to the extent of questioning the honesty of the person who is setting forth the evidence, so that the true facts need not be confronted.

"It was as a result of observing this display that I was motivated to write to Sydney Omarr, whom I had never met, and congratulate him not only for his very rational and knowledgeable approach to astrology but for his great patience in dealing with the types of accusations that Dr. Brothers had not so subtly laid against him in front of millions of people throughout the country.

"At no point in the encounter with Dr. Brothers did he lose his equanimity or composure, or his very rational perspective. The same, I think, cannot be said for Dr. Brothers."

Whatever else may be said about her, I feel that I owe a small debt of gratitude to the famous lady psychologist, for if she had not incurred the wrath of young John LaCorte, he would not have written that fan letter to Sydney, who turned it over to me—and that's how John got trapped into trying to teach me about the vernal equinox, the "precession" of the planets, and why Aquarius the water bearer is an air sign, not water.

Science Versus Astrology

Chapter 15

ASTROLOGY ON TRIAL

"I do not like the idea of prior condemnation, of condeming a subject without investigating it."

—DR. J. ALLEN HYNEK

CHAIRMAN OF THE DEPARTMENT OF ASTRONOMY
NORTHWESTERN UNIVERSITY, EVANSTON, ILLINOIS

As a slow-learning student of astrology, by now I have at least learned enough to know that this scientific art, as Sydney calls it, is a very complicated business, not mere fun and games or simple fortunetelling.

Unfortunately, the overwhelming number of practicing astrologers today know little or nothing about the historical and scientific basis of their subject, probably never even heard of Ptolemy's *Tetrabiblos,* and have no understanding of such basic and vital elements as mathematical equations and astronomy, the measurement of time by planetary movements, or the "precession of the equinoxes."

Neither do I understand them, but Sydney does. He is probably the most learned and most successful practitioner of his craft since Kepler and Newton, both outstanding astronomers in their day who were also astrologers. Unquestionably no one is better qualified to put would-be debunkers in their place. Partly because of his fluency and skill as a debater, but more importantly because of the vast storehouse of knowledge in his head, Sydney is the only astrologer intellectually equipped for verbal combat with some of the most outstanding astronomers in the country. He takes them on with zeal and usually comes out the winner.

When, as a boy of fifteen or sixteen, he first began writing about astrology, people would sometimes ask his mother, "What does your son do?"

She would reply, "He's an astrologer."

Then would come the raised eyebrow and "Oh. You mean an astronomer."

"She never bothered to correct them, and it was probably just as well," Sydney recalled. "Fortunately I learned about the prejudice against my profession at a very early age. That's one of the reasons I made up my mind to delve into astrology, to read everything and learn as much as I could about the subject."

One incident that made a deep impression on him occurred when he was living with a girl, Marian, a Gemini and his first love he calls her, and they were broke and tried to get a loan. Sydney found that he couldn't even apply for a loan, because he didn't have a "real" job. He was a free-lance writer who was writing articles on astrology. Marian was a teacher, but she was between teaching assignments and was assured of another job. She filled out the application for the loan and apparently everything was all set for the loan to go through. Then unexpectedly it was turned down. Sydney asked a friend with some influence to try to find out why. The friend got a look at the records and came back with the report: Marian's loan was turned down because she was "under the influence of a fortuneteller."

Sydney never quite got over that. Since then he has dedicated his life to disproving that astrology is fortunetelling, mystical magic, or mere ancient "superstition," as most scientists call it.

And in the process he has become so highly knowledgeable of the celestial operations he talks and writes about that even astronomers —at least some of them—grudgingly regard him with awe and respect.

In my own celestial sojourn during the writing of this book, one of my favorite stories, frequently recounted by other writers on the subject, concerns Isaac Newton's encounter with his contemporary Edmund Halley, discoverer of Halley's comet. This was at a time in the seventeenth century when astrology was being taught in major European universities, and Newton (1642–1727), famed for his principle of gravitation, was attending Cambridge University just so he could study the celestial science. When astronomer Halley made a disparaging remark as to the value of astrology, Newton gently rebuked him: "I have studied the subject, Mr. Halley; you have not."

With a change of names Sydney Omarr is in the unique position today of being able to say, justifiably, those exact same words to approximately 100 per cent of astrology's detractors.

This is why *Time* magazine once dubbed him America's "highbrow astrologer" in the ancient "science of the stars."

And it is why Sydney symbolizes for many observers a peculiar paradox: the rebirth of the ancient "superstition" of astrology at a time when science has relegated it to the graveyard of mythology.

Virtually all scientists today reject astrology as an unfounded superstition. Yet some academic doors have opened, and in spite of continuing hard-nosed academic-scientific-religious prejudice, astrology for the masses is booming and astrology for those seriously interested in the subject is experiencing a renaissance under the guise of new names—such as astrobiology.

Sydney's popularity, through mass media such as his syndicated astrology column, his best-selling books and astrological guides, and his frequent television appearances, has played a vital role in the renaissance of astrology.

But the road hasn't been easy. Over the years he has incurred the wrath and resentment of many so-called "authorities" and many media officials, especially in radio and television.

"Did you ever wonder why astrology is so popular and yet you never see a television program based on it?" he asks.

His Merv Griffin shows were—and are—an exception, but even these have had their ups and downs with the NAB code. This is the code of the National Association of Broadcasters, which in effect says, incredibly, that astrology must not be presented in such a way as to incite interest or belief in it.

"We talk about freedom of the press, freedom of the air waves, freedom of information. Forget about that freedom when it comes to talking about astrology on the air. The NAB code is absolutely illegal and immoral," Sydney declares. "I can't count how many times I've been told, 'Now, just don't make it look too good.' It's been a big fight from the beginning."

There was one significant exception: Herbert Scott, a man who recognized budding genius when he saw it—or heard it—and who gave Sydney his first break on the air waves on his own radio station, WPAZ in Pottstown, Pennsylvania, in 1951, was so impressed with his young protégé that he allowed him to do anything he wanted to do on the air.

Herb Scott is now the largest single individual owner of radio stations in the United States (most of them in the East: Pennsylvania, New York, New Jersey, and Delaware), and he recalls with awe and amazement how Sydney Omarr helped build up his stations' listening audience with his charm and ingenuity.

"His charm was unbelievable. And he was brilliant, absolutely brilliant, so competent at anything he did that I gave him carte blanche to do his own thing, whatever he wanted to do. If he wanted to talk about astrology it was all right with me. I didn't know what he was talking about and maybe neither did our listeners but they listened. I am not a believer in astrology but I am a believer in Sydney Omarr," said Herb Scott, sounding very much like another Omarr press agent. And with good reason.

He had just built his first radio station. There was no NAB code then, but Station WPAZ had its own problems, namely its competition, the local newspaper, which, in Scott's own words, "was fighting to keep the news from us."

He hired Sydney as a reporter and newscaster—*not* as an astrologer—specifically to help in the station's struggle to survive the media battle for news.

"I didn't know Sydney Omarr. I didn't know anything about him, but he called and asked for a job and I told him to come and see me. I knew immediately just by talking to him that he could do it. I hired him to do three 15-minute newscasts a day, and I warned him it would be tough. Besides the competition from the local newspaper, there wasn't all that much news in Pottstown. It was a small town, with a population of only thirty thousand.

"But Sydney dug in. He worked from 7 A.M. until 6 P.M. six days a week—and I was only paying him eighty dollars a week. It wasn't much even in those days," Herb Scott admits, "but I was just starting too, and it was all I could afford. It didn't seem to inhibit Sydney's enthusiasm or his talent. When there wasn't any news, he made his own news with local feature stories about people in the community. He seemed to have an intuitive knowledge that people liked to hear their names on the air, and he had a real flair for ferreting out news features and writing them and reporting them on his newscasts in a way that left listeners spellbound.

"He began to build up a great following. People would tune in to our station to hear Sydney, not the news. He was brilliant at improvising and writing features to fill in his newscasts, and he was tremendously popular. Everyone liked him."

Sydney soon was elevated to the status of news director for Station WPAZ (its first), though his forte still was features, often with an astrological twist.

"Astrology was quite a shocker in those days," Herb Scott recalled. "It was something foreign to most of us. I didn't understand it, but I knew that Sydney had something special. He was so far ahead of his time."

He was so far ahead, in fact, that on one of his newscasts he instituted a segment, "Cradle Call," during which he gave astrological forecasts for newborn babies.

"It was incredible and intriguing. I don't think anything like it has been done before or since. (The NAB code would prohibit such a show today.) Sydney was one of the most talented persons I've ever met, a gifted writer and an outstanding person as well. I personally feel he could have been a great success as a writer if he had not become an astrologer. And besides that," Herb Scott added, "he was quite a ladies' man in Pottstown. I remember he broke three or four hearts while he was there."

The Leo in Sydney relishes this sort of praise, but he is more grateful to Herb Scott for giving him his first break on the air with his real first love, astrology.

"If I hadn't given him his first break, someone else would have," says Scott. "That kind of talent doesn't go undiscovered."

It was a long jump from Pottstown's Station WPAZ to nationally syndicated and network shows and Sydney's ensuing confrontations with the NAB.

When he appeared on the Johnny Carson Show with Bette Davis, for example, a portion of the show was bleeped out because of the NAB code.

"I had just finished the part with Bette Davis. The show was going well and we were having a lot of fun," Sydney recalled. Then Johnny Carson asked me if there were any new developments in astrology. I told him about the recent research being done by John Henry Nelson at RCA, who was trying to find ways of determining when magnetic storms would occur, since these play havoc with world-wide communications. Nelson had the intellectual courage to admit that his research was astrological in nature. He found that by using Ptolemy's methods of relating squares and oppositions to human disturbance, he had some of the answers. He theorized that perhaps a key factor in the storms was the position of the planets in the solar system relative to the earth and to the sun. In effect, RCA was using the principles of the oldest science known to man, astrology, to forecast magnetic storms. All of this was bleeped out on the basis that it tended to excite interest or belief in astrology—something that is very specifically prohibited by the code of the National Association of Broadcasters."

Apparently only a very few people took note of the deletion. But among them was Jack O'Brian of the New York *Daily News*, who protested in his column the next day. He said he would like to have heard what the astrologer Sydney Omarr had to say about RCA's research on magnetic storms and he was sorry it was bleeped out.

"Usually there is precensorship," Sydney explained. "That is, they tell you what you should or should not do when you're discussing astrology. Keep it light and humorous. Don't try to influence or encourage the audience to take it seriously. It's okay to have someone who is very comedic on the same program to make the subject look silly, and it's okay to make silly predictions such as there'll be bedbugs in Ohio. I have nothing against humor and I always get my share of laughs by including funny anecdotes about my experiences and about the various signs. But once you begin to try to impart information about what astrology is, what its potential is, then you are in difficulty."

Because of his involvement with broadcasting, Sydney has found the NAB code to be the most annoying and harassing of all the hurdles he has had to leap in his profession as an astrologer.

It is a voluntary code (introduced in the 1950s), and some independent stations do not subscribe to it.

"Most who do subscribe to it break it anyway, because you're not supposed to present more than X number of commercials within a certain amount of time. But nobody pays any attention to that, because commercials mean money. However, when it comes to astrology, there are such strong restrictions that the subject can never be presented in a positive light," Sydney maintains.

Though Sydney was the only member of the American armed forces ever assigned full-time duty as an astrologer, and though he is in even more demand today on radio and television, the NAB technically bars his appearance on member stations with an antiquated code that says: *Program material featuring fortunetelling, occultism, astrology, phrenology, palm reading, numerology, mind reading, or character reading is unacceptable when presented for the purpose of fostering belief in these subjects.*

"Obviously the code is not always enforced," says Sydney. "But it *exists.* All radio and television stations subscribing to the NAB code could, under regulations of the Federal Communications Commission, *have their licenses to broadcast removed.*"

Sydney has done as much if not more than any individual to foist astrology on the NAB through his appearances on network television and radio and through his presentations of the subject in a manner that most certainly created interest and belief—so much, in fact, that his radio series on astrology in 1968 on Station KNX in Los Angeles (an affiliate of CBS) was perfunctorily canceled because he refused to follow the NAB's guidelines for his show, which were as follows:

A. It should contain an opening and closing disclaimer, which in effect points out that the program is for entertainment purposes only and that man determines his own fate. [Of course he does!]

B. The show should be kept as general, vague, and innocuous as possible with avoidance of any specifics or believable generalities regarding such sensitive areas as business, love, romance, loneliness, and so forth. The use of light spoofiness is strongly encouraged to help assure that the program material cannot be interpreted as being presented to foster a belief in astrology.

C. Techniques such as mystical hocus-pocus effects should be avoided.

D. Detailed technical references to signs of the zodiac that might lend credence to astrology as a scientific endeavor should be avoided.

The program, called "*Sydney Omarr's Almanac*," the first, last, and only one of its kind, met its demise through the dastardly NAB crime of lending too much credence to astrology. His approach was too serious, his knowledge too formidable, his percentage of accuracy in astrological forecasts too unbelievable for non-believers. A former chief of the NAB's Hollywood office boasted, "I finally got Sydney off the air; I got KNX to cancel him." He was most proud of his accomplishment.

Fortunately the setback for Sydney wasn't exactly devastating. He was destined—by the stars—to achieve other outstanding forensic victories on both radio and television.

But the NAB code has remained a prickly thorn in his craw. And no wonder. The "guidelines" set forth above applied only to Sydney's radio show on astrology.

The following "guidelines" on astrology programs were set forth in a letter by an assistant "code director" dated July 11, 1969, and are still applicable today:

1. The program should contain opening and closing disclaimers which, in effect, inform the viewer that the program is for entertainment purposes only, that the stars do not in any way control or influence man's actions, and the man, through his own efforts, determines his own fate.

2. "Astrology/horoscope" programs should not contain specific advice to individuals which, in effect, would encourage individuals to follow a particular course of action based on "astrology/horoscope" readings.

3. Descriptions contained in "astrology/horoscope" programs should be as general and vague as possible with special attention paid to the manner in which such sensitive subjects as love, loneliness, romance, medical matters, finances, business, etc. are handled.

4. To the degree possible, references to the fallibility of the "stars" and of "astrology/horoscope" character readings should be included in the program. A guest who indicates that what has been said about him or her is incorrect or indicates a disbelief in the subjects would be one way of approaching this aspect.

5. "Astrology/horoscope" programs should not contain material or devices which tend to be instructive in nature or support the credibility of the subjects. Technical descriptions of the signs of the zodiac, the elements, planets, their relationships and interrelationships, their effects on an individual's characteristics and life, should be avoided, as should detailed astrological charts, birthday books, etc.

6. When a professional astrologer appears on the "astrology/horoscope" programs, the individual should not be described in a manner which would tend to give credibility to his activities or the subjects. Additionally, the manner in which the professional astrologer is used in such programs would have to be reviewed to determine whether it is in keeping with applicable Television Code Standards.

7. To the degree possible, the use of light, spoofing material is strongly encouraged to help assure that the program cannot be interpreted as being presented to foster belief in "astrology/horoscopes."

8. References to famous individuals or descriptions of them based on "astrology/horoscope" readings could pose a problem under Code standards. The manner in which this is done, the things that are said about the individuals as they relate to "astrology/horoscopes" would be the determining factors. In general, straightforward descriptions of the general characteristics of the individuals would be acceptable under Code standards, provided that the descriptions in no way state or convey the impression that the "stars" had anything to do with the individual's success or characteristics.

Additionally, the description should in no way create the impression that the individuals involved believed in "astrology/horoscopes."

We would recommend that famous political figures (living or dead) not be used, if such sequences are contemplated, in order to preclude the possibility of viewers forming the opinion that the individuals believe(d) in "astrology/horoscopes." (From *Sydney Omarr's Astrological Guide for 1974*, pp. 11–13.)

•

These are the ridiculous handcuffs clamped on Sydney each time he makes a television appearance. Remember that the next time you watch him. But note also that he's sharp and sly enough to slip out of them at times and put in his erudite plug for astrology despite the NAB's blueprint for prejudice against it.

The so-called "guidelines" were ostensibly created to protect people from their own gullibility, from believing the charlatans or pseudo astrologers who might make wild claims on the air waves. But as Sydney points out, this is not only an insult to the listening audience but to the program directors and others who prepare the "astrology/horoscope" shows and book the guest stars.

The Merv Griffin astrology shows with Sydney have been notably successful and with a minimum of problems from the NAB code perhaps because of the intelligence and integrity of the shows' producers, as well as Sydney's. But as I have mentioned earlier, it is in his contract that any written material he reads on the show must first be approved by the producer.

He once was guest star on a Mike Douglas Show that simply never aired in some cities, including Los Angeles, because his readings of members of the audience were "too accurate." The show is pretaped and syndicated to stations in various cities where it is scheduled to be aired at a later date. Sydney was expecting to watch himself when the show aired in Los Angeles, but to his surprise there was no Mike Douglas Show on that date. The whole show had been canceled. He called the station and asked, "How come the Mike Douglas Show wasn't on today? I was supposed to be on it."

"That's why," he was told. "We had to take it off because of you. You were too accurate. They tell us that would break the code."

Who are "they?"

"They're hard to pin down," says Sydney. "Whenever I talk to the station manager or network representative or producer or program director, they're never the guilty party. They always say, 'Well, it's not my decision, it's somebody else.' You never really find out who the censor is, but the censorship is right there in the code."

There is an interesting Catch-22 situation regarding the subscription of the stations to the National Association of Broadcasters'

Code. The FCC (Federal Communications Commission) is the governmental agency in charge of licensing television and radio stations. It is the duty of the FCC to be sure that the air waves are used for the benefit of the American public and that the privilege of broadcasting is not in any way abused.

The FCC itself does not have very specific guidelines or criteria. These are to be found in the NAB Code. It is a peculiar marriage between the two. The code is "voluntary" and as such is not subject to scrutiny under the provisions of the Constitution that guarantee freedom of speech. The FCC states that subscription to the NAB Code is completely up to the station. But the stations know very well that if they do not subscribe to the NAB Code or if they violate at least certain provisions of the code, they are severely risking the possibility that their license will not be renewed by the FCC. The FCC says that it has nothing against astrology, for that would clearly be illegal. So they leave the situation ostensibly ambivalent, but in practice the stations know that they must be acutely aware of their astrological p's and q's.

The media is not the only area in which the federal government has arbitrarily intervened to limit or eliminate public access to knowledge of astrology and other forms of the mantic arts.

In the early sixties Sydney was approached by officials of the Post Office Department who threatened to prosecute him if he did not stop sending two of his books, *Thought Dial* and *Dreamscope*, through the mails. The one that mainly concerned Sydney was *Thought Dial*. He decided that it would be better to fight and establish his as well as the rights of others in matters of this kind.

He was willing to take on the time, expense, and inconvenience of the case because he knew he was right, and he felt that the line had to be drawn somewhere. This was a rather gigantic undertaking for Sydney, considering the fact that the government had unlimited funds.

Sydney at the time was working at CBS for his livelihood. He was taking a considerable risk financially. He realized that he could even lose his job if the case attracted adverse publicity. But to him the principle was much more important.

He had been told that if he continued to send *Thought Dial* through the mails he would be guilty of a felony—defrauding by means of the mails, because astrology was considered a fraudulent activity.

Sydney, of course, was infuriated. In spite of the state of his finances, he hired one of the leading attorneys who specialized in fighting book cases—usually smut-and-pornography books, though Sydney's *Thought Dial* certainly didn't come under that heading. The trial was all set to begin the following day when Sydney received a phone call. The government, with its unlimited funds, had flown out two men from Washington who wished to confer with him in his attorney's office.

When he walked in the door, one of them commented, "Well, he really doesn't look like that much of a villain."

In a short time he had convinced the gentlemen from Washington that the practice of astrology was not fraudulent.

They admitted they had no real grounds for prosecution and dropped the case against him.

But it was a trying time for Sydney, and he still regards the incident as an important test case for astrology.

"Since it involved the Post Office, they could pick their own jury, you know. And they had already decided that everything about astrology was a fraud. They even told me that they were going to stop all astrology books from being sent through the mails. I was perfectly willing to go to trial and to fight them if they hadn't backed down. No one really likes to be a guinea pig in a test case like that, especially when you have the government against you. It would have been an interesting trial. So what if I'd lost? Going to jail may not be so bad, but it would have been a tremendous loss financially. Attorneys don't work for nothing. It was one of the most trying experiences I ever had, because you feel so helpless when you're fighting the government."

But it was also a rewarding experience. Although perhaps difficult to evaluate, Sydney's action undoubtedly had some effect on limiting government meddling in mail-order astrology books (which incidentally are enjoying a booming business). And if the government had proved its case against Sydney, as well it might have with its unlimited resources, and established that astrology is a fraud, this could have set a precedent for future cases and surely would have changed the direction astrology has taken in terms of its increasing popularity in recent years.

FORTUNETELLING VERSUS ASTROLOGY

Sydney finally got his day in court on September 29, 1965, when he appeared as a defense witness for Kay Loring, former actress and professional astrologer, who had been arrested on a charge of fortunetelling by means of astrology.

Fortunetelling is a misdemeanor under the Los Angeles Municipal Code. Miss Loring could have taken the easy way out, pleaded guilty, and paid a fine of from fifty dollars to two hundred fifty dollars, depending upon the circumstances. Instead she chose to stand and fight before a trial jury. If found guilty, she could be fined up to five hundred dollars or imprisoned for not more than six months or both.

Sydney had no personal interest in Miss Loring. He didn't even know her. But remembering how his first love, Marian, had been turned down for a loan because she was "under the influence of a fortuneteller," he leaped at the chance to testify in court regarding the difference between astrology and fortunetelling.

It was Sydney's testimony that clearly won the case for her. She was acquitted after a historic two-day trial, probably the most colorful one of its kind since America's first and most famous lady pioneer astrologer, Evangeline Adams, was tried for "fortune-telling" in New York in 1914.

Many observers, including James Crenshaw, long-time Los Angeles newspaperman, author, and investigator in the field of psychic phenomena, believe the California jury that acquitted Kay Loring may have created historic precedent by establishing astrology as a "scientific art"—in accordance with Sydney's explanation.

Writing in the 1966 fall issue of *Fate* magazine, Crenshaw stated:

> Astrology, on trial in California, has won a vindication that may well set a precedent in other jurisdictions.
>
> In essence, the trial established:
>
> 1. That astrology has wide support for its representation as a "scientific art."
>
> 2. That its practice is not illegal per se.

3. That when properly practiced it does not involve fortunetelling.

Miss Loring, then forty-two, practiced astrology at her home in the Reseda district of the San Fernando Valley section of Los Angeles.

It was, therefore, two Los Angeles city police officers from the Van Nuys Division in the San Fernando Valley who made the arrest that led to Miss Loring's somewhat historic trial. They were undercover vice officers, a policeman and policewoman posing as a soon-to-be-married couple seeking advice.

The trial was held before a jury of eleven women and one man in the Van Nuys court of Municipal Judge Donald M. Redwine.

The specific charge against Miss Loring was that she "engaged in the business of telling fortunes by means of astrology."

This was in violation of Los Angeles municipal ordinance 43.30, which reads:

> No person shall advertise by sign, circular, handbill or in any newspaper, periodical or magazine, or other publication or publications or by any other means, to tell fortunes, to find or restore lost or stolen property, to locate oil wells, gold or silver or other ore or metal or natural product; to restore lost love or friendship and affection, to unite or procure lovers, husbands, wives, lost relatives or friends, for or without pay, by means of occult or psychic powers, faculties or forces, clairvoyance, psychology, psychometry, spirits, mediumship, seership, prophecy, astrology, palmistry, necromancy, or other craft, science, cards, talismans, charms, potions, magnetism or magnetized articles or substances, Oriental mysteries or magic of any kind or nature, or numerology, or to engage in or carry on any business the advertising of which is prohibited in this section.

Exemptions are provided in another section for ministers practicing such arts as a part of their religion, but in the trial before Judge Redwine, the issue was plain and simple: Had Miss Loring committed a misdemeanor by telling fortunes?

Defending Miss Loring was the well-known trial attorney Seymour Fried, who, in addition to his legal expertise, had been given a crash course in astrology by the man he called as his star witness, Sydney Omarr.

Recognized by the court as an expert, Sydney described in detail what astrology is and what is done by astrologers. He emphasized that there is no connection between astrology and fortunetelling. He said that astrology tries to give trends, cycles, and indications through observation of the planets and luminaries.

"How a person uses these trends, cycles, and indications depends on the individual," he said. "It depends on the ability of the astrologer and the intelligence of the client."

Sydney left no question in the courtroom as to his own ability as an astrologer. When the jury handed down its not-guilty verdict, Judge Redwine lauded them for a job well done. He termed the case "very unusual" and said he had never seen one like it in his eight years on the bench in Van Nuys.

Sydney's eyes still twinkle when he recalls the case with relish.

"It was great fun for me, though it must not have been fun for Kay Loring. First of all, they had to get my credentials to see if I was acceptable as an expert," he recalled. "I listed my occupation as a newsman and editor, not an astrologer. But I told them that I had spent all these years studying the subject and writing about it and had become known as an authority in the course of those studies.

"That was acceptable. Once the court had accepted my credentials and the prosecutor had accepted them, then the judge wouldn't let him cut me off. When the prosecutor objected to something I said, the judge told him he could not object because he had accepted me as an expert witness. You can't suddenly become a nonexpert in two minutes just because someone disagrees with you. I'm sure the prosecutor would never have permitted me to testify if he had known what I was going to say.

"You see, none of them knew anything about astrology, so they were rather startled when I began explaining it to them."

Startled is probably an understatement. The court must have been jolted when Sydney began reeling off references to Ptolemy's *Tetrabiblos*, St. Thomas Aquinas' *Summa Theologica*, the works of Kepler, Copernicus, and Galileo, the "precession of the equinoxes" and measurement of time by planetary movements, and his definition of astrology based on Carl Jung's theory of synchronicity:

> Astrology is that scientific art which treats of the synchronicity between planetary positions and mundane affairs including human character and potential.

"That's pretty encompassing, isn't it?" Sydney smiles.

He told them about RCA's astrological research in predicting magnetic storms and how both clock time and calendar time are the result of astrological calculations based on the earth's movement around the sun.

The principal purpose of Sydney's testimony was to dispute the implication that astrology is only one of various forms of fortune-telling. He explained something of the ancient history of astrology and the fact that vast amounts of data have been accumulated over thousands of years to prove that certain heavenly configurations can be correlated with events in the lives of men, families, and nations. Specific events cannot be forecast, he said, as alleged in the fortune-telling charge, but only their potentiality. Astrologers do not claim that any event is inevitable—only that in many instances the trends and portents point to a likelihood of events or conditions unless successful counteraction is taken.

He described astrology as both a science and an art—a science because it utilizes calculated astronomical data in setting up charts, and an art because the ability of the astrologer to interpret the data then comes into play to apply the data to a given situation.

Medicine, he said, is a similar "scientific art." Doctors use laboratory information and other scientific data to make diagnoses, but the success of the treatment depends upon the skill or "art" of the particular physician. In both astrology and medicine no inevitable events can be safely predicted, for there is always a margin of error, and the practitioner who insists upon being fatalistic—i.e., telling fortunes—runs the risk of being proved totally wrong.

Nature has a way of upsetting predictions—and then there is always the element of "free will" so often emphasized in the so-called occult sciences.

Nevertheless, Sydney explained, trends and cycles that can be interpreted by the competent astrologer often may be used to forecast conditions that may have certain effects upon an individual or a group coming into given conditions.

Defense attorney Fried emphasized throughout the case that astrology was not on trial, but it was necessary to educate the jurors not only concerning the legality of astrology but the theory of its practice, as distinct from fortunetelling, he said.

"The stars impel; they do not compel," he explained, using a well-known astrological maxim.

Following are excerpts from Fried's arguments to the jury, as recorded by James Crenshaw (who was also a defense witness at the trial) in his article "Astrology Wins in Court" in the 1966 fall issue of *Fate* magazine:

> 1. We learn that the hypothesis of the astrologers is that different effects will be produced by different configurations of the heavenly bodies.
>
> 2. Each sign represents approximately a month or a one-twelfth segment of the zodiac. The planets and the sun and moon, known as luminaries, are part of the zodiacal picture.
>
> 3. These heavenly bodies are constantly moving—a scientific fact.
>
> 4. Each month, each week, even each hour, they are in a different position, and by thousands of years of observations, it has been ascertained that certain positions of these heavenly bodies coincide with certain conditions.
>
> "Definite conditions seem to have prevailed in correlation with specific combinations and configurations," he continued. "Certain effects correspond to fixed positions of the planets in relation to the zodiacal signs and constellations, as well as to each other.
>
> "One versed in this art, by making a chart, which takes three to four hours of computations, can indicate the relative positions of the bodies in relation to the place and time a person was born. By tracing the movement of planets and luminaries, their relative positions can be deducted throughout the life of the individual—at the various ages of the person.
>
> "Key to all of this is the fact that astrologers do not and will

not attempt to tell what will happen in the future but only that which the planets and luminaries are tending to bring about. The reading reveals influences, not events."

In passing, he also noted that "prophecy" is an essential part of life as we know it today. Stockbrokers make predictions. So do politicians. Likewise, weathermen. But as in the case of astrologers, their forecasts, said the attorney, are "trends and portents" rather than actual events.

And that is not illegal. Nor is the practice of astrology as a "scientific art."

As a matter of fact, science itself is essentially based on the ability to predict specific results under certain conditions, particularly those encountered in the laboratory, the attorney noted.

He therefore concluded that Miss Loring had not engaged in the business of telling fortunes, as charged.

The jury agreed after less than two hours of deliberation.

Sydney had briefed the defense attorney well in the fundamentals of astrology, and Sydney's own testimony, although presented frequently in high-brow rhetoric that went over the heads of judge, jury, and prosecutor, played a major role in the jury's acquittal of Miss Loring on fortunetelling charges.

Evangeline Adams would have been proud of him!

EVANGELINE ADAMS

Of all modern astrologers, Evangeline Adams (1868–1932) was the most famous. Her book *The Bowl of Heaven* should be required reading for anyone interested in the subject. A direct descendant of President John Quincy Adams, she was a woman of great integrity, an artist when it came to interpreting horoscopes. She made astrology respectable, and she helped make America astrology-conscious.

To her studios in New York's Carnegie Hall came the great and near great—including the great financier J. P. Morgan.

Evangeline Adams was responsible for astrology being legalized in the state of New York after being haled into court as a fortuneteller. In 1914 an archaic law in New York State classed astrology with "acrobatic performers, circus riders, men who desert their wives, and people who pretend to tell fortunes." All in this category, according to the statute, were termed "disorderly persons."

Miss Adams had been plagued by undercover agents and charged with "fortune-telling" on several previous occasions, but in each instance the charges were dropped. Finally she dared the state of New York to put astrology on trial.

As she explained, "I had but one ambition: to legalize astrology in the state of New York. So when another enemy of the science came to me anonymously, secured a reading which she claimed was 'fortune-telling,' and haled me again to court, I went with a willing and determined heart."

She also went with a stack of reference books reaching nearly to the ceiling and "a mass of evidence that reached as far back as the Babylonian seers."

It isn't recorded how much of the history of this ancient science she told the crowded courtroom, but being a scholarly woman steeped in astrology, she must have given quite a recital, which could have gone something like this:

Astrology reached its zenith in Babylon between 625 and 538 B.C. Berossus, a priest, established a school of astrology on the island of Cos about 280 B.C., from where it spread through Greece. . . . Babylonian astrology was recorded on seventy clay tablets, the Illumination of Bel, found in the ruins of the library of King Ashurbanipal (669–633 B.C.) at Nineveh, Assyria, A.D. 1851. According to Professor A. H. Sayce, a student of this period, the Babylonian priests believed that predictable events were perfectly natural occurrences, determined by other natural occurrences, which could be correlated by a trained observer of the stars. "Hence, if a war with Elam had followed an eclipse of the sun on a particular date, it was assumed that a recurrence of the eclipse on the same day would be followed by a recurrence of a war with Elam."

According to Jess Stearn's research in his excellent book *A Time for Astrology* (also required reading for all students of astrology), the Babylonians used the rising planet, the first-house planet nearest the ascendant, as well as the sun and moon, to foresee the individual's life. If a child was born with the moon on the first house ascendant, he would have a bright, long life. With Jupiter on the ascendant, he would become rich as he grew old, and if Venus was rising, his life would be calm and his days long and favorable.

Jupiter on the descendant, which was in the seventh house, as opposed to the ascendant, was especially bad for the king, since Jupiter was the king of the planets. Other planets on the descendant had a correspondingly unfavorable effect, as they were manifestly opposed to the individual's personality.

Now, it seems fairly certain that Evangeline Adams was as well versed in the astrology of the ancient Babylonians as Jess Stearn or Sydney Omarr, but in all accounts of her history-making trial on charges of fortunetelling, the most dramatic and crucial test came when she demanded in the interest of science that she be allowed to cast a horoscope of anybody chosen at random and give a reading of that person.

Trial Judge John J. Freschi, entering into the spirit of the experiment, gave her the birthday, hour, and place of a person he identified only as "Mr. X."

Miss Adams consulted her ephemerides and table of houses, and drew the horoscope. Standing straight, speaking in a clear, confident voice, she gave her findings. The judge leaned forward. So did attorneys and spectators and newspapermen. . . . Finally the reading was over. Judge Freschi took a long look at the defendant. Then, unsmilingly, he announced his findings:

> The defendant raises astrology to the dignity of an exact science.
>
> She has given ample proof that she is a woman of learning and culture, and one who is very well versed in *astronomy* and other sciences. Her chart here, as made out, may be verified, as she stated, in the books and records of astronomers for years.
>
> In the reading of the horoscope the defendant went through an absolutely mechanical, mathematical process to get at her conclusions. She claims that astrology never makes a mistake, though astrologers do, and if the figures are correct, the information given is correct.
>
> The sincerity of the defendant's determination from her own perceptions and a study of authorities cannot be questioned. She certainly does seem to have a thorough knowledge of the subject. And in this, she claims no faculty of foretelling by supernatural or magical means that which is future, or of discovering that which is hidden and obscure; but she does claim

> that nature is to be interpreted by the influences that surround it.
>
> When the defendant prepared her horoscope of the complainant and calculated the relative positions of the planets at the time of her birth, basing this horoscope on the well-known and fixed science of astronomy, she violated no law.

As for the horoscope of "Mr. X," Judge Freschi said the reading gave him a new insight into the person's mentality and character. It turned out that "Mr. X" was his own son!

Today, as a result of that trial, astrology has been taken out of the Dark Ages and legalized in New York. It is no longer classified as "fortune-telling."

Chapter 16
THE GREAT DEBATES

> *"A true scientist is a searcher;*
> *he doesn't have a right to say*
> *that anything is impossible."*
> —SYDNEY OMARR

Sydney has put on his verbal boxing gloves for bouts with some of the most outstanding astronomers in the country, and he usually comes out the winner.

In his lifelong battle against academic and scientific prejudice, he still considers one of his proudest achievements to be the three-hour debate over Philadelphia's Radio Station WPEN in June 1951 with the famed astronomer Dr. Roy K. Marshall, then director of the Fels Planetarium and science editor of the Philadelphia *Evening Bulletin.*

Sydney was still a young upstart when the debate took place, only four years out of the Army, a fledgling astrologer earning his bread as a reporter and preparing horoscopes as a hobby at night.

Dr. Marshall at that time had quite a reputation as astronomy's public spokesman—with a special passion for attacking astrology, in his lectures, in the press, and on radio and TV. But he met his match in Sydney Omarr, whom a newspaper columnist later described as a "husky intellectual" and whose jabbing attacks, spiced with such words as "synchronicity" and *Tetrabiblos,* caused the famed astronomer to lose his scientific cool. He began pounding his fists on the desk and shouting that astrology was damned nonsense.

The upshot was a great coup for Sydney and astrology. The station's switchboard was swamped with calls. Telegrams and letters poured in for days afterward, all in favor of Sydney. The dominant note was one of protest against the manner in which the astronomer had ridiculed astrology and praise for Sydney's expertise as a sparring partner.

The debate elevated Sydney's stature as an astrologer within the scientific community. For the first time, science writers and editors took note of him.

Sydney still treasures a personal letter he received shortly after the debate from Pulitzer prize-winning science writer John J. O'Neill, then science editor of the New York *Herald Tribune* and himself an astronomer.

O'Neill admitted in his letter that for years he, too, had condemned astrology as "unscientific and totally irrational. . . . I condemned without making an adequate investigation of what I was condemning."

After making his own investigation, however, he came to the decision that astrology "is one of the most important fields for scientific research and one of the most neglected," he said.

"The human race should not tolerate further delay in bringing the full co-operative resources of science to extended researchers in this field," he continued. "We know very little about the array of forces that are impinging on the earth, but that little demonstrates a great urgency for further researches and the fascinating possibilities that await discovery. . . .

"Scientists today cannot look down on astrology; instead they must raise their eyes to take in the higher horizons that astrologers have preserved for them."

But Sydney's favorite and most widely quoted portion of the late John J. O'Neill's letter to him, which he regards as a historic milestone for modern astrology, is the last paragraph, couched in rather strong terms:

"Attacks on astrology without previous extensive investigations by competent individuals must, from now on, be regarded as a very antiquated, unscientific practice closely related to witch-hunting, and must be correctly diagnosed as a symptom of professional paranoia on the part of the individual doing the attacking."

Although written in 1951, after the widely publicized Omarr-Marshall debate, the letter is as applicable today as it was then, for the "great debates" between astrology and astronomy have continued and presumably will forevermore.

In the fall of 1975, for example, astrology hit the headlines with a resounding thud that reverberated for weeks in the broadcasting and news media.

A wire service broke the story: 186 SCIENTISTS CHALLENGE ASTROLOGISTS. The 186 scientists, including eighteen Nobel prize winners, had signed a statement emphatically disclaiming that there is any scientific basis for astrology and deploring the fact that "acceptance of astrology pervades modern society."

They were especially disturbed, they said, "by the continued uncritical dissemination of astrological charts, forecasts, and horoscopes by the media and by otherwise reputable newspapers, magazines, and book publishers."

In the ensuing brouhaha, Sydney Omarr's proud Leo the lion roared the loudest and with ferocious impact.

He brashly picked up the telephone and put in a call to one of the Nobel prize winners.

"I didn't know you had made a study of astrology, Dr. So-and-So," he said.

"I don't know anything about astrology but it is a lot of nonsense," Dr. So-and-So replied. He then recalled that he had read an article on astrology in the encyclopedia.

"It was probably written by an astronomer," Sydney informed him. "Most encyclopedias and lexicographers hire astronomers to write their definitions of astrology."

Dictionaries, for instance, Sydney points out, usually *define* words until they come to astrology. "Then they editorialize and call it a pseudo science."

In the wake of the widely publicized "challenge" by the scientists Sydney, of course, was swamped with offers from press and TV newshounds, who sniffed a good fight, to put on his verbal boxing mitts. This he did, with *élan* and great pleasure.

He was especially delighted to do battle again with an old astronomer chum, Dr. George O. Abell, chairman of the Department of Astronomy at the University of California at Los Angeles (UCLA). He had debated with Dr. Abell frequently, and although he hadn't made a convert of the astronomer to astrology, Dr. Abell was willing to admit that Sydney Omarr was "far and away" the most intelligent of the astrologers he had met.

This time, though, Sydney caught Abell with his zodiacal pants down, right on a Merv Griffin show.

The distinguished astronomer, of course, was one of the 186 signers of the anti-astrology proclamation, and to make his position even clearer he wrote a scholarly and scathing article against astrology for the Los Angeles *Times*. In order to prove to readers that he knew what he was talking about and to demonstrate his expertise in the subject, he drew his own horoscope and proceeded to give an astrological interpretation of himself that was facetiously amusing.

Sydney was more than amused. He was amazed and horrified when he saw it. The chairman of UCLA's Astronomy Department had his moon in the wrong position!

"This is a very serious mistake," Sydney explained. "Anyone who doesn't know how to place the moon in his own horoscope is an amateur, not an expert. What Dr. Abell did was to take the position of the moon right out of the ephemeris, and that isn't the moon that belongs in Dr. Abell's horoscope. The position of the moon has to be corrected or adjusted in zodiacal degrees according to the individual's time and place of birth.

"By lifting the moon right out of the ephemeris, without positioning it properly in his own horoscope, Dr. Abell made a mistake that amounted to four hours' difference in his birth time! That's quite an error, I would say, for anyone who claims to be an expert."

When confronted with these facts on the Merv Griffin show, the usually debonair and self-assured Dr. Abell, flustering between embarrassment and indignation, flippantly commented to Sydney, "Well, maybe I have a better ephemeris than you do."

Backstage after the show, Dr. Abell admitted to Sydney, "Most of my students accept astrology and that's the sad part of it. But what's even sadder is—I would wager that if a survey were taken among the students, more of them would know your name than would know the name of the president of the University."

This in fact was a mild understatement of the public's interest in astrology, as was forthwith brought out in a Gallup poll inspired by the then current clamor over the scientists' widely publicized proclamation. The Gallup poll found that the opinion of the 186 scientists, including the eighteen Nobel prize winners, made not one iota of difference to the American public, that an astronomical 32 million Americans believe in astrology and/or consult their daily astrology columns (of which Sydney's is the most popular) for counsel and predictions on what the stars have in store for them.

As Sydney long ago told that certain TV talk-show host, "I am going to become a household word." And he did. Millions of Americans, especially women, wake up and go to bed with Sydney Omarr. Astrologically speaking, that is.

Sydney views the intermittent public outcries of scientists as good therapy for them. "It probably makes them feel better. But their collective knowledge of astrology," he says, "should be catalogued under the heading: A Comedy of Errors."

In addition to Dr. Abell's displacement of his moon, Sydney discovered that another of the distinguished scientists had committed the greatest goof of all in drawing his own horoscope to accompany an article debunking astrology.

He omitted the planet Pluto!

"Of course it is the one farthest away (over three billion miles from earth) and the slowest (248 years to circle the zodiac), and it was the last one discovered (1930). But it *is* a planet and it's been there all the time even if we didn't know it," Sydney pointed out. "Anyone attempting to debunk astrology should at least be well enough informed to know the planets. He should know better than to leave out the planet Pluto. Not even a neophyte would do that."

One of the more obvious errors in the scientists' denouncement of astrology was the statement that ancient people "had no concept of the vast distances from the earth to the planets and stars. Now that these distances can and have been calculated, we can see how infinitesmally small are the gravitational and other effects produced by the distant planets and the far more distant stars."

To assume that ancient people had no concept of the distances between earth and the heavens is, as Sydney points out, a false premise to start with, as proved in such gigantic stellar-computer reminders from ancient civilizations as the great pyramids of Egypt and the famous prehistoric Stonehenge, built by Stone Age astronomers on the Salisbury Plain in England.

Though associated with primitive religious rituals, both Stonehenge and the pyramids were constructed as calendars, or astrological observatories, to record the positions of the sun and the moon, to determine the length of a year and the seasons. The amazing mathematical precision and accuracy of these ancient m... builders remains one of the scientific mysteries of all time, but their mathematical precision has never been questioned. Neither has it ever been duplicated by modern scientists with all their computer calculations.

As for the "infinitesmally small" cosmic effects produced by the planets and stars, it has been established, for example, that the effect of a photon does not diminish with distance (according to the Einstein photoelectric theory) and that the forces transmitted from space *do* have an effect on earthly activities.

As John J. O'Neill said in his letter to Sydney, "Astrology, properly defined, is the accumulated and organized knowledge of the effect on man of the forces reaching the earth from surrounding space. . . . We know very little about the array of forces that are impinging on the earth, but that little demonstrates a great urgency for further researches and the fascinating possibilities that await discovery. . . ."

In fact Sydney feels that a great deal of progress has been made and "fascinating possibilities" discovered since O'Neill wrote his letter, in 1951.

The recent work of an eminent French scientist, Michel Gauquelin, for example, lends statistical credence to the ancient "superstition" that planetary movements influence human characteristics. Gauquelin's monumental statistical research is summarized and analyzed in his two books *The Cosmic Clocks* (Regnery) and *The Scientific Basis of Astrology* (Stein & Day), and I recommend them as *must* reading for serious students of astrology. The latter especially is an eloquent testimonial to astrology, albeit strictly unintentional. Gauquelin actually set out to disprove astrology, but to his great chagrin came up with some "embarrassing and irritating" statistical evidence proving that various professional groups tend to be born under different signs.

Thus, more doctors and scientists, for example, are born under Mars or Saturn; more actors, journalists, and playwrights under Jupiter; more ministers and politicians during the rise and zenith of the moon.

Gauquelin spent years on his massive data-gathering survey, compiling mountains of statistics from thousands of birth records in six countries.

A careful reading of his books (they're rough going in spots but fascinating to anyone who has the patience to assimilate and digest them) would indicate that Gauquelin did an extraordinarily thorough and painstaking job in his research. It would seem that no one could question his statistical evidence—except, as might be expected, some of his fellow scientists, who refuse to recognize any scientific basis for astrology no matter how well documented.

As Sydney puts it, "The trouble with most of these scientists is that they're like ostriches with their heads in a rut and a red sign up that says: DON'T DISTURB ME WITH THE FACTS; MY MIND IS MADE UP."

He considers Gauquelin's work an inadvertently brilliant coup for the "scientific art" of astrology.

"The only trouble is, when these things [astrological trends] are accepted scientifically, they are no longer called astrology. They're given other names."

He tells of a man in Newport Beach, California, who was arrested for holding a class in astrology but then released and permitted to continue the class—so long as he didn't mention the word astrology.

Therein lies the clue to the contention: semantics.

For some reason, scientists simply don't like the word astrology, which literally translated from the Greek means "word of the stars." (*Astron*, star; *logos*, word.)

Gauquelin, therefore, refers to his own work as the "new science" of "astrobiology." His discovery that certain professional groups tend to be born under certain signs (i.e., especially doctors under Mars) is categorized as "planetary heredity." Laboriously he had to cast the horoscopes for thousands of persons (from their birth records) to determine the positions and movements of the planets at their hour of birth. But scientists abhor the word horoscope, a word that means literally "that which looks at the hour," and so Gauquelin has latched onto the obscure word "genethlialogy" as a substitute for horoscopy.

Sydney grumbles, "A rose by any other name is still a rose." Whether its name is astrobiology, cosmobiology, cosmic chemistry, cosmic biology, or cosmic clocks, the meaning is essentially the same as Sydney's definition of astrology: "synchronicity."

He isn't too much disturbed by the semantics, or the scientists' urge to discard the word astrology and substitute their own highfalutin label, so long as people know that it boils down to the same thing: the correspondence, coincidence, synchronicity (synchronization), or *timing* of certain planetary patterns with certain mundane actions, reactions, and events, and human, animal, and plant behavior and characteristics here on earth.

"The solar system," he explains, "can be regarded as a giant clock. Human activity corresponds to certain 'times,' which are available to us to see by consulting the 'clock.' An earth clock, for instance, might toll noon. At that time, many people begin their lunch hour. This does not mean the clock *caused* the people to go to lunch. We needn't be stymied because we can't explain *why* people go to lunch at noon, or leave work at five, or go to work at eight or nine in the morning. All we need to realize is that this correspondence works. The hands of the clock point to certain numerals and specific things happen, or correspond to those combinations of numerals. On an individual level we have our own personal schedules and we consult our calendars and our clocks. The solar system, in fact, regulates the calendar and the clocks.

"Human and animal activities, express a correspondence to the position of the planets. We need not look for *causal* answers. Jung has given us the word: synchronicity."

This means simply that certain mundane (wordly) events in the lives of people and nations (as well as plants and animals) seem to be synchronized with certain planetary movements—synchronized with and *not caused by* these movements, as Sydney has consistently emphasized. The synchronization of certain events or characteristics with certain planetary movements has been going on from the beginning of time, if we can believe the mound of empirical evidence that has accumulated through the ages and especially the reports of recognized science researchers in recent years.

Lunar Influences, or Cosmic Clocks: Dr. Frank A. Brown, professor of biology at Northwestern University, Evanston, Illinois, is well known for his experiments with the "cosmic clocks" of living organisms, particularly his discovery that the fiddler crab and the Long Island oyster have built-in "cosmic clocks" that respond to the position of the moon. In more recent experiments biologist Brown has found that rats also show peaks of activity very clearly related to the position of the moon—and that the growth of potatoes, carrots, and other vegetables varies according to the position of the moon by month and day.

Scientists have long been puzzled by the incredible palolo worms of the South Pacific, which the Samoans feast on during the last quarter of the moon in October and November.

I personally have a nodding acquaintance with the palolo, having once spent four months in Pago Pago that coincided with the "feast of the palolo," when the deep blue of the sea seemed to change color with the swarms of long, wriggly worms; and the Samoans, shouting with joy, rushed out in their fishing boats and came back with nets laden with their favorite delicacy. The palolos live in the coral reefs of the Pacific, rising to the sea's surface in October and then in great quantity in November, in the moon's last quarter, to shed their load of eggs and spermatozoa. This spawn comes up at low tide, early in the morning, for several days. The Samoans eat the worms raw. I delicately declined all invitations to palolo feasts during my stay in Samoa, so I can't vouch for how they taste. But scientists say that of all sea worms, the palolo (its scientific name is *Eunice viridis*) has the best known and most apparent lunar rhythm.

If animals, sea creatures, and plant life respond in various ways to the moon's influence, would this not also apply to humans?

It is widely claimed that the moon influences our moods and our reproduction and regulates the female menstrual cycle. Some doctors acknowledge that correlations exist between the moon and certain illnesses, such as tuberculosis. The continuing investigation into the intriguing mystery of lunar influences is in Sydney's opinion a giant step forward in breaking the barrier of scientific prejudice against astrology.

Sunspots: It is now established that the planets play a part in solar activity, including the phenomenon of sunspots, which follow an eleven-year cycle coinciding with the orbit of Jupiter.

Sydney feels that the research on sunspots and conclusive evidence of the sun's eleven-year cycle offer one of the best supportive claims of a scientific basis for astrology. The sun's vagaries in relation to the planets, for example, can alter the duration of a day, disturb the earth's magnetic fields, cause radio interference, and perhaps even induce earthquakes. Michel Gauquelin says the sun's eleven-year cycle is stamped and engraved everywhere on earth: on the water level of Lake Victoria, the number of icebergs, the famines in India, the quality of Burgundy wines, the number of rabbit skins taken by the Hudson Bay Company. And all because the weather, including variations in rainfall, is connected to the sun's eleven-year cycle. Moreover, the "sound of the planets" or the "music of the spheres," as it is also called, is now a recognized fact, the result of electromagnetic waves created by great storms in the atmosphere of Jupiter or Venus.

Russian scientists studying the eleven-year cycle of solar flares claim that the flares affect the human psyche, that coinciding with these flares is an upsurge of violence, an increase in mental illness and crime.

A. L. Tchijewsky, professor at the University of Moscow, was the first to establish a statistical correlation between the sun's eleven-year cycle and events on earth. He investigated the results of solar activity on epidemics, general mortality, and even on large-scale social movements such as wars, human migrations, and changes of government. He also was one of the first to emphasize the sun's predominant role in the production of ions in the atmosphere.

Professor H. Bortels, director of the Bacteriological Institute of Berlin-Dahlem, was one of the first and most persistent investigators of the new "cosmobiology." He established that atmospheric conditions altered the reactions of the micro-organisms.

Maki Takata, doctor and professor at Toho University, in Tokyo, discovered that blood serum, women's ovarian cycles, and certain physiological changes in men were the result of disturbance from the sun's eleven-year cycle. He concluded, "Man is a living sundial."

Giorgio Piccardi, director of the Institute of Physics and Chemistry at the University of Florence, conducted experiments in descaling boilers with "activated" water that led to the discovery that "cosmic forces" (sunspots and planetary movements) could alter the chemical components of water, the "liquid of life." (The human body is more than 60 per cent water.)

Such discoveries, Sydney contends, have contributed to the advancement of astrology by whatever name it is called.

A well-known American pharmaceutical company recently issued a newsletter titled *Astrology and Biology*, which began: "If astrology is stripped of horoscopy, then a reasonable case can be made for it. The central thesis may be simply stated: the heavenly bodies have distinguishable effects on biologic materials."

ighbrow *Intellectual Digest* of June 1973 printed an article, der the heading of *Scorpio Rising*, that began: "Astrology may have a scientific basis after all." It reported that a University of Colorado professor, K. D. Wood, had observed that Mercury, Venus, Earth, and Jupiter all raise surface "tides" on the sun that correspond with the eleven-year cycle of sunspot activity. The height of the tides depends on the relative positions of the planets. For example, when Earth and Venus are in either conjunction or opposition, they raise a tide about 50 per cent larger than the maximum tides caused by Jupiter, according to Wood.

From the positions of the planets in the past 220 years, the professor calculated the tidal fluctuations on the sun and compared them with the number of sunspots occuring in each period. He found that maximum and minimum sunspot activity closely correlated with the presumed ebb and flow of the planetary tides. "Since sunspots interfere with radio transmission, they may affect other activity on earth. If so," the *Intellectual Digest* concluded, "this data may support astrologers' claims of planetary influences."

Sydney regards all these supportive scientific speculations with Leo-grand tolerance and amusement. They merely reaffirm his own conviction that there is a correlation between the planets and what happens here on earth.

He is quick to remind you that astrology once was so highly esteemed that it was taught in many of Europe's leading universities, and he is hopeful that it will one day be included in the American college curriculum.

The crack in the door of academia is opening, and among the brightest young champions of astrology within the hallowed halls of higher learning is my technical assistant on this book, Dr. John J. LaCorte, an assistant professor of philosophy at California State College, Dominguez Hills, near Los Angeles. In addition to his regular courses, in the philosophy of religion, he has added another entitled The Philosophy of the Occult and Mantic Arts, which includes the study of astrology.

"Fortunately the chairman of our philosophy department has a very sympathetic approach toward the mantic arts," says John. (Probably because of his own intellectual approach.) "But I'm sure that in 90 per cent of all other philosophy departments in this country I would be shut down immediately for even mentioning astrology."

John is a protégé of Sydney's, and like Sydney he is also a fiery Leo. . . . Under the rule of the sun . . . strong-willed, forceful, idealistic, commanding, and confident. . . . Especially confident that astrology will soon be liberated from its yoke of academic prejudice.

"And one day," as Sydney says, "teachers of history will find it natural to point out that Napoleon was, of course, a Leo."

Chapter 17
ASTROLOGY AND RELIGION
(*To Each His Own*)

"*Astrology . . . has proved the existence of a universal intelligence. . . .*"

—SYDNEY OMARR

Is astrology anti-religious?

Is it in itself a religion?

Is the study of the stars contrary to a belief in God?

We could probably argue these points until doomsday—but don't worry. We're not going to.

Sydney wisely declines to become embroiled in this controversial aspect of astrology. He has settled the matter for himself within the dictates of his own conscience and he leaves it to you to do likewise.

"Religion is different things to different people and should be respected as something very private and personal between each man and his own God," he says. "To each his own."

Although his own background is Jewish, he has never accepted any one formal religion and is not a biblical scholar. But he has read reams of pros and cons on astrology by authorities quoting the Bible, all of which he regards with proper respect and the bemused comment, "I suppose if you really worked at it long enough you could prove or disprove just about anything you wanted to by quoting the Bible. But then where are you?"

From a purely personal viewpoint Sydney is convinced that astrology is not anti-religious or in conflict with any form of organized religion. He has discussed the subject with various leaders of the Catholic, Protestant, and Jewish faiths who have confirmed this conviction, though he is fully cognizant of the fact that thousands of parishioners have developed a prejudice against astrology either through their own lack of knowledge, religious bias, or "brainwashing" by local clergymen.

Modern astrology certainly is not a religion in the traditional sense, he emphasizes, although it has permeated all religions from ancient times. In fact it still complements all systems of religion that acknowledge God as a "universal intelligence."

"It seems to me," Sydney says, "that a study of astrology would strengthen one's religious beliefs. At least for me personally it has definitely proved the existence of a universal intelligence, a universal order correlated with the solar system. Because the solar system *is* orderly. It is predictable. It gives us our life rhythms, provides us with the stop and go signals of life. Somebody put it there. Somebody operates these stop and go signals of the universe: the seasons, the time for the cosmic clocks to start ringing. Astrology is a key to understanding the nature of the universe and man's relation to it. It is not a religion. It is simply a way of broadly looking at the world for a better understanding of ourselves and others and the mysteries of the universe. Is this contrary to a belief in God? I don't think so."

From an historical viewpoint, as Sydney points out, astrology is the oldest religion, and in ancient times it actually was a religion. The Chaldeans and Babylonians had their astrologer-priests and worshiped the planet-gods who supposedly ruled not only their celestial sphere but all earthly life as well. In Egypt the high priest of Heliopolis (the City of the Sun) was from the beginning of history honored with the title of "astrologer-in-chief." This post was held by, among others, Potipherah, the father-in-law of Joseph in the Book of Genesis. The ancient Egyptians worshiped the river Nile as a fertility god and believed that it was a combination (conjunction) of the bright star Sirius and the sun that caused the Nile to overflow its banks once a year, bringing everything in the arid soil to life again. Hence the beginning of the new year in Egypt coincided with the rise of Sirius in conjunction with the sun.

At one time, under the last of the Pharaohs, Egypt became one of the great centers for students of divination by the stars. The celebrated sage Ptolemy wrote his *Tetrabiblos*, the book that was to become the astrologers' bible in the ancient world, at Alexandria.

In China, more than two thousand years B.C., the worship of the heavens was associated with agriculture and then became an actual law of society.

In India, traces of astrology dating back to earliest times deeply pervade the various philosophies and religions. Astrological conceptions are found in all the religious writings of India, and belief in astrology is still very much a way of life in India today.

In Mexico, the ancient Mayas and Aztecs worshiped gods who reigned over both meteorological phenomena and animal life and had their dwelling places in the stars. Astrologer-priests concerned themselves with specific predictions of events or persons based on birth dates and the good or bad omens in their sacred calendar.[1]

Thus, in Egypt, China, India, and Mexico, astrology and religion were interwoven. The ancient Greeks and Romans also developed their own theories of planet-gods. The constellation known as the Seven Sisters, or the Pleiades, has been worshiped throughout history by various peoples.

With the beginning of Christianity, some of the first Church Fathers regarded these forms of astrology-religion as fundamentally wrong, immoral, and dangerous, because they were based on a number of gods or forces of nature who controlled men's destinies and allowed no freedom of will, instead of a single, all-powerful God, or Divine Providence.

Since God was sole master of men's fate, they argued, it was therefore impossible for the stars to be the cause of human events or to have any control over them.

However, the great Latin theoretician Plotinus came up with a theory that helped to circumvent any real war between Christianity and astrology and eliminate conflict between the two beliefs.

According to the French scientist Michel Gauquelin in his book *The Scientific Basis of Astrology* this was the basic postulate of the philosopher Plotinus: *Celestial bodies should be denied any claim to being the efficient cause of human events. The stars did not produce these events, they were only the signs which announced them.*

Of course, this is exactly what Sydney has been saying all along.

As for free will, he has constantly reiterated the fact that astrol-

[1] This brief résumé of the historical development of astrology-religion is based on Michel Gauquelin's accounts of it in his books *The Cosmic Clocks* and *The Scientific Basis of Astrology*.

ogy is not fatalistic, it does not eliminate free choice. Rather, it provides certain cycles, trends, guidelines, to use as tools in planning the course of your life within natural, cosmic rhythms.

"There are times when we should take a chance and times when we should not take a chance. But this does not mean you should stay in bed all day because you might slip in the bathtub. You have to use common sense in applying astrology to everyday life," he warns. "Astrology provides the guideline. But you can change it by being aware of it. If it pleases you, go along with it. If the road ahead is indicated as rough, do something about it. That's the purpose of astrology."

Sydney's theory of how the stars work as omens or indicators (not the cause) of certain events is fortified by the ingenious explanation of the great Plotinus, whose reasoning was that the stars work in the same way as birds of omen:

"Just as birds, whether they fly or come to a halt, tell us by their feathers and cries of events in the future of which they know nothing, in the same way it is possible to say that Jupiter is health-giving and Mars terrible, for happy events are signified by the one, and by the other unhappy events.

"They are, therefore," adds Plotinus, "like writings constantly being inscribed in the heavens, or, rather, inscribed there once and for all."

But how does this pre-established harmony between celestial motions and the earth below enable astrologers to produce accurate forecasts?

Plotinus puts forward this explanation by way of example: "Just as with a living being, by virtue of the single principle on which his nature depends, it is possible to assess one part by another; an examination of his eyes or some other part of his body allows us to estimate his ways." In the universe, therefore, the stars have no actual, physical influence. "The active cause is the soul, the inspiration of the great animating spirit" (Enneads, IV, 4).[2]

Gauquelin's summation of the astrology-religion conflict: "This world soul was only a step away from God himself, and the Church Fathers gladly made the transition with ease. Thus some of them, like Saint Thomas Aquinas, could announce with a clear conscience that they were convinced followers of astrology."

[2] From *The Scientific Basis of Astrology*, by Michel Gauquelin.

(In his *Summa Theologica*, the key theological work of the period, Aquinas made many references to the influences of the moon and the stars on the course of men's lives. His primary concern was whether they operated against the concept of free will. Apparently the teachings of Plotinus satisfied him on this point.)

Gauquelin continues: "Thanks to the ingenious doctrine of Plotinus, astrology and Christianity ended by making a sort of marriage of convenience, or at least a relatively peaceful coexistence. Later, some priests and even a number of Popes during the Renaissance were to countenance astrologers, on condition that they acknowledged that the stars they consulted were only signs of God's will, and not direct causes of human destiny."

For those interested in the current official status of astrology and the Church, Gauquelin puts it succinctly: *At the present time, the Church condemns the use of horoscopes, but does not reject the possibility of an astral influence on men.*

(For a more detailed analysis of modern astrology and religion, readers are referred to a pamphlet on the subject written by Ruth Hale Oliver, former president of the American Federation of Astrologers.)

The reason Sydney has never accepted any one formal religion is that he became aware of astrological influences at a very early age.

He recalls, "My parents dragged me to the synagogue until I was past thirteen. I had a Bar Mitzvah so as not to hurt them. But then I realized that all religion is based on astrology. I already had learned enough about the subject to realize that all religious holidays are based on the planetary positions."

For example:

—The Passover begins on the day of the first full moon after the vernal equinox, the beginning of spring and of the astrological year, when day and night are exactly the same length.

—The end of Lent, or Easter Sunday, is always the first Sunday after the full moon after the vernal equinox.

—It was the Emperor Constantine who decreed that the day of the sun, Sunday, should be the Christian Sabbath.

—In the Orient, the New Year begins at the time of the new moon after the sun enters Aquarius, and is termed Tet.

—The Jewish New Year is set by the new moon in Libra, the zodiacal sign of the scales and the law.

—The first day of Ramadan, which begins the most holy period of fasting and penitence for the Moslems, also is marked by this new moon in Libra.

"Thus we can quickly realize that the ecclesiastical calendar of the world's religions is linked astrologically with the major phases of the sun and the moon," Sydney says.

"There are special prayers in the synagogue for the time of the new moon and the time of the full moon," he adds. "And on the reverse side of the Government of Israel's official state medal there are the twelve signs of the zodiac as found on a mosaic floor in an excavated sixth-century-A.D. synogogue in Bet Alpha, Northern Israel.

"As for the Catholic religion, do you know that some of the finest rare astrological texts can be found in the Vatican Library? This is not surprising. During the fourteenth, fifteenth, and sixteenth centuries the greatest astrologers were Roman Catholic bishops. For one example, Marinus, a French bishop, was responsible for a method of calculating horoscopes which is still utilized today," Sydney says.

Ruth Hale Oliver wrote a booklet for the American Federation of Astrologers called *The Basic Principles of Astrology*. She points out that astrology has existed in pagan religions and within Christian religions and is a subject in its own right. Different religions and different philosophies may adopt astrology or may be opposed to it, but astrology still exists, independently of any other religious or philosophical concept. Thus it is not anti-Christian at all.

"I am not a scholar in the history of religions," Sydney emphasizes, "but in devoting my life to astrology, I have gained at least a cursory knowledge of its influence in many areas, enough to convince me that astrological concepts were not only the basis of ancient religions but infiltrated early Christianity as well, and are still alive today."

For example, many authorities are still trying to solve the mystery of the biblical Star of Bethlehem, which guided the three "wise men," or Magi, from the East to the birth of Christ. Two new translations of the Bible—one Catholic, the other Protestant—both translate "Magi" as "astrologers."

In both *The New English Bible* (1961) and *The New American Bible* (1970), the Magi are referred to specifically as astrologers. . . .

From *The New English Bible:* "Jesus was born at Bethlehem in Judaea during the reign of Herod. After his birth astrologers from the east arrived in Jerusalem, asking, 'Where is the child who is born to be king of the Jews? We observed the rising of his star, and we have come to pay him homage. . . .'

"Herod next called the astrologers to meet him in private, and ascertained from them the time when the star had appeared. . . ."

What was this star of Bethehem that the Magi-astrologers saw?

"Most likely a conjunction of Jupiter and Saturn," says Sydney. This is a speculative theory which agrees with that of most biblical-astronomy authorities. The great astronomer-astrologer Kepler, however, in A.D. 1606 saw the grouping of Jupiter, Saturn, and Mars and suggested that the star of the Magi might be that conjunction. Some modern astronomers say the star of Bethlehem was a comet. Others maintain that it was a supernova, or exploding star, which could account for its great brilliance.

And then there is the continuing controversy over when Christ was actually born. Almost all authorities agree that it wasn't December 25, as tradition has it. Therefore he wasn't a Capricorn, as many believe. The Mormons believe he was born in April under the sign of Aries. Others are equally convinced that he was born in October under the sign of Libra, or sometime between February 19 and March 20, under the sign of Pisces.

Sydney is content to leave such speculation to others. He hasn't even tried to cast Christ's horoscope.

"It would take a lot of time even if you knew His approximate birth date," he says. "But it hasn't even been settled yet what century Christ was born in, or whether He was actually a historical character. Astrology can't answer such questions. But perhaps," he adds hopefully, "it can make us more knowledgeable of how our religion—any religion—is definitely linked to the stars."

Chapter 18

MEDICAL ASTROLOGY
(The Moon and You)

> *"A physician who practices without knowledge of astrology is to be regarded as a fool."*
>
> —HIPPOCRATES

Astrologers like to point out that Hippocrates, the father of medicine, once said, "No doctor can be successful in the practice of medicine unless he knows the stars."

Possibly the most important breakthrough for astrologers is in that relatively new and specific area called medical astrology, which also includes psychiatry and psychology.

In ancient times, of course, medicine played an important role in astrology, which in its total concern with human nature naturally had an answer to all kinds of health problems. But modern medical scientists have relegated much of this to folklore, to the category of mere superstition.

Recently, however, modern medical research has come up with new evidence to support this ancient "superstition." Even the American Medical Association admits that the "planets influence our lives" (in its official publication *Today's Health* of October 1971), but the staid A.M.A., of course, denies that this has anything to do with astrology. As Sydney says, "A rose by any other name. . . ."

In spite of the A.M.A.'s official stand, there now seems to be irrefutable evidence that certain physiological and psychological functions and malfunctions are linked with planetary influences, especially the moon.

So all the talk about "lunacy" and the effect of the full moon on human beings may be more than mere superstition.

Researchers have found that people generally seem to be more emotional and less restrained during the time that the earth is positioned precisely between the magnetic influences of the sun and the moon.

The moon, of course, has a very obvious effect on the sea, as is shown in the tides, and also influences sea life, as noted in our Chapter 16, on "The Great Debates."

According to modern research, the moon also influences our moods and our reproduction, and regulates the female cycle.

Darwin argued, "Man is descended from fish. [*Descent of Man*, 1891] . . . Why should not the 28-day feminine cycle be a vestige of the past, when life depended on the tides, and therefore the moon? . . ."

Sydney says, "Astrologers long have known that there is a connection between phases of the moon and human emotions. Psychiatric admissions multiply during the full moon; the same is true of crimes of violence. Outbreaks of murder apparently are triggered by the moon tugging on 'psychological tides' inside the body."

Dr. Arnold L. Lieber of the University of Miami's medical school made a two-year study that definitely established a scientific relationship between phases of the moon and the murder rate in Dade County, Florida.

The study reveals that the county's murder rate begins to rise about twenty-four hours before the full moon, then drops back before climbing to a secondary peak at the new moon.

Says Dr. Lieber, "I feel that eventually we are going to show that any organism, human or animal, is an integral part of the universe and responds to changes like variations in solar and lunar cycles."

It is now a well-known fact, as Sydney points out, that people become more agitated or emotional during the full moon, as evidenced in the increased activity in police stations, fire departments, hospitals, and mental institutions.

There is a popular belief that madmen, the unbalanced, and the epileptic are more restless and nervous than usual when the moon is full, and that headache-prone people are susceptible to "lunar migraine."

One of the most promising areas of study in relation to astrology is the field of psychiatry and psychology. The psychiatrist Carl Jung often used astrological charts in the treatment of his patients and felt that in time such charts would be a part of all patient files and used as a diagnostic tool to determine the nature of the patient's disorder. Today more and more psychiatrists and psychologists are consulting astrologers for assistance in working with problem patients.

A person's birth chart, for example, can indicate whether there is a tendency toward alcoholism, homosexuality, schizophrenia, or suicide, according to recent studies.

A competent astrologer, interpreting an individual's birth chart, can provide information that might prove invaluable as warning signals or guidelines for remedial action.

Of course it doesn't always work that way, as Sydney is the first to admit. A famous movie star, very beautiful and very rich, once came to him for help during a period of deep despondency. She was also under the care of a psychiatrist, and in fact the psychiatrist, too, had enlisted Sydney's astrological advice in treating her.

In this case, neither psychiatrist nor astrologer was able to help. Her attempted suicide was splashed all over the headlines.

"Her birth chart had all the warning signals, but what I didn't know," says Sydney, "was that she was in love with her psychiatrist."

Most suicides, the records show, occur in late December or January, when the sun is lowest in the sky, although Marilyn Monroe, whose birth chart clearly revealed her suicide-prone nature, died in August (1962).

"We need a great deal more research to bridge all the gaps," says Sydney. "Astrology is an age-long body of knowledge that has stood up pragmatically as people have used it. Yet it has never had the money to test it, whereas millions of dollars in grants are given to all sorts of silly projects in the name of science. Such as the sex life of the grasshopper or something equally absurd."

One of the most significant contributions in the area of medical-astrology research is a study of how the moon influences postoperative hemorrhaging.

Sydney's statement that he would not advise anyone to have a tonsillectomy or a tooth pulled during the full moon because of excessive bleeding at this time is based on the research done by Dr.

Edson G. Andrews, an eye, ear, nose, and throat physician-surgeon in Florida, specializing in ophthalmology for twenty-seven years. He is a Diplomate of the American Board of Ophthalmology and has served as president of two county medical societies and of the Florida Society of Ophthalmology and Otolaryngology.

He gave a detailed description of his original research, along with a review of other evidence of the effects of the lunar cycle, in the *Florida Medical Association Journal* (May 1960).

A condensation is included here because Sydney feels that Dr. Andrews' research not only adds a new dimension to medical astrology but also may add another milestone in the long, hard road to freedom from the yoke of academic prejudice against the concept of planetary influences on human life.

What Dr. Andrews proved beyond a doubt, if statistics can be believed, is that people bleed more profusely under the full moon.

He did not set out to prove this. It was his nurse who gave him the idea. He had noticed, as many other surgeons have noticed, that at certain times the human body has a greater predilection to excessive bleeding than at other times. When his nurse suggested that perhaps the moon was an influencing factor, he brushed it off as "utterly ridiculous."

But, unknown to him, his nurse had kept a record of his bleeders on a calendar and proceeded to show him, much to his amazement, that their bleeding was, indeed, coincident with the full moon.

He then decided to collect additional data in a more scientific and complete manner:

"Physicians have all heard for years the many and various myths relating the phases of the moon with health, not only mental but physical, particularly with regard to bleeding. Who among you has not heard the story that most farmers will not consent to castration of their animals during a full moon for fear that they would bleed to death? Who has not heard a patient say he did not want to be operated on at such and such a time, as the signs were not right? Was all this fact or fiction?"

Dr. Andrews combed the literature, but nowhere could he find that any work had been done to prove or disprove these myths. The scientists all agreed that it was folklore and superstition and that there was no scientific basis for such hypothesis, "but unfortunately they had never bothered to collect any data to substantiate their claim. I decided to do so. . . ."

He kept records on all his tonsillectomy cases during the years 1956 through 1958 and found that 82 per cent of his cases of post-operative bleeding (enough to require "medical management") occurred in an interval between the first quarter and one day before the third quarter.

"What makes this observation even more astounding is the fact that there were fewer admissions during the time of the full moon, when we had the most bleeders. Perhaps laymen know more about this than we do and are reluctant to enter the hospital at this time."

He then did further studies in collaboration with other doctors, first with some data on tonsil and adenoid bleeders, then with patients admitted for peptic bleeding ulcer. The statistical curves followed the same pattern, always showing an astounding preponderance of hemorrhage at the full moon and a relative absence at the new moon.

"What does all this mean? Can these amazing observations be backed up by any scientific fact?" Dr. Andrews asks.

He cites the work of Dr. L. J. Ravitz, who, in experimenting on human subjects at Yale University and Duke University and in the Veterans Administration, found, on attaching electrodes to various positions in the body, that there were rhythmic, cyclic variations in electrical potential, which varied during the month, and that the greatest increase in potential was during the full moon. The same cyclic variations were found in plants.

In humans they coincided with swings in mood, as in a feeling of ill- or well-being. There was also a consistent variation in potential during each hour and during each 24-hour period. "These changes were more pronounced in severely maladjusted persons."

He also refers to the "remarkable research" of Dr. Frank A. Brown of Northwestern University, whose studies of rhythmic cycles in body temperature, blood sugar, blood count, metabolism, and intraocular tension in plant and animal life revealed the startling fact that the cycles varied with the lunar cycle, being lowest at the new moon and highest at the third quarter.

Dr. Brown's conclusion was, ". . . there is incontrovertible evidence that, excluding all known forces influencing living things, there is a cyclic information in the form of radiation penetrating all ordinary containers that impresses all living things corresponding to atmospheric and lunar periodicity."

In plain English this means that our physiology changes with the moon.

It has been known for a long time that the moon has an effect on the weather and that barometric pressure changes have a great deal to do with health. Various authorities have reported that:

–Nosebleed (epistaxis) may assume almost epidemic proportions at times of weather change.

–There are more coronary deaths, more migraine attacks, more convulsive attacks, and more asthmatic deaths during the passage of a cold front than at any other time of weather change.

–There is more somnambulism on moonlit nights, and more epileptic attacks during the full moon. (The word epilepsy comes from the Greek meaning "to seize upon from the moon.")

–The moon has a serious effect on the minds of persons afflicted with nervous disorders (a theory widely accepted by psychiatrists).

Dr. Andrews also mentions a few classic examples of how the moon affects animal life. Off Bermuda, shrimp swarm in the waters just before midnight on the day of the new moon, once a year, and then are seen no more. . . . Once a year, the grunion swarm onto the beach in California at high tide, which, of course, is moon-controlled. . . . The Australian reef heron lives thirty miles inland from its feeding ground on the coast; it feeds at low tide only and every day leaves its roost just fifty minutes before low tide to reach the coast at the proper time.

One of the most intriguing moon stories I have come across recently was a news report that certain phases of the moon affect the hooting cycle of screech owls! The study was made by a young University of California zoology student, Philip M. Jardim, who spent fifty nights in a redwood forest listening to the hooting of the owls, the symbols of wisdom. His subject was called "owl vocalization." He discovered that the high-pitched "vocalization" reached its highest frequency during the last quarter of the moon and that the hooting of the screech owls increased during the mating season.

Another odd bit, which Sydney himself contributes to the compendium of moon lore, is this:

When the moon is in a fixed sign, a person's dentures are more apt to remain in place. (How's that to chew on for cocktail chatter?) And tooth extractions are more difficult when the moon is in one of the fixed signs: Taurus, Leo, Scorpio, or Aquarius.

Besides Frank Brown's research in the relationship between the moon and the oxygen consumption of the potato, carrot, and many vegetables, other studies tend to support the farmers' widespread belief in the moon's influence on the health of their crops, especially melons and all vegetables of the cucurbitaceous family. But one study (Kolisko's *Moon and the Growth of Plants*) concentrates on corn and peas and offers further proof of the correlation between, on the one hand, moon phases and planting, and, on the other hand, the health of the crops. Over a nine-year period, it was found that corn planted two days before the full moon was definitely larger than corn planted two days after. Also, peas withered more quickly when planted at new moon.

It would seem, therefore, from all the evidence accumulated to date that the moon does have an influence on plant life, animal life, and human life, in terms of health and well-being.

Returning to Dr. Edson Andrews' research on bleeders and his medical-astrology survey of other evidence of the effects of the lunar cycle, he summarizes his findings as follows:

"It has long been known that bleeding is markedly increased during menstruation, and who would deny that menstrual rhythm does not match the lunar cycle? . . .

". . . I had always heard that there were more babies born on the full moon, but my obstetrical friends said there were not. Just because I was stubborn, I charted the births at Tallahassee Memorial Hospital for the same period, 1956, 1957, and 1958, and plotted them against the moon phases. Four hundred and one babies were born within two days of the full moon, 375 within two days of the new moon, and 320 within two days of the first quarter. Draw your own conclusions.

"Could all this be an inherent rhythm of the tides—a remnant of our prehistoric existence, dating back to our emergence from the sea? A doctor in England claims he has data to prove that at the ebb of the tide there occur more natural deaths than at any other time. . . .

"It would seem that we do have evidence that prolonged bleeding at the full moon can occur and pretty good evidence that it is possible for human physiology to be so altered that it might explain periodic, prolonged bleeding. . . . It might be well to investigate this possibility in more detail before we say 'just superstition.'

"There is a large and widespread folklore about the moon, and somewhere beneath it may lie a few sparks of yet unknown truth. Folklore, even of the silliest sort, has sometimes proved to have a valid, if misunderstood, basis. The ancient practice of smearing wounds with nasty, moldy substance looked ridiculous until Sir Alexander Fleming discovered penicillin. The nature of the moon's influence is unproved; possibly the inherent protoplasmic rhythms may have lunar periodicity.

"If all this sounds too much like sorcery, let me, in conclusion, quote from Spencer: 'There is no bar to knowledge greater than contempt prior to examination.' I hope this stimulates someone better qualified than I to analyze in greater detail the amazing association of the full moon and the increased incidence of bleeding. Meanwhile, because these data have been so conclusive and convincing to me," the doctor ends on a light note, "I threaten to become a witch doctor and operate on dark nights only, saving the moonlit nights for romance."[1]

Astrology and Childbirth: Many medical-astrology investigators have turned their attention to that happy biological event: birth. They have come up with some interesting conclusions. First of all, they have established that births do not occur with the same frequency throughout the year.

On an average, there are more births during the months of May and June than in November and December, which means—counting back nine months—that there are more conceptions in August and September than in February and March.

The reasons given are astrological in nature, relating to the movement of the earth around the sun, which causes the seasons.

Summer and the holidays, it seems, are more favorable to sexual

[1] Excerpts from the report by Dr. Edson Andrews appear through the courtesy of the Florida Medical Association.

relations than the end of winter, probably for all sorts of material and psychological reasons.

But doctors have recently added a biological motivation to these: the number of hormones helpful to procreative power may increase and diminish in the course of the year.[2]

Specialists in pediatrics have produced statistics to support the theory of hormones and the yearly cycle of procreative power.

Even the French skeptic Michel Gauquelin, who set out to disprove astrology in his book *The Scientific Basis of Astrology*, seems impressed with the "cosmic clocks" that regulate childbirth:

"At the time of their birth, the weight of babies born in May and June is on average higher than those born in the depths of winter. So the strongest children seem to be those who are conceived at the time when the procreative tendency is strongest. Therefore, one can say up to a point that the month when a child is born does provide some indication as to the robustness of his constitution. If you were born in, say, June, you have a better chance of having good balance and being tall and strong, and even having well-developed mental faculties."

(Sydney says that Gauquelin has the makings of a very fine astrologer in spite of himself.)

"Another statistic even goes so far as to show that human geniuses have most often been conceived, in April, and most often died in May."

Gauquelin adds a word of warning: "Naturally, the correlation here is a weak one. Young couples who . . . wish to bring a future genius into the world ought not to confine their procreative activities exclusively to April, for a great proportion of these couples would risk being disappointed!"

He also answers the question that has undoubtedly puzzled millions: Why is it that most babies seem in a hurry to be born at the end of the night or at the beginning of morning?

". . . The alternation of day and night not only controls our everyday activities, which are conscious and organized, but also, and to an even greater extent, the whole of our biological system. . . . The succession of day and night is the main clock, the most powerful cosmic 'time-keeper' of the neural and hormonal activity of our bodies. Now, it is a hormone factor which appears to set off the be-

[2] *The Scientific Basis of Astrology*, by Michel Gauquelin.

ginning of labor in a woman. It is closely linked with the universal 'time-keeper' of 24 hours. Hormones determining the term of confinement are secreted in greater quantities during the night, and so birth generally begins toward the end of the night rather than in the middle of the day."

In the past few decades, as Gauquelin points out, induced confinements have become fashionable, and doctors can put the normal time of the confinement forward or back by the use of drugs and injections. This has the advantage of allowing births to take place more conveniently, during the day.

"But the hour when the baby is born may also indicate its future health. In fact, confinements which have naturally started at a time which is physiologically often the best, that is, around midnight, are quicker and easier. Hence the saying that the child of the morning is generally more welcome than the child of the afternoon."

And scientists say astrologers are looney for asking for our hour of birth? Anyway, I'm relieved now to know that I was born around midnight, which insured my future good health, and to have this corroborated by due process of scientific medical-astrological forecasting.

Astrological Birth Control: Dr. Eugene Jonas, a Czechoslovakian gynecologist, claims to have a method of astrological birth control that is 98 per cent effective and may even replace the pill. A detailed account of his work is included in the book *Psychic Discoveries Behind the Iron Curtain*, by Lynn Schroeder and Sheila Ostrander and need not be repeated here. Jonas is a leading member of the Astra Research Center for Planned Parenthood in Nitra, Czechoslovakia. The Czech doctors who belong to this organization have one thing in common: they prescribe birth control based on the positions of the sun, the moon, and the planets.

The Jonas method is based on the theory that fertility throughout nature is related in some way to the waxing and the waning of the moon. Basing his analysis on the angular relationship between the sun and the moon in a woman's chart, Jonas is able to determine a fertility and non-fertility cycle he claims is much more accurate than the traditional Catholic-approved rhythm method of birth control.

Let's say, for example, that your sun is in the early degrees of agittarius while your moon is in the early degrees of Leo. This means that there are approximately 120 degrees between these two heavenly bodies in your chart. Dr. Jonas maintains that this is the basic stellar configuration upon which one can determine fertility. In other words, every time the sun and moon are 120 degrees apart, this is the period when the woman is most likely to conceive.

Suppose the sun is in Libra this month. Well, each time there is a distance of 120 degrees between the sun and the moon, then you could conceive. With the sun in Libra, this would occur when the moon is in either Aquarius or Gemini.

Personally, I think I would find this all too complicated to bother with—or even to explain without the help of my assistant and astrological interpreter, John LaCorte, who blithely says, "Of course you would need to use an ephemeris to determine the exact times of astrological fertility. Or you might consult a professional astrologer."

Sydney says please don't consult him; he has enough problems without adding the burden of birth control.

Moreover, very little research, if any (as we write this none has surfaced), has been done in this country concerning the effectiveness of the Jonas method. So be careful! Be sure that you have all the information available before you undertake this method of birth control.

Dr. Jonas also claims that the sex of a child, whether it will be male or female, can be predetermined astrologically. In other words, you can have your choice of a boy or a girl, whichever you prefer, if you play your stars right.

Further extensive research in astrological birth control and predetermination of sex could open the door to an entirely new area of medical-astrological knowledge, which might be called "astrological eugenics."

Medical Astrology and Palm Reading: Strange as it may sound, some doctors are now turning to palm reading for clues to human ailments. A report in *Time* magazine of January 28, 1966, in the Medicine section and headlined "The Telltale Palm," begins: "Palm reading as a form of fortunetelling is as phony as it is ancient. As an aid to medical diagnosis, it is as promising as it is new."

Life magazine in its Medicine section at about the same time carried the same story, headlined "Doctors Turn to Palm Reading."

Both stories focused on the recent work of Dr. Ruth Achs and

Dr. Rita Harper, pediatricians at New York's Downstate Medical Center, who discovered that palm prints of newborn babies are indeed fraught with meaning—as indicators of birth defects and hidden abnormalities. Dr. Achs and Dr. Harper made their study of handprints from babies whose mothers had German measles early in pregnancy. They found that the disease had left its imprint on the babies' palms.

But other studies by British and American medical "palmists" have linked abnormal palm prints with other disorders, including mongolism, mental retardation, heart defects, hearing impairment, the absence of fingernails or toenails, webbing between the fingers and toes, and possibly phenylketonuria, or PKU.

Finger and palm prints are known to be definitely linked with genetics. They are fully determined in the first four months of life in the womb, when the fetus is most liable to damage from viral or other harmful agents. The study of the association between palm prints and disease now comes under the heading of a new science called dermatoglyphics.

I don't know whether they call it dermatoglyphics in Japan, but there have been reports that Japanese medical "palmists" can tell by the lines in your hands if you have a tendency to cancer or ulcers.

"Of course," says Sydney, "the human hand is a complete study in itself. (The study is known as cheiromancy.) A person's birth sign often indicates the shape and size of the hand. All of these mantic arts and sciences, when combined, can give us a better understanding of ourselves and can be invaluable aids especially in the fields of medicine and psychology."

Sydney, of course, was an expert in palmistry at a very early age. In fact, when he was barely twenty, he published a tiny, pocket-size compendium of astrology, numerology, and palmistry, containing an intriguing "Astro Hand Chart," which he had worked out himself. So far as anyone knows, it has never been done before or since.

If nothing else, his Astro Hand Chart makes a good parlor game. The concept is simple (he says).

The idea is that you can guess a person's birth sign by the size and shape of his hand, and presumably, if you know enough about astrology, numerology, and palmistry, you go on from there—as Sydney does.

First, you must know that all twelve zodiacal signs fall into four groupings of the elements: earth, fire, air, and water.

The earth signs are Taurus, Virgo, Capricorn.

The fire signs are Aries, Leo, Sagittarius.

The air signs are Gemini, Libra, Aquarius.

The water signs are Cancer, Scorpio, Pisces.

Now for the matching shape of the hands:

Earth signs have square hands.

Fire signs have cone-shaped hands.

Air signs have triangular hands.

Water signs have oval hands.

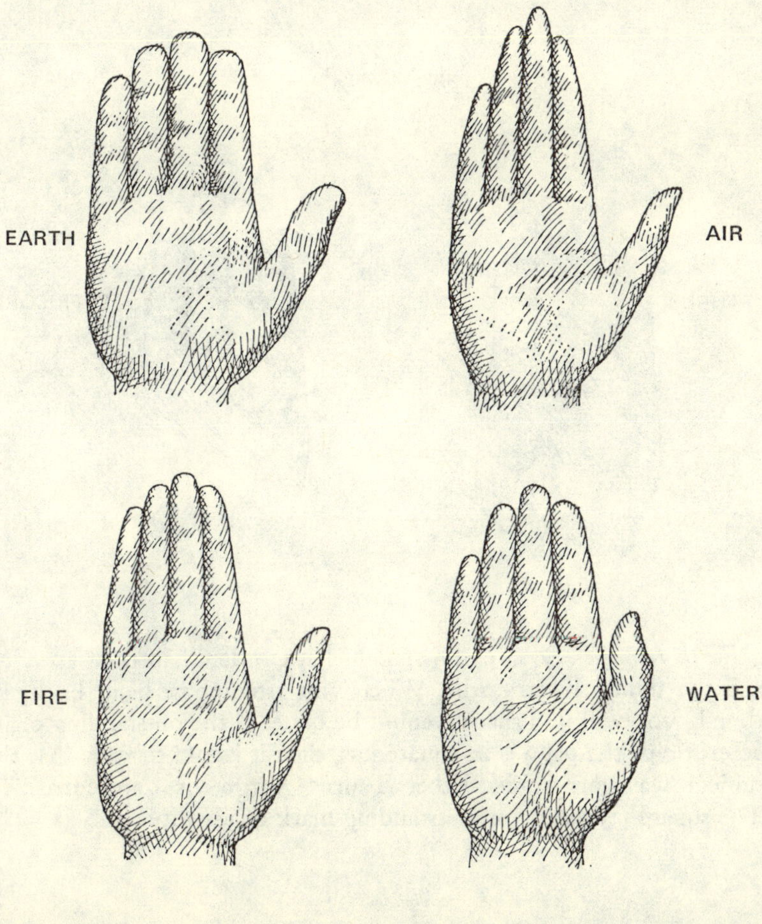

Since the twelve zodiacal signs fall into four groupings, Sydney calls each grouping a trinity and ascribes common characteristics to each trinity. Here are the charts drawn by Sydney to illustrate the shape of your hand according to your zodiacal sign.

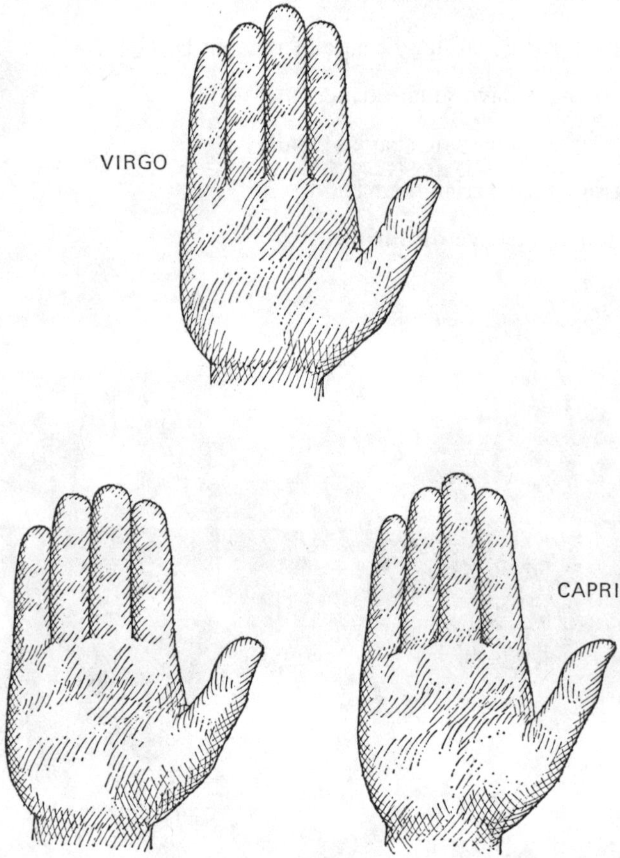

EARTH

Earth trinity: Square. Their palms are wider than they are long and the thumb is very stiff. When you attempt to bend back the thumb, you will find that it cannot be done. If the outstanding characteristic of the palm is its squareness, then it is safe to state that the subject was born under either Taurus, Virgo, or Capricorn. . . . The square jaw is also an outstanding mark of identity.

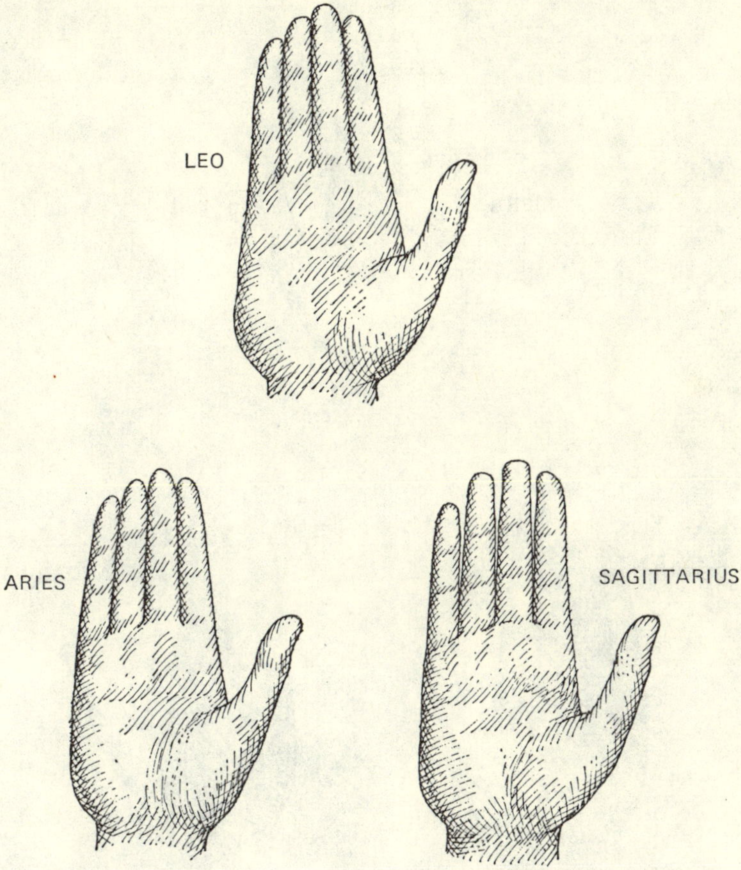

FIRE

Fire trinity: The hand is cone-shaped. This group can also be distinguished by high foreheads. There is a tendency for the hairline to recede, giving them an intellectual appearance.

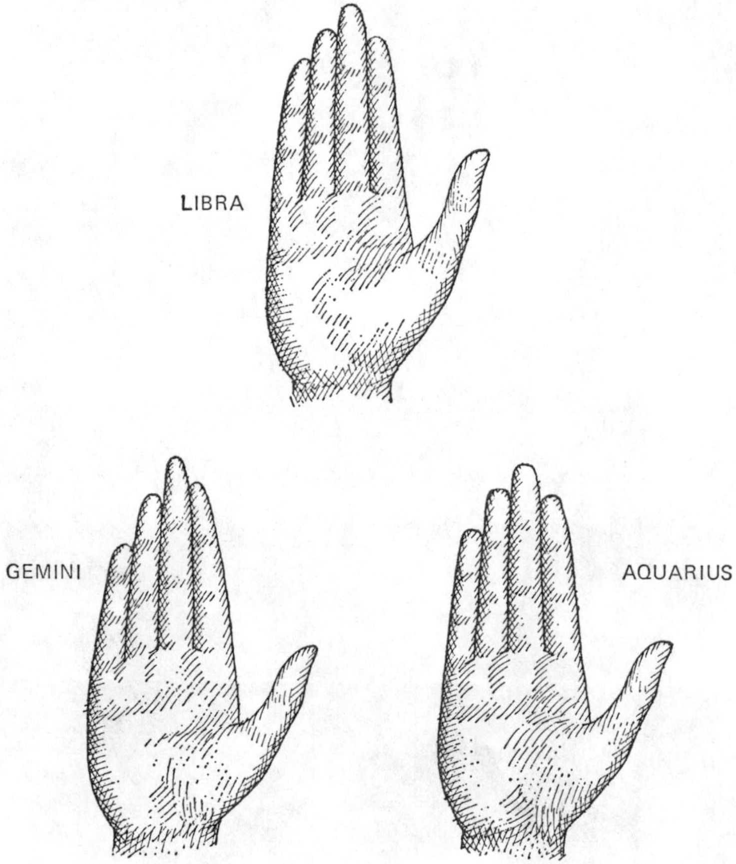

AIR

Air trinity: Represents the triangular hand type (thinner than the conic), best symbolized by the signs Gemini, Libra, and Aquarius. Narrow palms and long fingers mark their hands, which are probably the most graceful of the palm types. The hand is usually long and thin, with more lines on the palm than are to be found in the other groups. These people are the quiet, intellectual type, with poise and self-assurance. There is an expansiveness about them; they seem able to capture the pulse of the public. They sense trends and are often world leaders.

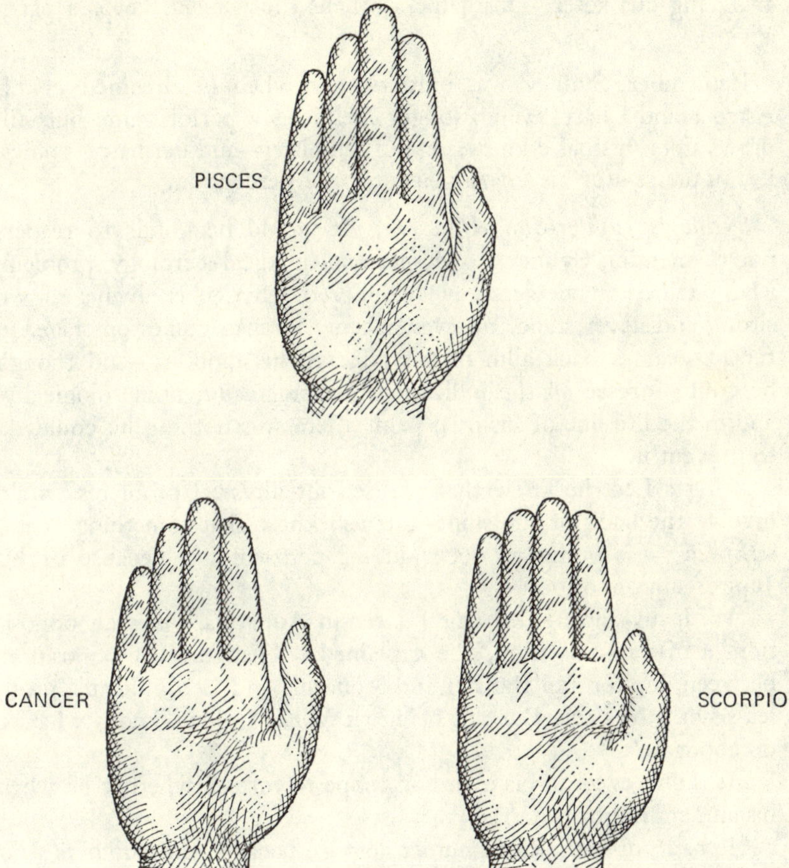

WATER

Water trinity: Those born under the signs Cancer, Scorpio, and Pisces have oval hands. The palm is inclined toward fleshiness, the fingers thick. It is a soft hand, with the mounts, or lumps on the palm, highly developed. It is almost a mixture of all four types. This group is impressionable, almost psychic. These people seem to be able to read your thoughts.

"Your skill in this game will increase with practice. You will not only be able to identify zodiacal signs but will develop a knack of analyzing character. This game sharpens the wit and keeps a party alive!"

Remember, Sydney was only twenty when he dreamed up his Astro Hand Chart. He no longer uses it as a parlor game but still draws upon his basic knowledge of palmistry—and dermatoglyphics, if you please—for his amazing accuracy of perception.

Sydney's Jupiter-Sun Affliction: It would be unfair to readers not to mention Sydney's own personal medical-astrology problem. Many television viewers have wondered why he is always shown sitting and never stands up even when a woman comes on stage. In recent years a back ailment has affected his mobility—and though he could foresee all the indications astrologically, numerologically, and in the life line of his own palm, there was nothing he could do to prevent it.

Being a Leo, he knew that any serious physical problems would involve the back or the spine. He also knew that something "catastrophic" was going to occur in his personal life because of his Jupiter-sun opposition.

"With my sun in Leo and Jupiter in Aquarius, that's an opposition—a major opposition," he explained. "That kind of opposition, between Jupiter and the sun and Aquarius and Leo indicates problems with the back. But not being an M.D., I didn't know what to do about it."

He didn't even do his own horoscope to foresee whether or when his ailment might be cured.

He had put his faith in numerology, especially the numbers four and eight, which he calls his "fadic" numbers (derivative of fate), because they keep recurring in his birth chart. He was convinced that his forty-eighth year would be a crucial time for him, and if he could get through his forty-eighth birthday (August 5) and the rest of the year (1974), he would have passed the critical period. (He did.)

But as for looking into his own horoscope, he said, "I'd rather defer on that. It's tough for me to do my own. Doctors don't do their own diagnoses. It's very difficult to be strictly objective about yourself."

Although he can give excellent advice based on his horoscopic charts for others, he is the first to admit, "I'm not very good at following the advice of the stars for myself."

He was hospitalized once for three weeks in a hospital unit he describes as more like a Beverly Hills hotel bungalow, and he behaved accordingly—with extracurricular activities including wine, women, and song. (The unit was closed down soon after he left.)

"I don't think all that carrying on did the state of my health any good," he says.

In sickness and health, in romance and marriage, he is as human and as fallible as the next guy.

"But it's the humans who err, not the stars," he insists. "We would all be better off if we would just listen to the message they give us."

From ancient times, astrologers have believed that various parts of the body are ruled by the twelve zodiacal signs. These areas are considered the weak spots of the body and are most susceptible to injury or some type of malfunction if they correspond with the sign you were born under.

Following is a list of the signs with the parts of the body they rule and helpful hints for your good health.

ARIES rules the head; a common Arian complaint is headaches.

TAURUS rules the throat and the neck. Watch out for laryngitis, strep throat, mumps, swollen glands, thyroid problems, etc.

GEMINI rules the nerves, arms, and shoulders. It also rules the lungs, and many Geminis are prone to bronchitis.

CANCER rules the stomach. Cancerians tend to internalize their troubles and woes, and many of them end up with ulcers because of it. The breasts are also associated with Cancer.

LEO rules the heart, spine, and back. Tensions for Leos often manifest themselves as backaches. Leos must also be careful not to overexert themselves, because of the danger of heart attacks, especially in later years.

VIRGO rules the nervous system and the intestinal tract. Virgos and Cancers have much in common in that both signs are very sensitive to the types of foods that are ingested.

LIBRA rules the kidneys. When tensions upset the Libran's need for balance, serious kidney difficulties may arise.

SCORPIO rules the sexual organs and the need for the expression of sexual energy. If this is suppressed, the energy sometimes manifests itself in very destructive ways.

SAGITTARIUS rules the liver, hips, and thighs. Sagittarians need a lot of physical and mental activity. Without it, liver problems may develop, or there might be an increase in weight, especially in the hips and thighs.

CAPRICORN rules the knees, bones, and teeth. Capricorns are very susceptible to calcium deposits in their joints (arthritis). They should be sure to have a sufficient amount of calcium in their diet.

AQUARIUS rules the circulation, the shins, and the ankles. Aquarians are susceptible to fractures and broken ankles.

PISCES rules the feet, and Pisceans are very sensitive to their feet. If their feet are uncomfortable, their entire well-being is threatened. Also, they are very sensitive to all kinds of drugs.

MISCELLANY: A general rule of thumb is: Never have an operation on a day that the moon is in a sign ruling the part of your body to be operated on. For example, do not have a head operation when the moon is in Aries.

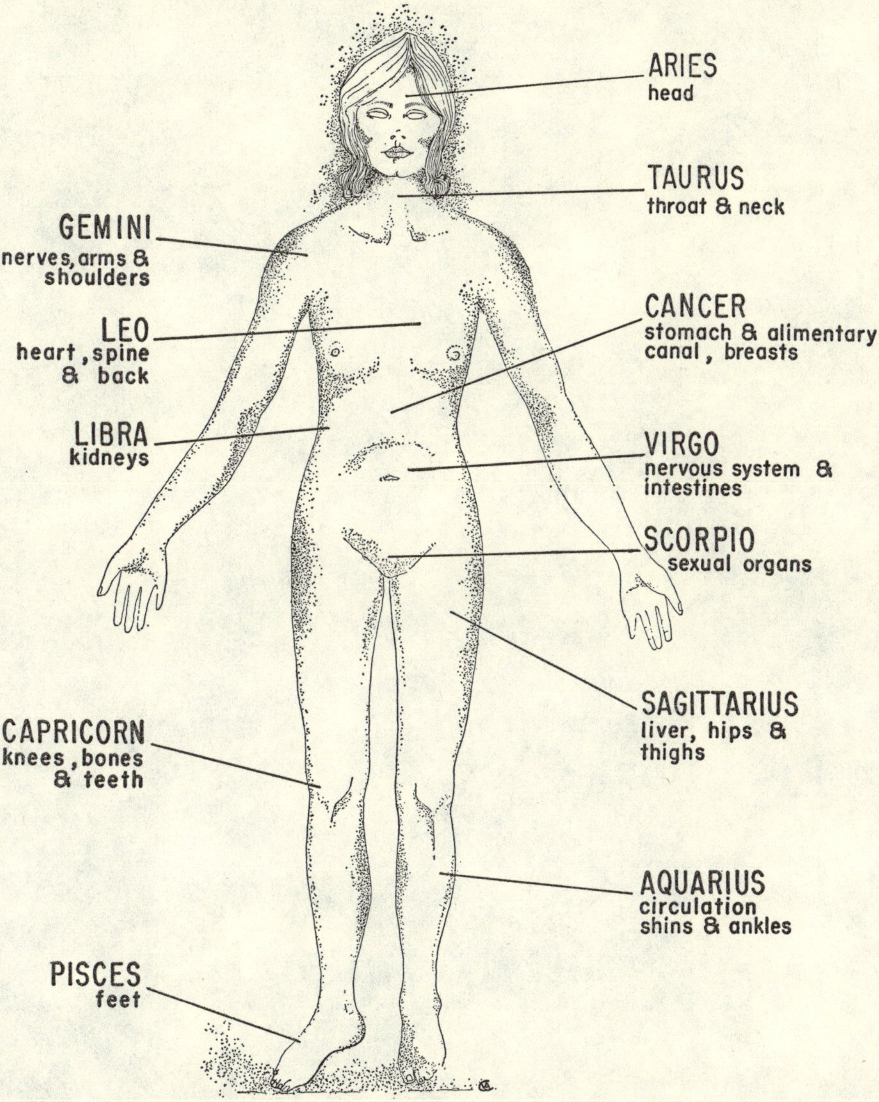

DRAWING BY VINCE CAMERON AND DIANE EHLERS

How to Do It Yourself: With Astrology

Chapter 19

HOW TO . . . AND WHEN TO . . .

(The Answers Are All in the Skies)

"Astrology is astronomy brought down to earth and applied to the affairs of man."

—RALPH WALDO EMERSON

We have come a long way since man first looked at the sky and pondered its mysteries.

The sun, the moon, the stars—all became objects of worship, of fear, of hope, in man's eternal quest to pierce the veil of our tomorrows and to know what the future holds.

The sun rises and sets, the moon waxes and wanes, and the planets in all their celestial splendor speak a universal language to those attuned to their cosmic message.

Just as ancient astrologers found their answers in the skies, so modern science, almost in spite of itself, has given rebirth to a new "cosmology" that adds validity to primitive man's myths and superstitions about the stars.

The essence of astrology—or cosmology, if you prefer—is *time*.

And all time, from birth to death, from clock to calendar, from sowing to reaping, is either controlled by or correlated with the movement of the planets.

The music of the spheres has its own tempo, its adagio and allegro, its upbeat and downbeat rhythms which affect not only the fate of men but all elements of nature: winds, rains, storms, tides, earthquakes.

Astrology has continued to survive not only because of man's fascination with the immutability of the stars and their cosmic rhythm that pervades all of nature but because the stars can be brought down to earth and applied to the affairs of man, as Emerson said.

And as Sydney says, "In astrology everything begins with time. It isn't only what you do or how you do it that is important, but *when* you do it. Time is the essential element, the heartbeat of astrology. All practical applications of astrology are based on divisions of time, days and hours, months and years, seasons and cycles. All are governed by planetary positions. From ages past we know that there is a time for everything. . . ."

A time when the fish bite and the corn grows tall . . . a time to plant crops or to have your teeth pulled . . . a time to mate and marry . . . a time of procreative power . . . a time to have sex if you want a healthy and robust baby, or even a child genius (but don't count on it!) . . . a time of animal migrations, population movements, political and economic crisis, epidemics, wars, and revolutions. . . .

Statistical studies of the cycles of such social phenomena indicate that they have occurred at peaks of solar activity. The eleven-year cycle of sunspots, for example, has even been linked to such mundane affairs as the number of road accidents and mining disasters.

"If we know even a little bit of astrology," Sydney says, "if we study the recurrent patterns of time cycles and trends, then we can learn how to put astrology to use in our everyday lives, to prevent some things from happening and prepare ourselves for others."

Astrological Almanac of Crime: In the area of crime, for example, a knowledge of astrology might even save your life. Specialists in crime analysis have noted correlations between, on the one hand, crime and accidents, and, on the other hand, planetary positions; as previously noted, according to Roy Wilson, a veteran in the Charlotte, North Carolina, police department, the astrological chart of every murder victim he has studied clearly indicated that trouble was on the horizon.

Astrologically speaking, forewarned is forearmed, as Sydney says, so he has drawn up his own astrological almanac of crime, which might help you avoid trouble on your own horizon if you know even these few generalities:

Many murders occur in January, June, and August. Fewer murders occur in February, November, and December. Danger periods for infanticide are in February and May; few cases occur in December. Specialists in poisoning are active in May, idle in September. Death threats are made in August, few in February, or November. Active months for perjury are February and December. Forgeries multiply during April, October, and December. Forgers also are active during the first days of every quarter and the last days of every year. Thefts flourish during December and January.

Outbreaks of murder appear to be triggered by the moon tugging on "biological tides" inside the human body, according to Dr. Arnold L. Lieber of the University of Miami's medical school. Dr. Lieber reports that a two-year study has established a sound, scientific relationship between phases of the moon and the murder rate in Dade County, Florida. The study shows that the county's murder rate begins to rise about twenty-four hours before the full moon, reaches a peak at the full moon, then drops back before climbing to a secondary peak at the new moon. Dr. Lieber asserts, "I feel that eventually we are going to show that any organism, human or animal, is an integral part of the universe and responds to changes like variations in the solar cycle and the lunar cycle." (From Sydney Omarr's *Weekly Astrological Guide for Sagittarius*, 1976, page 10.)

If Sydney had his way, courses in astrology would be included in all high school and college curricula–if competent teachers could be found. Anyone, he says, can learn the basics of astrology, just as we learn English and math, and a basic knowledge of astrology can be useful in practically all areas of life.

Medicine, Psychiatry, and Psychology: In Sydney's opinion, one of the most important areas of research is medical astrology, and many of the numerous potentials in this field have already been mentioned in our chapter on "Medical Astrology." In addition, planetary influences have been linked to heart attacks, lung diseases (especially tuberculosis), schizophrenia; to diphtheria, typhus, and cholera in Europe; and to the death rate of smallpox victims in Chicago. A knowledge of astrology can be useful as an aid in the diagnosis of physical and mental illnesses, the prevention of excessive bleeding in tonsillectomies or peptic ulcers, and perhaps even in eugenics, if the Czech doctors' findings in astrological birth control are confirmed. Already there is enough firm evidence of the correlation between planetary influences and the state of our biological ill- or well-being to justify further research. And Sydney is convinced this is one area in which astrology could make an important contribution to the future of mankind.

Education, Teaching: If you are a teacher of English literature, for example, you will be a better teacher if you understand the astrological references in Shakespeare, Chaucer, or Tennyson. . . . And if you're a history teacher, you should be aware of Ben Franklin's leanings toward astrology. *Poor Richard's Almanac*, one of the most popular publications of its time, of course had an astrological basis. However, the first almanacs were printed in the fifteenth century in France—as soon as printing was invented. They contained all kinds of astrological advice and forecasts about subjects such as sowing time and the kind of weather the year would bring. Some almanacs specialized in health topics. They indicated propitious times to bathe, shave, purge oneself, or let one's blood. And they also explained the astrological origins of disease.[1]

Religion: There are many astrological references in the Bible, as well as many biblical stories that can be interpreted astrologically (e.g., Jonah and the Whale, Joseph's Coat, the Star of Bethlehem). As Sydney says, "To each his own . . . interpretation." But a knowledge of astrology may give you a better understanding of the Bible and help you clarify its relation to all religions.

Weather Prediction: It is now known, of course, that the sun, the moon, and the stars all have an effect on the weather, that their strange effects, which seem to influence all of life on this sphere, can now be forecast. Possibly nothing has done more to convince non-believers than John H. Nelson's work at RCA in forecasting radio interference based on the motions of the planets.

Prediction of Earthquakes: Some astrologers claim they can predict earthquakes, but don't believe them, says Sydney. His approach to this earth-shaking question is a cautious one.

"I feel that eventually we may be able to make earthquake predictions, but this will come from working with someone in another discipline, like a geologist. Once we define and understand what an

[1] *The Scientific Basis of Astrology*, by Michel Gauquelin.

earthquake really is, then, like all things, it will relate to astrological terms. Then we can find the answer. But astrologers can't do this alone. They must work with geologists to arrive at a valid conclusion."

Astrologically speaking, he explains: "Astrologers traditionally have associated the planet Uranus with earthquakes. The Uranus cycle is seven years; the planet remains in each zodiacal sign for that length of time. Now scientists at the National Oceanic and Atmospheric Administration reveal they have found a definite link between major earthquake activity and an 'earth wobble,' which reaches its maximum every seven years. The next major 'wobble' is due to occur in 1978."

Air Pollution: Sunspots correlate to planetary aspects. Many experts believe that *major periods of air pollution occur during minimum sunspot activity*. If this is checked out and found to be valid, then we may have a breakthrough in solving the horrendous problems created by air pollution, Sydney believes. A research program should get under way and not be delayed merely because it was the brainchild of an astrologer, he warns.

Politics, Oil Crisis: There are countless ways in which astrology can be applied to political affairs. For example, the oil crisis. It is a well-known fact that Sheik Ahmed Zaki al-Yamani, Saudi Arabia's Minister of Petroleum and Mineral Resources, is a fervent believer in astrology. "The moon and stars *do* influence human behavior," he insists.

"Therefore," says Sydney, "our State Department is very stupid to have this knowledge and not to utilize it. Everybody in the world knows that Neptune is oil [well, not quite!], and with Neptune in Sagittarius, and with Sagittarius being the international sign of long-distance communications and foreign countries, oil will be the major trouble factor until Neptune gets out of Sagittarius. Neptune went into Sagittarius only a couple of years ago, and it stays in Sagittarius for fourteen years . . . and since Yamani, the man who controls most of the world's oil, is such a passionate believer in astrology, it seems to me that it only makes sense for our State Department officials to inform themselves astrologically and negotiate with him accordingly. All we would need to do is to check th pects of Neptune to know when the rough times are coming, and then to reason with him, . . . just as in World War II, when it became known that Hitler's henchmen were utilizing astrology, the British consequently employed their own astrologer to tell them what Hitler's astrologers were doing. . . ."

On a personal note, Sheik Ahmed Zaki al-Yamani happens to be a great fan of Sydney's, corresponds with him, and once telephoned him from Switzerland, in early January 1976, soon after he had been held hostage by a terrorist group and then released. Sheik al-Yamani wanted Sydney's astrological advice on various matters and invited Sydney to come to Switzerland for a personal consultation. Because of his physcial ailment and consequent immobility, Sydney explained, he could not accept the invitation, to which Sheik al-Yamani replied, "Then I will come to see you." At some point in their transatlantic conversation, Sydney absent-mindedly said, "Excuse me, sir, but I don't like to run up your telephone bill." The sheik, one of the world's wealthiest oil czars, nearly broke up with laughter.

Exactly why Neptune is oil, or why Neptune in Sagittarius means trouble in the oil fields, is still one of those astrological mysteries beyond the comprehension of a slow learner. But, again, I'm willing to take Sydney's word for it.

And while we're on the subject of Neptune, Sydney says: "Persons with Neptune in the sixth house are more sensitive to drugs than most, have a distinct tendency to nervous disorders, and are attracted to work which makes them privy to secret information. They often deal with associates who are considered strange and poetic. Very often, this horoscopic signature corresponds with hospitals, institutions. The native [subject] succeeds by working behind the scenes."

As an example, Sydney cites mystery writer Ian Fleming, who reportedly worked with the British during World War II, planting an astrologer on the staff of Rudolf Hess. A phony horoscope indicated to Hess that he should make his now-historic flight to Scotland. Fleming also was instrumental in having astrologer Louis de Wohl commissioned a captain in British Intelligence for the purpose of analyzing what astrologer Karl Krafft might be advising the Nazis.

Since Rudolf Hess supposedly made his infamous flight to Scotland on the advice of astrologers, Adolf Hitler, according to Sydney, ordered astrologers in Germany rounded up and hurled into concentration camps.

"Despite popular misconceptions," Sydney insists, "Hitler was no friend of astrology."

Whether he was or wasn't makes little or no difference to the over-all role of astrology in the political arena.

Business and Finance: Just as there are good times to plant and sow, there are good times to invest, to sign contracts, to make business deals. The up-and-down patterns of planetary influences pervade all nature, including business and finance on a national or international level (e.g., a national economic crisis), and on a personal level. In fact, so permeating is astrology in our lives today that many major business decisions are based on charts of the heavens.

"The use of astrology by companies has been going on for many years, and if anything it is on the increase," Sydney points out. "The birth date we use is the date of incorporation. There are good periods and bad periods for signing contracts, for starting a new business, or merging with another firm. Astrology can be used to determine how executives would be likely to react to each other, or at what time a new deal would be most likely to go through smoothly. It is also used by many companies in deciding which key people to hire. Most business firms, however, do not like to admit publicly that they consult astrologers. But I think this is going to change," Sydney adds hopefully, "as soon as we get through this period of academic prejudice against astrologers."

One businessman who doesn't at all mind admitting that he consults Sydney regularly is Joseph Chrenko, an insurance executive with the Monarch Life Insurance Company in Los Angeles. He is general sales manager of the firm. Joe, who happens also to be the real-life "Hungry Joe" character in Joseph Heller's best seller *Catch-22*, claims that he has doubled or tripled his business since he began utilizing astrology combined with Sydney's Thought Dial technique a few years ago. He uses it in the hiring and firing of personnel and in planning sales programs. He is particularly enthusiastic about the numerological tips he has learned from Sydney, always asks job applicants to give him their birth dates and three numbers, and says the results have saved him "a lot of ulcers."

In interviewing prospective salesgirls, for example, he can tell from "numberizing" them which ones are most likely to create the most problems, so he doesn't hire them.

"I am convinced that Sydney Omarr's system is far more valid than the usual evaluation tests given by most business firms," Joe Chrenko told me.

Two of Sydney's greatest admirers—and astrology's strongest defenders—are authors Jess Stearn and Henry Miller, who are not at all reluctant to admit publicly that they have consulted him on business as well as personal matters.

Jess Stearn has related his own personal experiences with Sydney in his book *A Time for Astrology*. And Henry Miller, the highly revered, awesome, and controversial author of *Tropic of Cancer*, certainly leaves no question about where he stands on the subject, as evidenced in his glowing introduction, "The Astrologer Seen Through the Eyes of a Friend." He was equally and unabashedly glowing when I called on him for a personal interview. (See Chapter 25).

Business and economic fluctuations run in cycles, and as Sydney points out, the general economic state of affairs in the nation is reflected in the individual's business affairs. Sydney and other astrologers could accurately forecast the nation's big economic squeeze that hit its peak in 1975, just as they were able to forecast the crash of 1929—on the basis of the economic cycles that are manifest in the horoscopic chart of the United States. But individuals also have business and economic cycles in their own charts, and each individual's chart is different.

This is why, for example, some people made money at the height of the depression. Their cycles were up, while the national cycle was down.

"Everything in astrology depends on timing," Sydney emphasizes. "That's why a knowledge of cycles is so important. In fact that's what astrology is all about, ultimately: the study of cycles."

All clock-and-calendar time has an astrological basis that must be obvious to everyone. For example, it takes a year of time for the earth to travel around the sun. A month is the interval of time between two moons. The four weeks in a month are equal in time to the four quarters of the moon. There are twelve months in a year, as there are twelve signs of the zodiac. And those who know French plus a modicum of astrology must be aware that each calendar day of the week is dominated by a planet: Sunday by the sun, Monday by the moon, Tuesday (mardi) by Mars, Wednesday (mercredi) by Mercury, Thursday (jeudi) by Jupiter, Friday (vendredi) by Venus, Saturday by Saturn.

There are twice-twelve hours in a day, as there are twelve astrological houses.

The symbolism of the "astrological houses" is of vital importance to the proper interpretation of a horoscope, Sydney tells me, but somehow it gets all mixed up with the position of your rising sign, or ascendant, at the time of your birth, and the calculation of the ascendant is too complicated for amateur dabblers in astrology. I leave this to the experts.

But since the second house of your chart governs business and finance, and the fifth house romance and love, obviously, as Sydney says, we need to know the symbolic meaning attributed to all the twelve houses of astrology in order to familiarize ourselves with our own time-dominated cycles and understand our relationship to the stars.

The planets also have their own symbolism governing various human characteristics and events. And then there is the symbolism of the "aspects" of the planets. The "aspects" are the angles formed between the stars as seen from earth, and astrologers attach great importance to these "aspects." In other words, a trained astrologer must be able to keep track of all the combinations of aspects, signs, planets, and houses, as well as the *transits* of the planets. And to decipher all of these elements correctly into a total astrological picture, or horoscope, is, as I have said, a very complicated business.

For those who desire further details, I refer you again to Sydney's book *My World of Astrology*. These chapters are meant only as general guidelines in bringing the stars down to earth, as Emerson put it, and applying them to useful purposes in everyday life.

Chapter 20

HOW TO PICK A MATE
(Getting the Yin-Yang of Your Love Straight in the Fifth House)

"Taurus, Scorpio, and Virgo men are the most difficult."

—SYDNEY OMARR

People consult astrologers on all kinds of problems, but the three most common ones are, predictably, love, money, and health—in that order.

Just as the second house, as we have seen, symbolizes money, fortune, goods, and possessions, so the fifth house, apparently the most important in the zodiac, symbolizes pleasures, amusements, games, love, creativity, children.

True, the seventh house symbolizes marriage and partnership, but the fifth house is where it really begins, the house of fun-and-games sex and love, physical attraction. It's most important to have your fifth house in order, your creative juices flowing, your love life in shape.

"Once that's in shape it's pretty hard for anything else to be out of shape," Sydney says.

There are a number of astrological ways of doing this.

First and foremost, if you're a woman, you must know where your man's Mars is in relation to your Venus.

It is also extremely important to know where your partner's moon is. It's a good omen when the moon in a woman's chart falls on the sun in a man's chart. This means compatibility. But woe to those whose moon falls in Scorpio!

And then there is Saturn, the troublemaker. You would not want

Saturn on your sun, your moon, or your ascendant, and you certainly wouldn't want Saturn in your second house, which has to do with finances.

If you have Jupiter in the fifth house, you are inclined to be impulsive and fall in and out of love quickly, and you can be sidetracked by an eccentric member of the opposite sex.

November is probably the worst month to plan your wedding date, especially that part of the month that falls under the sign of Scorpio (October 23–November 21). From ancient times the people of India have had an innate suspicion of Scorpio. In India, civilized people are not supposed to mate or marry or even have intercourse during the period when their sun is in Scorpio.

Sydney doubts that anyone is going to endure abstinence completely, no matter where Scorpio is in relation to his or her sun or moon. (In India it's even worse if one's moon is in Scorpio!)

"It's important to know the position of the moon in relation to your sign if you want a close personal relationship," Sydney says. "The moon is a strong tie between two people."

As for sex under a full moon? "I don't know whether it's better astrologically, but more people do, more mating animals do; the mating instinct seems to be activated during the full moon. . . . And of course the grunion run more under the full moon," he is quick to slyly remind you.

If all contemplating marriage would spend the money for a professional astrologer to cast their horoscopes (it would cost much less than the reception or the honeymoon) or spend the time to study and compare their own, do-it-yourself horoscopes, they would have a better understanding of the pitfalls, the plus and minus factors, the up and down trends of their astrological "aspects"; it could cut down on the divorce rate, Sydney is convinced.

"For example," he says, "if you're going through a very upsetting kind of aspect in your chart, it doesn't mean that this is the end of the world. If you can look at your chart and understand it astrologically, then you will know that this malefic aspect is going to pass in a year or two (because that's about as long as any affliction from the planetary transits will last), and you don't need to talk about breaking up or getting a divorce until that planetary transit is past."

According to Sydney, there are basic things to look for in your prospective partner.

Generally speaking, he says, persons born two signs apart tend to have lasting marriages—or, to put it another way, with one sign between. For example, Leo and Libra, or Leo and Gemini, or Sagittarius and Aquarius, or Capricorn and Pisces would be more compatible than those who are three signs apart (two signs between), such as Leo and Scorpio, Taurus and Leo, Aries and Cancer.

Taurus is the most amorous sign. Leo (the ego) is a Lothario. Virgo has an instinct for chastity.

Taurus, Scorpio, and Virgo are considered the three most difficult men in the zodiac. A female Cancer is the best sign to handle a Taurus (the bull) male. Virgo females seem to get along with troublesome Scorpio men. But Virgo men are demanding, intellectual, perfectionists—and they shy away from sex.

This is merely a brief glimpse into the vast potential of astrological matchmaking. In Sydney's opinion the Mars-Venus conjunction is of prime importance.

"When horoscopes are compared and there is a Mars-Venus conjunction [when there is no gap between the planets and they are side by side in the zodiac], it follows as night follows day that there will be a great physical attraction between the man and the woman. Any biology teacher will tell you that Mars symbolizes the male and Venus the female, and if we don't get our Mars and Venus straight in our fifth house, then nothing will be straight. What it boils down to is getting the yin-yang of your love straight."

Do As Sydney Says, Not As He Does: Sydney is the first to admit that his yin-yang of love in his fifth house isn't in such good shape. His first and only marriage lasted about six weeks (he isn't sure).

The trouble was: he's a Leo with Mars in his seventh house (which means a marriage usually takes place very suddenly, quickly, without much forethought or plans, which it did), and she was a Virgo with her Saturn on his ascendant, or rising sign, Libra.

"It's a very destructive type of relationship and we both knew it. We had consulted our charts and we knew it was a terrible time to get married, especially for Jeraldine. She was in a number-seven year numerologically, and she had the sun, Venus, and Mars conjunct in her tenth house, with her Saturn opposing those three vital planets, squaring her moon in Gemini and giving a bad aspect to her rising sign, Sagittarius. It was a terrible period in her life. Almost anything that she would have tried would not have worked at that time, especially marriage.

"But I went out and had a few drinks and decided that I was going to marry her anyway and see whether astrology would prove wrong or not. Besides," Sydney admits, "I was attracted to her."

The moral is: Astrology was right, the marriage was wrong.

Today Jeraldine says, "It is difficult living with a genius." But they have remained the best of friends.

The Leo's charm with the ladies is legendary, and if Sydney marries again it will probably happen suddenly, as it did with Jeraldine, because he has Mars in his seventh house.

"But I would be very careless to have an affair with a girl whose Saturn is on my sun or moon or ascendant or falls in my second house, because then I would know that my finances are going to suffer. . . ."

Not only does Sydney have the typical Leo's lengendary charm with the ladies, but he's also the luckiest of Leos, because he has Jupiter in his fifth house.

He may have problems with his yin-yang of love with Mars in his seventh, but with Jupiter in his fifth he is assured of a vast abundance and multiplicity of sexual encounters.

Gloria Swanson once told Sydney's sister Ruth, "Your brother is fascinating. He is handsome, positive, and at the same time so charmingly shy."

Ho, ho! Miss Swanson obviously didn't know about Sydney's Jupiter in his fifth house.

His first meaningful encounter was at age ten in Atlantic City with a young lady named Teresa, a Pisces, who hit him over the head with her shoe (naturally, it had to be a shoe, since Pisces has some zodiacal connection with the feet) when he refused to disclose how he made her dime disappear.

Then there was Molly, a Scorpio, his grammar-school puppy love, who shoved him off his bicycle when he boasted of another favorite female.

Next was Connie and a brief fling at "experimental love" at age eighteen during army basic training in Wichita Falls, Texas. The breakup came when Connie disclosed her birth date and he discovered her Saturn was on his sun.

His first "try at the real thing" was at age twenty-one with a nice girl named Flo, a student in one of his journalism classes in Philadelphia. They were about to run off and get married and start a small-town newspaper, but unhappily her Venus squared his Mars so he called it off.

Then there was his very serious, truly genuine first love, Marian, the Gemini schoolteacher who was turned down for a loan because she was "under the influence of a fortuneteller" (Chapter 15). Before and after Marian there were numerous meaningful encounters: with Ann, Elsie, Patricia, Belle, Charlene, Mary, Marie, Alice, Alicia, Betty, Bettina, Margaret, Monica, Adriana, Elaine, Pearl, Anita, Georgiana, Zelda, Robin, Renee, Adelle, Rebecca, Joan . . . and on ad infinitum. Amazingly he remembers all their signs, but nothing came of these encounters because of their Mars-Venus collisions.

His second love was Valerie, a Capricorn with Scorpio rising, whom he was courting until he met Jeraldine, his third love, a Virgo with Sagittarius rising, her moon in Gemini and her Saturn on his rising sign Libra. (Don't ask me how he keeps them all straight!)

Both Valerie and Jeraldine—and probably all the others—still adore him. One of them happily told me he's one of the world's greatest lovers.

Sydney claims both hold a special place in his heart. He accepts their compliment with modesty and a mirthful twinkle in his eye. "Well, it's only because I'm lucky enough to have Jupiter in my fifth house." His fourth love is upcoming, and probably a fifth, sixth, and seventh . . .

Keeping Your Fifth House in Order: In astrology everything begins with time, and the time for love and marriage depends on your horoscopes. You can be physically attracted to someone, but you might not be coming together at the right time for a marriage. Or if you happen to believe in reincarnation, maybe it's not even the right lifetime, Sydney quips, though as far as he's concerned, astrologically speaking, any time is the right time for sex and love.

Following are his helpful hints in this category from some basic characteristics of the signs of the zodiac.

ARIES: Sex, for an Aries, is a matter of sudden impulse rather than deliberation. The Aries is rash, impetuous, headstrong, impulsive, warm, passionate, and creative. But without love and romance, the Aries has little interest in sex. Once committed, however, the Aries gives his or her all. The physical side of relationships is extremely important: feeling, touching, embracing. Children mean much to the Aries; he or she regards sex as something that can and should lead to offspring. Sex, for you, Aries, is no plaything. HINT: But learn to cope with that green-eyed monster.

For Men Only: Aries is not the kind of woman you can lead around in circles. She can be temperamental, headstrong, proud, and arrogant. She is Martian, fiery in nature, spirited to the point of being domineering—if you let her. You can win your way with this woman by being diplomatic, but don't let her think you're an easy catch, and be wary when she becomes bossy. An Aries woman wants a man, not someone looking for a mother.

For Women Only: The man born under Aries can be dominant, inventive, and very impatient. His temperament is fiery, his drives are strong, his ambitions are great. His capacity for love is enormous. He can be militant, determined, and obstinate. Once he gets rolling—even down the wrong road—he tends to keep in motion and in the same direction. He is often brilliant but often adventure-seeking and erratic. HINT: Try to keep his chin up. Once he begins to sag or lag, he is heading for defeat.

TAURUS: The love pattern is strong. Taurus is sensuous, has a lusty approach to sex and a great capacity for love—but can be too demanding. Taurus appetites are strong, as reflected in their sexual drive and love of fine food and physical comforts. Taurus is passionate, affectionate, warm, and hungry for love—and not shy about speaking up when the partner is lacking. HINT: Don't take offense, Taurus, when this pattern is reversed. Be more flexible.

For Men Only: Taurus women are generally hungry—for experience as well as for food. They like the good life, are earthy in temperament, and there is a tendency for them to become careless in the way they look. Don't be a stuffed shirt, but don't put up with curlers in the hair. This lady is seductive but pleasantly lazy. She may be troublesome at times, but she is generally worth it.

For Women Only: Ladies, if you are looking for perfection, you can bypass the Taurus man. Don't try to corral him; he won't stand for being fenced in. He wants plenty of room. He doesn't want lectures, he wants love, but he isn't always easy to live with. He likes luxury, but he wants you to be practical about it. He is earthy in temperament, enjoys the basic things: eating, sleeping, loving, fighting, mating. HINT: He can be very stubborn. When he makes up his mind, don't try to change it.

GEMINI: Sex symbol Marilyn Monroe was a Gemini. The mercurial side of Gemini can cause utter confusion in the sex area. Gemini is restless, seeking, probing, curious, searching for that "ideal" of sexual gratification that goes hand in hand with mental satisfaction and creative fulfillment. HINT: You *think* too much, Gemini, and therefore your creative forces are blocked. Give that motor-like mind of yours a rest. Relax and let nature have its way.

For Men Only: Gemini women have an infectious laugh, but they also have a disturbing habit: they laugh at the wrong times. This can be very annoying, especially at a romantic moment. Some men find Gemini impossible, but if you're not careful, she grows on you. She can be seductive and charming, lovely, witty, and daring and at times devastatingly funny. On occasion she can even be reasonable! HINT: Treat her lightly, don't take her too seriously. Develop your own sense of humor. This is a must if you're dealing with a Gemini.

For Women Only: Gemini men are versatile, alert, charming, and blessed with loads of energy. They may tire you out. They are airy in temperament, idealistic, elusive, quick with the hands, artistic, and restless. They can talk their way into and out of almost anything. HINT: Listen to them but remain skeptical; and keep that Mona Lisa smile on your face. That definitely helps.

CANCER: The moods of others have a direct effect on the emotions of Cancer people. They are prone to jealousy and possessiveness, have a tendency to attract clandestine relationships, sometimes use sex as a means of changing patterns or habits or renovating a way of life. When love does not go well, they often turn to food and gain weight and then become involved in an unhappy love affair, which only adds to their weight—and other—problems. HINT: You can be responsible, discriminating, and loyal without shutting the door to sexual fulfillment.

For Men Only: Cancer women are lovely but often lonely. Being of the water element, they are highly emotional, have a tendency to brood and worry, require constant reassurance and affection. If you can give the Cancer woman real love, if you are willing to make a home for her, she will usually prove faithful, loyal, warm, and exciting. Besides, she is a good cook! But she demands sincerity, and don't try to fool her. If you are looking for a woman who can make a home for you, she is for you. HINT: But never, never take her for granted.

For Women Only: Be sympathetic with the Cancer man, but don't spoil him. He is more emotional than the average man, and he is not the easiest man to love. He is an idealist. His standards are high. He wants and needs a good home. He appreciates women and the finer things of life. But he is a moody man and he can't tolerate whining. HINT: The Cancer man fears ridicule, and the quickest way to lose him is to laugh at him.

LEO: Those born under the sign of Leo tend to fall in love with love rather than with a partner. They attract numerous affairs of the heart and they are intrigued by the drama of sex. They are impulsive, impetuous, and excellent at what sexologists term "love play." They want to be adored, revered. They want their partner in sex to gasp with excitement at almost every gesture. Loving is living, and they tend to fall in and out of love easily. HINT: You could become a lazy lover, Leo. You need more emotional involvement.

For Men Only: Leo women have a flair for the dramatic [like Mae West]. They abhor the humdrum, the ordinary, the routine or the sameness of anything. They like to be in the spotlight. They are not always exhibitionists, but they certainly do want you to be aware of them. Stand up when a Leo lady enters the room. Smile in a special way. Her nature is fiery, passionate. Her personal magnetism is strong. HINT: It's all right to be jealous—as long as you don't let her know it. Stay cool and calm.

For Women Only: Leo men are fiery and romantic, tend to be fixed and non-flexible. A Leo man is never satisfied merely to be great; he wants to be told so. He is attractive to women, seems to draw them like flies. He is fascinated by subtle women. A Leo man can be taken advantage of; he enjoys being the center of intrigue. He is a natural showman, a man of tremendous pride, likes to be praised and complimented. He wants you to be independent but to completely depend on him. He is a rather impossible person. [Famous Leos include Aldous Huxley, George Bernard Shaw, and Sydney Omarr.]

VIRGO: Love is a very serious matter to Virgos. They take nothing for granted, tend to worry about affairs of the heart, prefer marriage or a formal engagement. They would rather suffer in marriage than seek pleasures illicitly. They have a built-in sense of guilt about pleasures not condoned by legal action. They analyze, deduct, form conclusions, theorize. They are often so theoretical that they don't enjoy sex. HINT: Stop theorizing. Love openly, freely, without being too concerned about bank accounts, your standing in the community, or Dun & Bradstreet ratings.

For Men Only: Virgo women are discriminating, often regal, and sometimes tiresome in their pursuit of cleanliness. They are mercurial, earthy in nature, energetic, full of plans and ambition. The Virgo woman is ambitious not only for herself—but for you. She's a natural fighter and her goal is truth, so don't beat around the bush with her. HINT: Never underestimate a Virgo woman. She knows what it's all about.

For Women Only: The Virgo man is demanding; he asks that you prove yourself, that you be willing to sacrifice when necessary. He knows the meaning of work and the value of money. He is the kind of man a woman can depend upon for security. But he will not tolerate deception. He is not a pretentious man; often you will have to help him build up his confidence. HINT: But he is a good bet for a long, solid relationship.

LIBRA: If you were born under Libra, there is an abundance of romance in your life, but love is not always smooth. Love for a Libra usually means carrying a burden, taking on added responsibility, sometimes accepting a love partner whose character is below your standards, or whose social and educational background doesn't measure up to yours. But Libras are romantic, and most Libras feel it is better to have loved and lost than not to have loved at all. HINT: Don't be flattered into accepting an inferior product.

For Men Only: Libra women possess great charm and are generally intellectual, idealistic, sensitive, and have a great awareness of beauty. If you want to win this lady, avoid coarseness. Appeal to her sense of justice, of good and beauty. She needs love and affection. Her principles are paramount in her life; she is not likely to compromise. This woman balances one thing against the other; she appreciates money and luxury but compares these advantages to character and stability. HINT: Her moods can be all the way up or all the way down, and you may as well get used to that idea.

For Women Only: The Libra man is considered high-strung. In reality, however, it is not so much his nerves but his sense of awareness, his keen convictions, his drive for justice and independence. His natural bent is toward intellectual subjects and the arts. He is nobody's fool. He has a better sense of humor than you might think at first. HINT: He prefers a woman with an even temper.

SCORPIO: Those born under Scorpio (the scorpion) are very much sexually oriented, have strong creative drives but often lack confidence and so are constantly trying to prove themselves. This can lead to frenzied sexual activities. Scorpios are possessive—and proud of it; they are jealous—and pugnacious about it. They can love and hate and nurse grudges and use sex as a weapon. This is a great temptation with Scorpios. HINT: Relax and stop trying to prove yourself.

For Men Only: Scorpio women are emotional, affectionate, passionate, and have a tendency to marry younger men. They have an air of mystery about them and are often considered psychic. A man involved with a Scorpio woman is not always going to have an easy time of it—but it will be exciting and he will know he's alive. The Scorpio woman is forceful and dynamic, dominating, and even explosive. HINT: She likes secrets, so don't try to know all there is to know about her.

For Women Only: Don't expect your Scorpio man to say one thing and mean something else. He is forceful, direct, independent, aggressive, and he likes results. He is very physical, yet also emotional. He requires love in its poetic sense, yet he can be animal-like, even brutal. Nothing halfway here. He works hard, plays hard, and at times his appetite appears insatiable. HINT: Ladies, do not attempt to reform your Scorpio man!

SAGITTARIUS: Lucky Sagittarians! you have a sense of humor about sex, which is more than can be said for most people. You believe in the double standard, whether you openly admit it or not. You are basically conservative, but your qualities of selection leave more than a little to be desired. You choose, but not wisely. You can get what you want, but you don't always want what is good for you. You seek love, but you can get trouble instead. You are more affectionate than passionate, but you would not like this to be known. You are intense, but not necessarily sensuous. You are more intellectual than daring. HINT: Keep your sense of humor and don't let complications defeat you.

For Men Only: The Sagittarius lady is an idealist. Honesty and frankness are keys to her character. She is loyal, proud, refined, sensitive—often disturbed by minor matters. She is fiery in temperament; her outlook is universal, philosophical. She gives the impression of being shy. Yet she can be very exciting. This woman is difficult to resist. But you must state your business with her, your intentions. Don't attempt cover-ups or false promises. HINT: She is drawn to men who are kind to animals.

For Women Only: The Sagittarius man is open, trustworthy, dislikes petty persons. He thinks quickly and likes to learn—by reading, experimenting, traveling, writing, questioning, examining, probing. HINT: You can intrigue him by asking provocative questions. He admires individuality in a woman.

CAPRICORN: In the sex and love area, Capricorns are vulnerable and deadly serious. They want to call the shots, outline the programs, decide when to stop and go, control the when, where, and how of tender, intimate moments. They can be vindictive, and they don't easily forgive anyone who takes advantage of them. Love can turn into hate. The person who once was an object of affection can become one of scorn. Capricorns are not really the kind to play games in the emotional arena. HINT: You think too much!

For Men Only: The Capricorn woman may appear aloof, cold, disinterested—but the fire of passion runs through her. She is an earthy woman, with energy and strength. She is apt to be cautious. But she can accept challenges, is disciplined, and possesses great determination. She usually finishes what she starts. HINT: Let her express herself; she deserves to be heard.

For Women Only: The Capricorn man is earthy, possesses a keen sense of awareness, can be depended on to help the underdog. He busies himself in helping others instead of putting his shoulder to the wheel in connection with his own problems. Ambition is keynoted in Capricorn's chart. He may deny it over and over again, but this is an ambitious man. Tact is important in dealing with him. HINT: Let him talk about himself (which he likes to do), but if you're looking for quick rewards, forget him.

AQUARIUS: Those born under the sign of Aquarius are very much aware of touch, feeling, tenderness. The Aquarian is sensitive and needs to be regarded as an individual, not as a sexual object. A special problem with Aquarians in the sex area is a restlessness, a need to be understood. Yet, paradoxically, at times they seem intent on hurting people they love. They are generous and giving, but not as passionate as they might be. (You certainly wouldn't mistake them for Scorpios!) Basically they are rather innocent, and in their innocence are apt to insist on their own terms. HINT: Like most persons, Aquarius, you need love. Don't be so stubborn!

For Men Only: Man, this Aquarius lady can be as fixed and determined as anyone you've ever met! She is idealistic and airy in temperament, so you should take her bluster and pugnaciousness with a grain of salt. Remember, she lives in a dream world and she likes to have her own way. When she is right, let her. But she'll lead you in circles if she can get away with it. Don't let her. She has a finely honed intuition, can usually sense what the future holds, expects you to be dashing and daring. HINT: Never a dull moment with this one.

For Women Only: Sometimes, ladies, this man's mind is so much on the future that he tends to completely overlook the present. Make yourself a part of his plans, for he has a tendency to make dreams come true. But he needs someone to have faith in him. He can be exasperating. But he is willing to pioneer, to accept challenges, to lead a life of adventure and risk. HINT: Go along with him. Never a dull moment!

PISCES: It is no easy task analyzing a Pisces person in relation to sex and love. Their views are all grandiose. Sex is moonlight and violin music. The Pisces is ruled by emotions and can make as many or more mistakes than most of us. Pisces people have a tendency to become involved in clandestine affairs. It's all part of romance, intrigue. But they're happier married than single. HINT: Elizabeth Taylor is a Pisces—with her moon in Scorpio!

For Men Only: Your Pisces lady is apt to be possessive and has a tendency to take over. But she is lovely, poetic, emotional in temperament, giving and generous. You will want to shield her, protect her, but time and again she will prove that she is tough and able to take it. The next moment, she becomes the gentle, dependent, leaning Piscean. One of her great assets is a sense of humor. Another is her psychic power. HINT: Don't let all this deceive you. She has plenty of practical common sense.

For Women Only: The Pisces male is imaginative, highly creative, and a dreamer—but not a schemer. When he decides he loves you, it is with all his heart. He has flashes of insight that often prove not only correct but ultimately profitable. He is not the easiest man to be with, but may well be one of the kindest and most considerate. He is a sensitive soul, so go slow, be subtle, take it easy. HINT: If you can't stand dreamers, then find another man!

There. You see how simple it is to get the yin-yang of your love life in the fifth house in order–if you know how to read horoscopes.

Learning to interpret and compare horoscopes helps sharpen your creative and intuitive sense, Sydney says, as well as helping you to set your own love life straight and on its right course.

If, for example, you spot Mars on the ascendant of a chart, you will know that this means your man is direct, aggressive, and pugnacious. (And often has a scar on the face or forehead.)

BONUS HINT: November is the worst month for domestic problems.

There's that Scorpio again!

Chapter 21
HOW TO PICK A HORSE
(The Horseplayer's Horoscope)

"I'll bet everything he bets.
So I can't go wrong."
—JESS STEARN

Author Jess Stearn once said to Sydney, "If you astrologers are so smart in predicting the future, why don't you make a bundle on the horses?"

Sydney calmly replied, "Well, I have."

"That's fine," said Jess. "How about doing it with me, showing me a bit of action?"

"Okay. But I can't do it right now," Sydney said.

"Why not?" Jess asked.

"I have to wait until the moon is in Aquarius," Sydney explained.

"Hey, now, wait a second! How do you know that?" Jess was skeptical.

"How do you think I know it?" Sydney countered. "I've discovered it from going to the track. I always have better luck when the moon is in Aquarius."

So when the moon went into Aquarius, the two of them went to the races—Jess, a stubborn Taurus, with Leo, the show-off.

"It was really a day to remember," Jess recalled as we sat and sipped apple juice together at his Malibu Beach pad, with the waves pounding in.

He was telling me about his long friendship with Sydney and his rather awesome respect for him as an astrologer—despite his own Taurus-like and journalistic skepticism. The truth is, this bullheaded Taurus is very fond of the gentle-miened Leo the lion.

And the two of them, as Jess told it later, were like the Marx Brothers at the races.

"Sydney made all the arrangements, because he had been there quite frequently. We took a table, but he kept jumping up to go over and look at a horse or a jockey," Jess recollected. "He would come back and say, 'That horse's name is Royal Sputters—or something. Royal—that's Leo,' he would say. Then he would look for a jockey who was a Cancer, or whose moon was in Cancer, or something. I didn't understand it, but I figured whatever he was betting would win because the moon was in Aquarius, and though he's Leo and I'm Taurus, I'll bet everything he bets. So I can't go wrong. If he wins, I win.

"Well, he picked the first horse, and I didn't see how that horse could possibly finish the race, much less win. Right? So I just said, 'I can't bet that horse,' and he said, 'Do it your own way, Taurus.'

"That's what I did. I used the racing form and he used astrology. Every two hours the signs changed, but he knew how to keep track of them. The upshot was that he won five races in a row and I didn't have a winner all day."

After one of the races, Jess recalled, a very dignified little old lady, who had been watching them with interest, came over to their table and asked, "Are you psychiatrists?"

"No, only psychos," they told her jokingly. "Why?"

"Well, I knew you must be something," she said, "from the way you're concentrating, like you're trying to study the minds of the jockeys and the trainers and even the horses."

She was alluding mainly to Sydney, of course. When concentrating on the planetary influences, he has a tendency to be about as mirthful as a funeral director, even at the race track.

But he's pretty good at picking horses, and maybe you can improve your luck by following his system.

Following is a reprint of his system published in *Argosy* magazine of May 1974 but still applicable today with a few updated changes:

THE HORSEPLAYER'S HOROSCOPE

Anyone who tells you he goes to the race track because he likes the fresh air, the green grass, the blue sky, and the beauty of the horses in motion is a liar, or at least a purveyor of half-truths. He really goes to the track to win. When you've won, the air is perfume, the grass is the color of emeralds, the sky is cloudless, and every horse moves like a ballet dancer. When you've lost, it might as well be the middle of December in Caribou, Maine, and every horse has the grace of a mongrel dog. My purpose in writing this piece is to introduce you to a system of picking the horses that is so precise that you can win consistently and have more time to enjoy the air, the sky, the grass, and the horses.

A system? you say. Everyone has a system and not one of them works! This one does. It works because it is based on the most powerful influence on human luck and destiny: the stars.

By now you are laughing even harder. A betting system based on astrology? But think for a moment; all gambling involves risk and all risk involves luck. Luck is controlled by the stars. I have been using the "Money Horse" system for thirty years with great success. You too can make money and enjoy the track more. Here's how it works:

There is one "Money Horse" and one "Money Race" for each day of the month at any track in the world. The numbers for the horses and the races are predetermined by the positions of the stars and the planets in conjunction with the sun. Only a master astrologer and numerologist can calculate which numbers apply for each day. I have provided a list of Money Horses and Money Races for the month of May. That and a list of entries for any given day are all the information you will need.

When you get to the track, check the entries for the Money Race of the day. Let's say, for instance, that it's May 6. The Money Race for that day is the second race. Now look for the Money Horse, number 3. This number does *not* refer to post position, but, rather, to a numerological translation of the horse's name. Each letter of the name has a corresponding number from 1 to 9, as follows:

A	B	C	D	E	F	G	H	I
1	2	3	4	5	6	7	8	9
J	K	L	M	N	O	P	Q	R
1	2	3	4	5	6	7	8	9
S	T	U	V	W	X	Y	Z	
1	2	3	4	5	6	7	8	

Using this alphabet key, assign numbers to each of the letters in the name and add from left to right. Reduce all totals to a single digit. Thus, if the total is 24, add the 2 and the 4 for a final total of 6.

Let's say, for example, that we find a horse named Charley's Aunt entered in the second race on May 6. Using the alphabet key, we translate the name in this fashion:

C H A R L E Y' S A U N T
3+8+1+9+3+5+7+1 1+3+5+2

=48=4+8=12=1+2=3

So Charley's Aunt is the Money Horse for the second race, the Money Race on May 6. (See Money Chart)

Here's how the "Money Horse" system worked in February at Santa Anita. My calculations had already indicated that the Money Race for February 7, 1974, was the seventh. I had also determined that the money horse for that race was one whose name added up to number five. At the track, I found one horse in the seventh race who filled the bill:

S P I N L I G H T N I N G
1+7+9+5 3+9+7+8+2+5+9+5+7

=77=7+7=14=1+4=5

Without reference to past-performance tables, the condition of the track, the jockey, the odds, or any of the usual indicators, I calmly bet ten dollars across the board on Spin Lightning. He won and paid \$48.80, \$15.80, and \$6.20. My ticket was worth \$117.90. It was a lovely day at the track.

It is important to note that I bet Spin Lightning across the board —to win, place, and show. This "hedge" is vital to your success with the Money Horse system. I learned my lesson long ago, when, at the age of 15, I first devised the system. With my first, illegal ten dollar bet at a track, I managed to pick the Money Horse, but lost. I bet him to win and he came in third. He was in the money, but I wasn't. The system is designed to indicate the horse most likely to finish in the money, not necessarily the winner. There are too many other factors to contend with in successfully picking winners, so don't always bet to win.

As an adjunct to the Money Horse system, it is useful to familiarize yourself with the zodiacal signs of the jockeys. This provides insight in two areas: character traits that are most apt to bring home

MONEY CHART

DATE	MONEY HORSE	MONEY RACE
May 1	*No. 8*	*Ninth*
May 2	*No. 7*	*Third*
May 3	*No. 6*	*Fifth*
May 4	*No. 5*	*Seventh*
May 5	*No. 4*	*Ninth*
May 6	*No. 3*	*Second*
May 7	*No. 2*	*Fifth*
May 8	*No. 7*	*Third*
May 9	*No. 9*	*Fourth*
May 10	*No. 8*	*First*
May 11	*No. 7*	*Third*
May 12	*No. 6*	*Fifth*
May 13	*No. 5*	*Seventh*
May 14	*No. 4*	*Ninth*
May 15	*No. 3*	*Second*
May 16	*No. 8*	*Fifth*
May 17	*No. 3*	*Seventh*
May 18	*No. 2*	*Sixth*
May 19	*No. 8*	*Ninth*
May 20	*No. 7*	*Third*
May 21	*No. 6*	*Fifth*
May 22	*No. 5*	*Seventh*
May 23	*No. 4*	*Fourth*
May 24	*No. 5*	*Seventh*
May 25	*No. 2*	*Fifth*
May 26	*No. 3*	*Fifth*
May 27	*No. 2*	*Sixth*
May 28	*No. 8*	*Ninth*
May 29	*No. 7*	*Third*
May 30	*No. 6*	*Seventh*
May 31	*No. 5*	*Seventh*

a winner and the times when a jockey is most apt to have Lady Luck as a companion. It is my purpose here to provide you with a racing edge, to give you an idea, astrologically speaking, of when some jockeys can expect to get the "breaks."

This kind of information can be especially useful when the Money Horse system comes up with more than one possibility. For instance, if Charley's Aunt was not the only horse whose name added up to three in our hypothetical second race on May 6, it would be useful to know if the jockey for Charley's Aunt was a Capricorn. Capricorn's have their best chances of success in May. Capricorns are also at their best with older horses, at longer distances, on off tracks or slow tracks. So if Charley's Aunt is a bit long in the tooth and is entered in a mile-and-a-half race on a slow track, and a Capricorn is riding him, the odds of his finishing in the money are greatly enhanced.

You will find that this system is a lot easier to use than your own struggles with past-performance charts, breeding guides, and the like.

So familiarize yourself with jockeys' zodiacal signs. Our reference table will help you find the birthdays of many outstanding jockeys. This information, combined with the specifics in the Money Horse table, should give you many happy days with the fresh air, the green grass, the blue sky, and—more importantly—the horses at the track.

SOME PROMINENT JOCKEYS' BIRTHDAYS

Larry Adams	June 13, 1936	(*Gemini*)
Braulio Baeza	March 26, 1942	(*Aries*)
Chuck Baltazar	May 22, 1947	(*Gemini*)
Eddie Belmonte	February 5, 1943	(*Aquarius*)
Walter Blum	September 28, 1934	(*Libra*)
Angel Cordero	May 8, 1942	(*Taurus*)
Earlie Fires	March 19, 1947	(*Pisces*)
Bill Hartack	December 9, 1932	(*Sagittarius*)
Eddie Maple	November 8, 1948	(*Scorpio*)
Laffit Pincay, Jr.	December 29, 1946	(*Capricorn*)
John L. Rotz	December 16, 1934	(*Sagittarius*)

Willie Shoemaker	August 19, 1931	(*Leo*)
Ron Turcotte	July 22, 1951	(*Cancer*)
Bob Ussery	September 3, 1935	(*Virgo*)
Miguel Valenzuela	December 25, 1934	(*Capricorn*)
Jacinto Vasquez	January 4, 1944	(*Capricorn*)
Jorge Velasquez	December 28, 1946	(*Capricorn*)
Manuel Ycaza	February 1, 1938	(*Aquarius*)

A HINT: During the month of May, Willie Shoemaker, a Leo, is most likely to be a winner on the eighth and ninth. Braulio Baeza, an Aries, should do exceptionally well this month on the twenty-sixth and twenty-seventh.

THE JOCKEYS' HOROSCOPE

ARIES (*Mar. 21–Apr. 19*): Aggressive and headstrong. Chances are best on a horse who starts fast and sets the pace. Most favorable month for winning is August.

TAURUS (*Apr. 21–May 20*): Determined. A smooth rider who comes from behind and rides well in mud and on grass. Has sixth sense about pacing. Best month is September.

GEMINI (*May 21–June 20*): Active. Finds openings on crowded tracks. Good bet for upsets, long shots and daily doubles. Most favorable month is likely to be October.

CANCER (*June 21–July 22*): Dependable. Ideal for fillies and mares as well as older horses. Best month for being in the money is November.

LEO (*July 23–Aug. 22*): Flamboyant. At his best in stakes races, but may let down in races he takes for granted. The ideal rider for the champion horse. Best month is December.

VIRGO (*Aug. 23–Sept. 22*): Analytical. Very aware of time; makes moves with clockwork precision, but can become too mechanical. Most favorable month is likely to be October.

LIBRA (*Sept. 23–Oct. 22*): Gives you an even ride with no surprises. Has good insight into a horse's capabilities and potential. Fine for favorites. Best month: February.

SCORPIO (*Oct. 23–Nov. 21*): Intense. Does not do well with rank horses, but give him a sound horse and he makes you feel your money is in the bank. Best winning cycle is March.

SAGITTARIUS (*Nov. 22–Dec. 21*): Understands and talks to horses. May ride for upsets; can talk a nervous animal into a great stretch run. Best month is April.

CAPRICORN (*Dec. 22–Jan. 19*): Reliable. Best with older horses in longer races and is a good off-track rider. Liable to have best winning cycle in May.

AQUARIUS (*Jan. 21–Feb. 18*): Exciting rider with unorthodox style. Loves the dramatic finish, the long-shot win. Shows the horse who is boss. Best month for this rider is June.

PISCES (*Feb. 19–Mar. 20*): Apt to know more about the horse than its trainer. Good bet for long shots, in the mud, and on off tracks. Look for him to do well in July.

Harry Egner, publisher of *Argosy* magazine, was so impressed with Sydney's system of beating the horses that he issued a "Certified Statement" to that effect under the heading "ARGO-NOTES FROM THE PUBLISHER." It was printed in the same issue (May 1974) in which "*The Horseplayer's Horoscope*" appeared. It is as follows:

CERTIFIED STATEMENT

This is to certify that I, Harry Egner, publisher of *Argosy* magazine, have witnessed the use of Omarr's star system of beating the horses for one week, and attest to the fact that those editors so following it won money. Furthermore, I certify that they made selections *every day* from different tracks throughout the country and bet accordingly.

Signed,

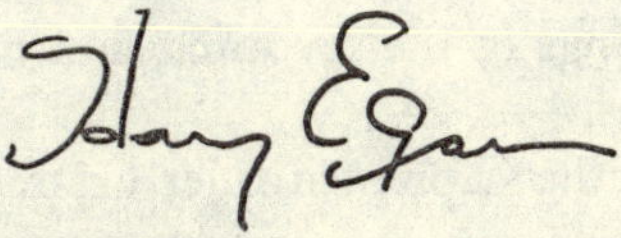

Harry Egner
Publisher

In addition to his *Argosy* article, Sydney has these helpful hints on

HORSES AND JOCKEYS

When the moon is in Aries, the Aries jockey will be the rider who finds special openings. His timing and judgment will be good. The Pisces jockey will bring in the favorites, and the Sagittarius jockey will bring in the upset winners. All this is when the moon is in Aries.

When the moon is in Taurus, the Taurus jockey is the one who finds the openings, brings his horse through, and gives a steady ride. The Aries jockey brings in the favorites, and the Capricorn jockey brings in the upset winners.

When the moon is in Gemini, the Gemini rider finds the openings and gets what we call racing luck. The Taurus jockey brings in the favorites. The Aquarius jockey brings in the upsets.

When the moon is in Cancer, the Cancer jockey has racing luck. The Gemini jockey brings in the favorites. The Pisces jockey brings in the upset winners.

When the moon is in Leo, the Leo rider has racing luck, the Cancer jockey brings in the favorites, and the Aries jockey brings in the upset winners.

When the moon is in Virgo, the Virgo rider has racing luck, the Leo rider brings in the favorites, and the Taurus rider brings in the upset winners.

When the moon is in Libra, the Libra rider has racing luck, the Virgo rider brings in the favorites, and the Gemini brings in the upset winners.

When the moon is in Scorpio, the Scorpio rider has racing luck, the Libra jockey brings in the favorites, and the Cancer brings in the upset winners.

When the moon is in Sagittarius, the Sagittarius rider has the racing luck, the Scorpio jockey brings in the favorites, and the Leo rider pulls in the upset favorites.

When the moon is in Capricorn, the Capricorn rider has racing luck, the Sagittarius rider brings in the favorites, and the Virgo brings in the upset winners.

When the moon is in Aquarius, the Aquarius rider has racing luck, the Capricorn rider brings in the favorites, and the Libra rider brings in the upset winners.

When the moon is in Pisces, the Pisces rider has the good timing and racing luck. The Aquarius rider comes home with the favorites. The Scorpio rider comes in with the upset winners. . . .

If you study the horoscope carefully, you can see the pattern. If Pisces is the rider with racing luck, the rider who brings in the favorites is only one sign behind (Aquarius) and the upset winner three signs behind (Scorpio).

Doesn't a horse's horoscope have anything to do with it?" I asked.

"No. The last time a horse gave me his birth date it turned out he was lying about his age," said Sydney. "So it's best to stick to a system that's simple."

It's simple when you know how. Now all you have to do is pick the winners.

Now that you have had a trial run in learning to pick the horses by Sydney's star system, based on charts for a past racing season, are you ready for a little surprise?

Our editors have given us leeway on our deadline for this portion of our book so that Sydney could consult the stars and bring you a last-minute updated revision of his astrological calculations for the spring of 1977, when the Triple Crown races begin with the Kentucky Derby in the first week of May and then continue through the Preakness and the Belmont Stakes.

For all those horse players who are usually desperate for new "systems," it should be emphasized that Sydney's star system remains basically the same. So, best you review and digest what he has told you thus far, so you will understand it.

In addition, as a special book bonus, we are providing here the Money Horses and Money Races and the numbers that apply for each day of the May–June racing season of 1977. Only a master astrologer and numerologist can make these calculations. Sydney has worked them out especially for you. Happy winnings!

SPECIAL BULLETIN
SYDNEY OMARR'S MONEY HORSES
FOR MAY–JUNE RACING SEASON–1977

DATE	MONEY HORSE	MONEY RACE
May 1	*No. 5*	*Seventh*
May 2	*No. 4*	*Ninth*
May 3	*No. 3*	*Second*
May 4	*No. 2*	*Fourth*
May 5	*No. 1*	*Sixth*
May 6	*No. 9*	*Eighth*
May 7	*No. 2*	*Eighth*
May 8	*No. 7*	*Third*
May 9	*No. 6*	*Fifth*
May 10	*No. 5*	*Seventh*
May 11	*No. 4*	*Fifth*
May 12	*No. 3*	*Ninth*
May 13	*No. 2*	*Fourth*
May 14	*No. 1*	*Sixth*
May 15	*No. 6*	*Fourth*
May 16	*No. 3*	*Seventh*
May 17	*No. 7*	*Third*
May 18	*No. 5*	*Fourth*
May 19	*No. 5*	*Second*
May 20	*No. 4*	*Fourth*
May 21	*No. 3*	*Sixth*
May 22	*No. 2*	*Eighth*
May 23	*No. 1*	*First*
May 24	*No. 2*	*First*
May 25	*No. 1*	*Seventh*
May 26	*No. 7*	*Third*
May 27	*No. 6*	*Fifth*

DATE	MONEY HORSE	MONEY RACE
May 28	*No. 5*	*Seventh*
May 29	*No. 4*	*First*
May 30	*No. 3*	*Second*
May 31	*No. 2*	*Fifth*
June 1	*No. 4*	*First*
June 2	*No. 3*	*Second*
June 3	*No. 2*	*Fourth*
June 4	*No. 1*	*Third*
June 5	*No. 9*	*Eighth*
June 6	*No. 8*	*Ninth*
June 7	*No. 7*	*Third*
June 8	*No. 6*	*Fourth*
June 9	*No. 5*	*Seventh*
June 10	*No. 4*	*First*

Each day, there is one Money Horse. For June 3, for example, the horse whose NAME totals 2 in the FOURTH race is our Money Horse selection for that day.

To discover the name of the Money Horse, use the Alphabet Key. Under each letter in the horse's name, place the number given under the corresponding letter in the alphabet key.

Example:

H I L L R I S E
8 9 3 3 9 9 1 5

Now, add from left to right. All totals are reduced to a single digit between 1 and 9. Thus, if a total is 24, you would add the 2 and 4 for a final total of 6.

Now, take the example of HILL RISE:

H I L L R I S E
8 9 3 3 9 9 1 5=47=4+7=11=1+1=2

You simply add from left to right. You would do this for each horse in the Money Race until you discover which horse was *IN THE MONEY* for that day. If more than one horse in the race totals the money number, take your choice. If no horse in the Money Race totals the money number, skip your selection for that day.

Remember: *Selections apply to all tracks.*

If You Want to Fight, You'd Better Be a Capricorn

It will be recalled that Sydney has been picking winners in the boxing ring since his early youth. Boxing is still his favorite sport. He hasn't worked out any special system for picking fighters to put your money on as he has with horses.

Personally, he isn't interested in betting on any sport. To him the challenge lies solely in picking winners through his expertise in astrology and numerology.

"If you enjoy a sport, you shouldn't bet on it," he says scowling. "I only do it with the horses sometimes to show people like that stubborn Taurus Jess Stearn I know how.

"Now, with boxing, that's such a great sport that I would never tell anyone how to bet on it. But," he added slyly, "I can tell you how to spot an up-and-coming contender or a future champion. It is very important that he has the qualities of Saturn, that his zodiacal sign is Capricorn."

As Sydney has stated earlier, more heavyweight champions have been born under Capricorn than any other of the zodiacal signs.[1]

He points out that the only two ever to regain their championship titles, Muhammad Ali and Floyd Patterson, were both born under Capricorn, as were the only two former champions ever matched to fight each other, George Foreman and Joe Frazier.

Foreman, an astrology buff himself, won the heavyweight boxing championship at the Olympics held in Mexico City. Sydney had predicted in his astrology column that he was going to be a winner because he was a Capricorn. Later, Foreman told Sydney that he had read the column, paying special attention to his sign, and that this had given him a lot of the confidence he needed for winning.

One of Sydney's biggest thrills in his lifetime as a boxing enthusiast occurred when Muhammad Ali telephoned him from New York during his three-year period of excommunication from the sports world. He had refused to be drafted because of his religious beliefs.

[1] Jess Willard, December 29, 1881; Floyd Patterson, January 4, 1935; Muhammad Ali (Cassius Clay), January 17, 1942; Joe Frazier, January 17, 1944; George Foreman, January 10, 1948.

He was stripped of his championship title and banned from the ring. He called Sydney to ask about his prospects for the future. Sydney told him that he was going to be vindicated, that he would win his case in the courts and his title would be restored. (The prediction proved to be accurate.)

Sydney recalls their conversation with amusement.

"At first he seemed elated by what I told him. I thought I had raised his spirits somewhat. He said, 'Hey, man, that's fine, that's great.'"

But then, apparently to keep Sydney in his place or to remind him of who was the greatest, he said, "Well, look, man, I don't know about all this astrology stuff. Can it predict rounds like I can?

"I know who I am and what I am. I'm a Capricorn. I know when I was born and where I was born–in Louisville. I even remember the number on the hospital door and I remember as I was being born I came out yelling, 'I am the greatest, I am the greatest.'"

Sydney let him rant and rave to his heart's content. "After all, it was his nickel," he shrugs philosophically. But he was pleased when Muhammad Ali won his title back, as the stars had indicated he would.

On a more recent occasion, Muhammad disregarded Sydney's gentle warning against engaging in a wrestling match in Tokyo—and was kicked so badly that he wound up in a hospital with blood clots in his legs.

Sports fans will remember the big event of June 1976, the wrestling match in Japan during which I-am-the-greatest Ali got clobbered.

Sydney had warned in his columns that this Capricorn was "planting the seeds of self destruction."

"He is sensitive, spiritual, sincere about his religion," he said, "but he has a distinct martyr complex. It is this which might lead to his undoing. With his sun in Capricorn and Leo rising, he has a subconscious desire to suffer. He is stringing a rope across his path and is probably going to trip on it."

Everyone knows what happened in Tokyo. As this is written, only a few weeks after the fiasco, Ali-the-greatest is still incarcerated with his blood clots in a hospital in Santa Monica, within blocks of the big luxury apartment building where Sydney lives with a commanding view of the blue Pacific.

As a dedicated devotee of boxing, Sydney still bristles at Ali's brashness in booking himself for a wrestling match.

"It is a travesty on boxing for any boxer, expecially a heavyweight champion and especially a Capricorn, to go into the ring with a wrestler. Wrestlers are allowed to do all sorts of things. Those kicks in the legs were Ali's undoing, because he's a Capricorn with Saturn qualities and Saturn holds sway over our bone structure, especially the bones in our knees and legs."

Saturn, you will remember, is one of the so-called "malefics," or "bad guys," in the zodiac, the same satanic planet that rules former President Nixon's sign, Capricorn (Chapters 3 and 4). Sydney knowledges the fact that it is frequently a troublemaking planet, but he doesn't denigrate it to the extent that most astrology writers do.

"Saturn is not all evil," he is quick to remind you. "It exerts an influence of will power, discipline, tenacity, perseverance, pugnaciousness, resilience, and staying power that is very important for a fighter to have.

"A fighter must give up the luxury of Venus for the bleakness of Saturn. He must give up the good life for the hard road of work and training. He must be able to withstand adversity and ride with the tide. He must understand the meaning of time, or timing—the importance of a two- or three-minute rest period between bouts, or, on a broader scale, getting into the fighting ring of life when the timing is right.

"If a fighter isn't determined to train, then he cannot hope to become a champion.

"The same lesson applies in all our lives, whether we are in sports, business, the arts and sciences, or whatever we choose to do. Saturn has to be there somewhere in your chart. There is no success without Saturn. Wherever Saturn is on your chart, that is your testing ground. You might have popularity power with Venus, but it's Saturn that gives you lasting power."

And this, in the zodiacal nutshell, is why Sydney says if you want to bet on a champion fighter, pick a Capricorn.

The reason it applies especially to boxing, he says, is that boxing is not like other sports, such as football or baseball, in which there are so many people on a team.

"Boxing is a microcosm of the kind of lives we lead, the confrontation, the fight between two people. Eventually it happens to all of us, and if we don't have Saturn on our side, then we may as well give up."

Chapter 22

HOW TO PICK A PET

> *"A Pisces dog or cat*
> *makes a very fine house pet."*
>
> —SYDNEY OMARR

Actress Kim Novak is an animal lover. She is also a great believer in astrology. She is Aquarius with Pluto in the sixth house, which indicates danger from large animals. This is unfortunate, since she has a special passion for horses.

Once, she was hauling a new horse from Beverly Hills to her oceanside estate at Big Sur, above Carmel, California, when the horse jumped from the trailer, went through the roof of her car, and landed right beside her on the seat. Fortunately she was unhurt, but at various times since then she has consulted Sydney before buying a horse to see how the horse's horoscope related to her own.

Yes, animals have horoscopes, too, and that is why some people get along better with one pet than with another. Your sign and that of your pet should be harmonious. Or at least you should be aware of what to expect from animals born under the different signs.

Many astrologically oriented persons pick their pets by astrology.

Kim Novak, however, has a special problem.

"She has to be careful at all times, because she has that Pluto in the sixth house. It's a great quandary for her, because she loves animals so much," Sydney says.

"But Kim's awareness of this possible danger from large animals is a big advantage. Knowing of the danger, she can be more cautious or take special precautions in handling them. She is at least aware that she should never be careless around them, especially her horses."

The sixth house relates to—among other things—"small animals" or pets. Actually, large animals usually fall in the ninth house, but this might include anything from cows and buffalo to alligators and orangutans—the sort of animals that are not usually regarded as house pets.

Horses aren't exactly house pets either, but they frequently *are* pets and so are often included in the sixth house, which has an emphasis on pets.

"If you have a malefic [evil planet] in that house, whether it be Mars or Pluto or Saturn, then you would not be deliriously happy with pets. They might become a great responsibility," Sydney says. "It's fine for someone like Kim Novak, who loves animals and is aware of the potential dangers as indicated in her horoscope. But, in general, I would advise anyone not to get a pet if you have a malefic in the sixth house."

Personally, I was rather reluctant to accept the idea of pets having horoscopes. So I decided to spring a surprise test on Sydney.

I presented him with the birth dates and places of three dogs: Lady Day, a great Dane who belongs to my assistant, Vera; Louie, a droopy-eyed spaniel and celebrated show-business partner of stage and television performer Bob Williams (you've seen Bob and Louie!); and Gogi, my own French poodle, who died some years ago.

Sydney knew nothing about any of these dogs.

Lady Day is a Capricorn, born January 8, 1971, near Dallas, Texas.

Sydney's reading on her: "If this dog were a human, you would never have to take up a benefit for her. She would always be in a position of handling responsibility. She would make herself invaluable to those who support her. I assume this is a female dog, because her name is Lady. Without doing an actual horoscope, I can tell certain things from her birth date and from numerology.

"Numerically, her number is nine. She was born under Capricorn, which is Saturn, but born on the eighth, which is also Saturn. This dog appears to have the weight of the world on its shoulders. It cares about the family and thinks it has certain duties to perform. And she does them. This is a very serious, very responsible dog. It would be a wonderful seeing-eye dog.

"The only problem with this dog is she has a tendency to be arthritic. She might have bone or calcium problems—but a vet would have to interpret that."

He had hit it right on the nose, describing Lady Day perfectly. Vera had bought the dog for the specific reason of taking care of her and guarding her house. She is indeed a very responsible dog, and so serious that she even looks as though she has the weight of the world on her shoulders.

"One more thing," Sydney added. "Besides the problem of calcium and bones, she has another problem. Vera should be very careful with her, because she tends to gulp. She has Gemini on the cusp of her sixth house. I don't know how you tell whether a dog eats too quickly, but Gemini on the sixth house has to do with the lungs and just going too fast, perhaps choking. It would be nice if there was a way of regulating her meals so she doesn't gulp."

I don't know anything about great Danes and I had never seen Lady Day eat. But when I checked with Vera, she confirmed that she feeds her bone meal (which is like calcium) every day to offset problems and that Lady Day gulps to the extent of putting away approximately four and one half pounds of dinner in less than one minute. How much closer can you get?

Sydney's reading on Louie, born October 25, 1967, in Van Nuys, California, and his master, Bob Williams, was equally intriguing. Louie is a Scorpio. Bob, who was born on December 22 at 1:00 A.M., is right on the cusp of Sagittarius, going into Capricorn.

"In this case, I think it's very important that Bob Williams is a Sagittarius," said Sydney, "because Sagittarians are more compatible with animals, and Louie, being a Scorpio, needs someone with special understanding.

"The numerological interpretation in this case also is very important, because Bob Williams was born on the twenty-second, and we have found that usually those persons born on the twenty-second of any month were either psychologically or literally separated from one or both parents at a relatively early age, and on their own. This person [Bob Williams] was probably a little revolutionary, you might say. He broke away and did something that would be considered very unusual. [That he did!]

"His birth path is number eight, and that is associated with money, Saturn, responsibility. Louie, the dog, has a number-five birth path, but they have a great deal in common. They have an innate understanding of one another. Neither one fits into a pigeonhole. The dog, being born on the twenty-fifth, also is Neptunian. That has to do with television, motion pictures. He is the kind of dog who really takes lessons to heart. He's supersensitive.

"Yes, this dog would have a special affinity for Bob Williams. I would say they almost read each other's mind. I have a feeling that this dog was on his own very early in life, too. Bob Williams and Louie have shared many life experiences. They have a special relationship, which is not true of most people and their dogs. This dog is taught mainly through affection, not discipline. They seem to have a perfect understanding."

Sydney was uncannily accurate in his description of Bob and Louie, even to the details of both being on their own at an early age.

Bob and Louie do a stage act together, in night clubs and on television, which many consider one of the finest and funniest in show business. Louie listens attentively to his master's gentle commands and then, being a wily Scorpio, proceeds to do just the opposite. They have a quite remarkable rapport. If Bob and Louie understand each other, they are probably the only ones who do. I have asked Bob numerous times how he trained Louie. He has always said that he didn't train Louie—that Louie just *knows* what to do.

Sydney, incidentally, doesn't know Bob and Louie, has never seen them perform. What he knows about them he obtained from the stars and numerology.

Neither did he know my poodle, Gogi, an Aquarius, born on February 10, 1962. But, again, he was amazingly accurate and specific.

"This dog, I would say, had a great deal of innate pride and bearing. He was very aristocratic. He had tremendous independence of thought and action, and also he was extremely intuitive. And certainly he was harmonious for you, because he was Aquarius and you are Sagittarius. You were very close and compatible. He went everywhere with you, and you carried on talks with that dog almost as though he were a human being. He was terribly intuitive. He knew what you were saying and he could almost talk back, like the two of you were carrying on a conversation. You could look at that dog and he seemed to be telling you something, sending you messages, and so forth.

"I think you always felt that you were learning lessons from him, that he was teaching you. That's because the dog had an eleven birth path. Remember, in numerology eleven is one of the two master numbers, and for a human being that signifies a teacher. But in this case the dog was teaching you.

"Also, he was born on the tenth, and that means independence and a tremendous amount of pride. He was a showman about it. He knew he would get his way around you by utilizing his intelligence and intuition. In this respect he was almost human. You've heard people say that some dogs are smarter than people. Well, in this case I think sometimes you were the learner and your dog was the teacher."

Almost everyone who knew Gogi invariably remarked that he was "aristocratic," very "intuitive," and "almost human"—three of the descriptive terms Sydney used.

As for the teacher-learner situation, it was Gogi who taught me to fetch the ball, to trot behind him on the other end of the leash, and we could never carry on a conversation around him if we didn't want him to understand. For a while we tried spelling out certain words until we realized he apparently knew how to spell, too. At least he knew what the words were.

With only birth dates and numbers to go on, Sydney had given an absolutely perfect description of all three dogs. When I told him this he quipped, "Maybe, instead of seeing clients, I should see dogs."

In a more serious vein, he admits that he is not especially an animal lover, has never had much to do with animals, and hasn't had too many people consult him about animal problems. But astrology can be helpful to those millions of pet owners—or potential pet owners—who might like some general guidelines in choosing a pet for themselves or their children.

"The same astrological aspects that apply to humans would also apply to animals. For example," Sydney explains, "I would say, generally speaking, that a person with a malefic in the sixth house [like Kim Novak] would have to take special precautions in connection with pets, while a person with Jupiter, Venus, or the sun in the sixth would be more likely to derive pleasure from pets. I suppose this is one of the reasons astrology has lasted: it shows the interrelation of everything, the planetary influences on all twelve of the zodiacal houses, which cover all departments of life, from work and play, sex and love, romance, marriage, money and health—and even pets."

Following is Sydney's brief summary of helpful hints for picking your pet by astrology. (In general it would apply to either dogs or cats.) It is based on the twelve sun signs:

ARIES: The Aries dog would be the most independent, headstrong, Martian, and aggressive. The Aries animal has a tendency to get scratched and cut, have a scar on the head. An Aries dog would snap, the cat scratch. They are susceptible to abrasions. (Ruled by the planet Mars.)

TAURUS: The Taurus dog would be the most placid, but always collecting. Might come home with an old shoe or grasshoppers, or whatever.

GEMINI: The Gemini dog or cat would be the most restless and active.

CANCER: The Cancer dog or cat would be the most domesticated of the animals. Would love the home and eat a great deal.

LEO: The Leo dog would be a showman, of course. (Sydney once did a TV show with a dog from "The Brady Bunch." He was a typical Leo dog, tried to steal the show from typical Leo Omarr.)

VIRGO: The Virgo dog or cat would be the most finicky and the neatest. If your cat was born under Virgo, you would almost never have to worry about the cat litter. On the negative side, Virgos can be so finicky they probably wouldn't use the feeding dish twice. You would have to wash it out with each feeding or they would turn up their nose. Virgos are very sensitive about what they put in their mouths. They have finicky digestive systems.

LIBRA: A Libra dog or cat would be the most graceful, and would love flowers and music. It would have an innate sense of beauty.

SCORPIO: A Scorpio animal would be the most difficult one to have around children. A Scorpio dog, or even the cat, might be too intense and hard to handle. Scorpio is associated with Pluto, which indicates a tendency to be revolutionary and rebellious. You wouldn't want this kind of animal around children. Eventually they might make fine pets if you learn how to handle them, but they would also be very sexual, always trying to mate with other animals —more so than the average—and they might not be the easiest to cope with as pets. If you're specifically picking a pet for your children, you wouldn't want a Scorpio.

SAGITTARIUS: The Sagittarius animal also might be a little rough for children, unless you have a large yard. This animal loves the outdoors and requires the outdoors for proper exercise, which is more important to him than to animals born under other signs. So it is best not to pick a Sagittarian for a pet unless you have lots of room.

CAPRICORN: As previously mentioned with Vera's Lady Day, the Capricorn dog is very serious, sometimes to the point of appearing morose, and always seems to have a great sense of responsibility (the Saturn influence). They should make fine pets as well as guard dogs and seeing-eye dogs.

AQUARIUS: An Aquarius pet would be the most unorthodox, because Aquarius is Uranus, which signifies the unorthodox, the adventurous spirit. With an Aquarius pet (human or animal) life is never dull. An Aquarius kitten, by the way, should be the most fun to have because of its monkeylike antics.

PISCES: A Pisces dog or cat makes a very fine house pet, even for a handicapped or confined person. Pisces are generally sensitive, sympathetic animals whose weak points are their feet. They don't necessarily like to be on their feet that much, and so they don't mind being confined in an apartment or small area, and they don't require a lot of exercise, as the Sagittarius animal does. Another thing: the Pisces is extremely sensitive to strangers; almost psychic, in fact. He can sense when a stranger doesn't like his master or their household, and instead of trying to make friends immediately, as the Sagittarius or Gemini dog would, he will probably just crawl under the bed or a table and stay there until the unwelcome guest goes away.

Happy pet hunting!

Chapter 23

HOW TO COOK WITH ASTROLOGY

"If you were born under Capricorn, you have food tastes that might be considered somewhat peculiar: vinegar, sour pickles, artichokes, rutabagas, cabbage."

—SYDNEY OMARR

As an extra fillip, Sydney can even help you improve your cooking with astrological guidelines. His book *Cooking with Astrology* (with Mike Roy) contains helpful hints on everything from the soup kitchen to elaborate dinner parties, all planned around the zodiacal signs.

And there are people crazy enough to take this seriously. I have been to some of their parties.

Personally, I prefer to stay as far away from the kitchen as possible, since only the malefic planets seem to rule over that basic (and lethal) kitchen weapon, the can opener.

But if you'd like to try your culinary skills in accordance with your sun signs, here are Sydney's suggestions (not mine):

ARIES: If you're an Aries, you should be adventurous, daring, and dominant as a chef in the kitchen. You're best at foods with tantalizing flavors. Spices, paprika, tomatoes, and beets, the red and tang of chili sauce—this is your dish. The Aries cook is a great chef, doesn't like lingering in the kitchen, is fast, direct, and versatile, and likes food with eye appeal—reddish in color.

TAURUS: Could be called a meat-and-potatoes type. Loves heavy creams, hearty salads, cauiflower, has a tendency to concentrate on quantity. HINT: You need more variety. Avoid the temptation to overeat.

GEMINI: In the kitchen Gemini is active, quick, experimental, burns up a great deal of energy, serves so many snacks that by the time the entree is served, appetites have waned. Indecisive in planning meals, because they want to try a bit of everything; fond of garnishes, decorations, variety in meals. Coleslaw is a specific Gemini dish. Also beer and gingerbread (not necessarily together).

CANCER: Many great chefs were born under Cancer. Of all signs, this is the one most closely related to food and the pleasure of dining. The Cancerian is nearly always a good cook, a gourmet, an artist in the kitchen. Specialties are soups, prime rib roasts, jams and jellies, foreign dishes. Food is a living adventure if you're a Cancer.

LEO: The flamboyant type in the kitchen. Leo prefers flaming dishes, cooks not only with fire but with showmanship. Makes fine use of herbs and spices; desserts are on the showy side. Every meal is a banquet—that's Leo's style. Leos have a special touch: the egg becomes an omelette, a slice of bacon is transformed into an appetizing garnish; shrimp, crab, and oysters are magically turned into Neptune's delight; steak and potatoes become a piquant vision of color. Even bread and cheese and a bottle of beer can be as heady as caviar and champagne with a Leo—who is also expert when it comes to barbecues. With Leos, food and sex are closely associated, and all those good things in life. (Tsk, tsk, Sydney!)

VIRGO: You may not be the greatest cook in the world, Virgo, but you are an expert at camouflaging. Even if some of your dishes lack the showmanship of Leo, they are substantial, pretty to look at, and tasty. You are not exactly wild about being confined to the kitchen. Cooking, for you, is associated with health, well-being. But your meals are versatile. Your preparation of salads can be the talk of the town. Vegetables are never more attractive than when you prepare them. You are not afraid to experiment. And you enjoy baking your own bread. You are a discriminating shopper.

LIBRA: Food for you, Libra, is a work of art. Your tastes are refined. You care very much about appearance. Your touch is delicate. You prefer subtle flavors and your meat sliced thin. Food, for you, is variety. Snails suit you fine; butter sauces appeal. You seek balance: some of this, a little of that; everything piquant, stimulating to the palate. That's Libra—tart, delectable, fine. You delight in delicacies. *Haute cuisine.*

SCORPIO: Your food tastes run along unorthodox lines ranging from sauerkraut to oysters. Limburger cheese could also be a favorite. Your sensuous nature is aroused by the smell of food cooking—seafood and chicken, as in paella; steak and cheese well aged; steamed clams, thick soups, and dark bread; salads heavily laced with garlic. The Scorpio likes foods associated with aphrodisiac powers; also food that makes you come alive, "wake up," and brings a sparkle to the eye and a slight burn to the tongue.

SAGITTARIUS: A Sagittarian can be daring in the kitchen [not me!]; an original touch is essential. Snails are surely a part of the Sagittarius repertoire; so are desserts with exotic names. Sagittarians would be the first to try grasshoppers. [Not me, Sydney] . . . You find pleasure in barbecuing and are as much at home with a picnic basket as at an elaborate banquet. You are fond of spreads—cheese, butter, sauces, sausage, sweet and sour cream. You make an excellent meat loaf. You have a penchant for foreign dishes.

CAPRICORN: If you were born under Capricorn, you have food tastes that might be considered somewhat peculiar: vinegar, sour pickles, artichokes, rutabagas, cabbage. And food that comes from the earth: mushrooms, truffles. Capricorns also like string beans and tongue with mustard or horseradish. Of all the signs, Capricorn is the one most likely to accent cold rather than hot soup, and is partial to milk, puddings, soups, and foods that contain spinach and eggs.

AQUARIUS: Light and airy—that's the way Aquarians like their food. Angel-food cake is a favorite dessert. Heavy foods are depressing. They prefer vegetables to meat—especially cucumber, yogurt, eggplant, potato salad, and avocado. They could become experts at whipping up a tangy guacamole. They have a fondness for fruits and cold cuts, lots of lemon and lemon peel, cheese, oranges, and tomatoes. The dishes that an Aquarian serves would probably be easy to prepare—but you could be hungry less than an hour after you've dined.

PISCES: It is not surprising that tastes in food reflect the Pisces character: subtle, delicate, exotic, unique, selective. Seafood would be a favorite; also soups, especially of the fish variety. The Pisces is fond of celery. In the meat department the choice is likely to be veal or veal kidneys, although lamb kidneys might also be high on the list. Food cooked and wrapped in paper fulfills the poetic requirements of the Pisces. Fish and chicken can be done this way. The Pisces also enjoys cooking with steam, and is fond of olives. Mixed in salads or combined with other foods, olives are a special treat for Pisceans.

And while on the subject of eating habits, Sydney has learned from restaurant owners that the patrons who most consistently demand "doggie bags" are those born under the earth signs: Taurus, Virgo, and Capricorn. The customers who seem to be the hungriest are those born under water signs: Cancer, Scorpio, and Pisces. The most "delicate" eaters are those born under the air signs: Gemini, Libra, and Aquarius.

Those who eat first and fast and ask questions later are the fire signs: Aries, Leo, and Sagittarius.

And how are you doing with your diet?

In summary, if you want to plan an astrological dinner for twelve around all the zodiacal signs, here is Sydney's synopsis:

> Taurus eats and Cancer cooks; Pisces prepares—and the candlelight and glamour belong to a combination of Leo and Pisces. The surprise invitations are the forte of Aquarius. Gemini plans and prepares the hors d'oeuvres. Dining is an art as well as a pleasure; Virgo knows it and keeps bothersome details within bounds. Capricorn enjoys but wonders about costs. Aries takes over direction, while Libra instigates sparkling conversation. Scorpio tells stories about the wine and its age and origin. Sagittarius expounds on eating habits of the world. In this manner, dinners for twelve could become an astrological adventure!

Being a Leo, Sydney prefers the dramatic and romantic approach to gourmet cooking and dining, as you can see from the above.

But for diet and nutrition nuts there are also very specific, cut-and-dried guidelines to the body's food needs for each zodiacal sign.

ARIES: Needs foods containing potassium phosphate, such as beets, celery, lettuce, cauliflower, watercress, spinach, onions, mustard, radishes, carrots, cucumbers, dates, apples, walnuts, and lemons.

TAURUS: Needs foods containing sulphate of soda, which is found in spinach, beets, Swiss chard, cucumbers, cauliflower, onions, cabbage, pumpkin, and radishes.

GEMINI: Needs foods containing potassium chloride, found in green beans, asparagus, beets, carrots, cauliflower, sweet corn, celery, apricots, peaches, plums, and pineapple.

CANCER: Needs calcium fluoride, found in milk, cheese, yogurt, kale, watercress, red cabbage, pumpkin, onions, oranges, lemons, egg yolks, raisins, and rye bread.

LEO: Needs magnesium phosphate, found in almonds, rye bread, lettuce, apples, plums, figs, lemons, coconut, cucumber, blueberries, walnuts, and onions.

VIRGO: Needs foods containing potassium sulphate, such as chicory, endive, whole wheat, oats, rye, cheese, almonds, and lean beef.

LIBRA: Needs foods with sodium phosphate, found in carrots, asparagus, beets, yellow corn, brown rice, figs, apples, strawberries, peaches, blueberries, almonds, and raisins.

SCORPIO: Needs foods with calcium sulphate, found in onions, asparagus, kale, garlic, watercress, mustard greens, cauliflower, leeks, radishes, figs, black cherries, and prunes.

SAGITTARIUS: Needs foods containing silica, to be found in edible skins of fruits and vegetables, figs, strawberries, prunes, Scotch oats, parsnips, unpolished rice, and ripe cherries.

CAPRICORN: Needs foods containing calcium phosphate, such as cabbage, asparagus, spinach, lentils, brown beans, celery, almonds, cucumbers, barley, egg yolks, lean meats, whole wheat, strawberries, figs, blueberries, and plums.

AQUARIUS: Needs foods with sodium chloride (salt that can be assimilated by the body), to be found in cabbage, spinach, asparagus, celery, radishes, carrots, corn, lentils, ocean fish and shellfish, strawberries, apples, and figs.

PISCES: Needs foods containing phosphate of iron, found in raw foods such as lettuce, strawberries, radishes, cucumbers, almonds, walnuts, and raisins.

Don't ask me to explain *why* nuts and raisins and egg yolks go with certain signs. They just do, according to the high priests of astrology, who have boned up on the planetary influences on the body's nutritional needs. I'm sure that nutrition nuts such as Gloria Swanson, an Aries, and Carol Channing, a Pisces, who notoriously turn up at even the most formal dinner parties wearing their little basket of health-food goodies like a charm bracelet, can give you plenty of reasons why diets of sunflower seeds and vitamins are good for you.

Personally, I would find this rather boring. But when I said as much to Sydney, he reminded me, "Well, medicine started with astrology, and good nutrition is part of good medicine, and nutritionists have found that certain food ingredients and vitamins go better with certain signs."

He startled me by adding, "Matter of fact, I've just signed a contract with a health-food company for a new product: Sydney Omarr's Astrology Vitamins. There'll be a different kind for each sign."

Chapter 24
HOW TO DRESS BY ASTROLOGY

"*If pants are IN . . .*
she *will put them OUT. . . .*"
—MR. BLACKWELL, ON JACQUELINE KENNEDY ONASSIS

Have you ever wondered what accounts for the charisma of Jacqueline Kennedy Onassis? Or the mystique of Elizabeth Taylor Burton? Or the enduring aura of enchantment that still surrounds the remembered images of Marilyn Monroe and Judy Garland?

It all starts with the stars in their subconscious heavens.

With a basic knowledge of astrological precepts anyone can soon figure out why people look and dress the way they do. In fact some can even guess another person's sign instantly by observing certain physical characteristics and manner of dress.

Try it yourself sometime, and more likely than not you'll find that the person born under Aries the ram, ruled by Mars, has a penchant for red and usually wears hats or headgear of some kind (because Aries governs the head); Taurus the bull has a short, thick neck and often wears ascots; Gemini the twins, ruled by Mercury, often has a double personality, mercurial tastes in fashions, and expressive hands; Cancer the moon child has a moon-shaped face and should never wear turtlenecks. And so on.

Nowhere are the planetary influences reflected more obviously, though usually subconsciously, than in a person's physical features, gestures, bearing, and manner of dress.

According to astrological precepts, the different parts of the body are ruled by each of the twelve signs of the zodiac as follows:

ARIES (ruled by Mars) governs the head, face, brain, upper jaws, eyes.

TAURUS (ruled by Venus) governs the throat, neck, Eustachian tubes, cervical vertebrae.

GEMINI (ruled by Mercury) governs the shoulders, arms, lungs, nervous system.

CANCER (ruled by the moon) governs the breasts, stomach, elbow joints.

LEO (ruled by the sun) governs the heart and back.

VIRGO (ruled by Mercury) governs the abdominal area, small intestines.

LIBRA (ruled by Venus) governs the kidneys, loins, lumbar region.

SCORPIO (ruled by Mars and Pluto) governs the generative organs.

SAGITTARIUS (ruled by Jupiter) governs the hips, thighs, and liver.

CAPRICORN (ruled by Saturn) governs the knees.

AQUARIUS (ruled by Uranus) governs the calves and ankles.

PISCES (ruled by Neptune) governs the feet and body fluids.

How do these translate into fashions? First we must know some of the other basic astrological precepts for each sign, such as the symbol, element, colors, gems, and metals with which the signs are associated.

Thus:

ARIES the ram. Ruler: Mars. Element: fire. Color: red. Gems: amethyst, diamond. Metal: iron.

TAURUS the bull. Ruler: Venus. Element: earth. Colors: blue and pink. Gems: moss agate, sapphire, emerald. Metal: copper.

GEMINI the twins. Ruler: Mercury. Element: air. Color: yellow. Gems: beryl, agate, aquamarine. Metal: quicksilver.

CANCER the crab. Ruler: the moon. Element: water. Color: violet. Gems: moss agate, pearl, emerald. Metal: silver.

LEO the lion. Ruler: the sun. Element: fire. Color: orange. Gems: ruby, diamond. Metal: gold.

VIRGO the virgin. Ruler: Mercury. Element: earth. Color: gray or navy blue. Gems: pink jasper, sardonyx, hyacinth. Metal: quicksilver.

LIBRA the balance. Ruler: Venus. Element: air. Color: indigo blue. Gems: diamond, opal. Metal: copper.

SCORPIO the scorpion. Ruler: Mars and Pluto. Element: water. Color: deep red. Gems: topaz, malachite, opal. Metal: iron and steel.

SAGITTARIUS the archer. Ruler: Jupiter. Element: fire. Color: light bue. Gems: carbuncle, turquoise, topaz. Metal: tin.

CAPRICORN the goat. Ruler: Saturn. Element: earth. Color: green (also black and dark gray). Gems: white onyx, moonstone. Metal: lead.

AQUARIUS the water bearer. Ruler: Uranus. Element: air. Color: electric blue. Gems: sapphire, opal. Metal: uranium.

PISCES the fish. Ruler: Neptune. Element: water. Color: sea green. Gems: chrysolite, moonstone. Metal: tin.

Don't ask me the how or why of all these signs, symbols, and various associations. They are not original with me or with Sydney. They are part of the basic classical precepts of astrology, but Sydney has become perhaps the world's foremost expert at interpreting them in terms of individual personal characteristics and tendencies in relation to or as reflected by the stars and planets.

Again, as Sydney says, "We don't know how or why astrology works, but it works. You can see it even in the way people walk and talk and what they wear—or don't wear. Brigitte Bardot is a Libra. You can tell it by those curves and contours."

Let's go down the list of some famous personalities and see how they reflect their zodiacal signs.

ARIES: Two of my favorite Aries people, for example, are Bette Davis and dancer Ann Miller, and I associate both of them vividly with the color red. The last time I interviewed Bette Davis (she was in Hollywood shooting a television show), she was wearing a stunning red tweed suit and pillbox hat to match. On another occasion, in her Bel Air hotel suite, she was dressed in red pants and pullover sweater and a plaid cap with sun visor—even inside. Miss Davis usually wears headgear of some kind, is famous for her big, popped-out eyes. (Aries governs the head, upper jaws, eyes.)

Ann Miller's fabulous fashion wardrobe is predominantly red; the cardinal fiery sign suits her to a T; she has plenty of amethysts and diamonds, frequently wears head coverings such as turbans and twists of veil. And she is almost as famous for her brilliant baby-doll red lips as she is for her tap dancing.

Annie refused to go along with the dark, dull, pale, or opaque look in lipstick fashions, preferring to keep her lips a shiny, kissable scarlet red . . . and always a brush of red rouge on her upper jaws . . . a true Aries, the sign of the warrior or pioneer. (Marlon Brando is also an Aries.)

Interestingly enough, our editor on this book, Eve Roshevsky, whom we have never met, tells us she's also an Aries, who even has red hair! She also always wears hats, recently bought herself one to match her scarlet nail polish and lipstick, and has an opera cape with a thread of red running through it. "I feel very good in scarlet. It really gives me a lift," she says. But she didn't know this was due to her Aries personality until Sydney told her.

TAURUS: Alas, Taurus women usually don't give two hoots for fashions. Queen Elizabeth II and Queen Juliana of the Netherlands were both born under the sign of Taurus and neither has ever been on anybody's "best dressed" list. Television's deliciously zany comedienne Carol Burnett is one of the entertainment world's best loved and most admired personalities, but her Taurus sign didn't do much for her fashion-wise. She once had the dubious honor of making Mr. Blackwell's "Worst Dressed" list. Mr. Blackwell is that bluntly outspoken adversary of the fashion industry who flaunts his fury at their "Best Dressed," as we have mentioned earlier, by naming his own annual ten "Worst Dressed"—with outrageous comments.

Carol Burnett was Number 6 on Mr. Blackwell's "Worst Dressed" list in 1971.

His comment: "Mass confusion purchased from a Park Avenue garage sale."

Carol's comment: "Haw! Haw!"

A typical Taurean, with a short neck, Carol often wears scarves and ascots.

One of the country's richest men, W. Clement Stone, insurance tycoon and philanthropist, also a Taurean, has a short, typical Taurus-the-bull neck, which is nearly always adorned with a dashing silk ascot or bow tie. Other famous men born under Taurus were two former U. S. Presidents, Ulysses S. Grant (April 27, 1822) and Harry S Truman (May 8, 1884).

GEMINI: In Sydney's opinion Marilyn Monroe and Judy Garland were both outstanding classic examples of the sign Gemini the twins, a mutable, airy sign: restless, versatile, clever, exuberant, expressive, with definitely mercurial personalities, quicksilver whims, and a two-in-one, double image. Marilyn Monroe was the screen's greatest sex symbol, Judy Garland one of its greatest talents. But behind the celluloid and footlights each was a vulnerable girl child who never grew up and whose life ended in tragedy. . . . The late President John F. Kennedy also was a Gemini, which is why news of his alleged sexual flings in and out of the White House didn't surprise astrologers. . . .

On the surface Geminis are generally delightfully quick-witted, exuberant, very active and agile (they move better in loose-fitting sports clothes), but there is usually a more serious side to them. Bob Hope, Beatrice Lillie, Cornelia Otis Skinner, and Rosalind Russell were born under Gemini. So were Igor Stravinsky, Cole Porter, and Burl Ives.

Personally, Gemini is one of my favorite signs. Most Geminis I have met are extremely likable, perhaps because there are two to choose from (the twins). As one of them said to me, "I like being a Gemini. I figure if somebody doesn't like one of me, maybe he'll like the other."

CANCER: Among physical characteristics of the Cancerian, the bony structure generally is the most striking feature. The arms are long in proportion to the body; the shoulders are broad, the hands and feet large. The skull is of a generous size, with an overhanging brow, high cheekbones, a pronounced lower jaw, expressive mouth and smile. The eyes are often short-sighted, deep-set, and wide apart; the eyebrows distinctly marked, sometimes almost meeting, with a decided downward curve, just over the bridge of the nose.

In women the structural characteristics are softened to a less bony build, and many female Cancerians have considerable grace of movement. They more than make up in expression for any lack of regularity in features. Kirsten Flagstad and Gertrude Lawrence were born under Cancer. So was New York socialite Mrs. William S. Paley, who for years was on the fashion industry's "Best Dressed" list.

She isn't particularly proud of it. "God help us, I got stuck with it thirty years ago and I've been trying to live it down ever since," she told me.

Calvin Coolidge was a Cancerian and the only President to have the same birthday as the United States—July 4—but a different year, 1872. Ernest Hemingway, Louis Armstrong, Nelson Rockefeller, and Van Cliburn also were born under Cancer.

LEO: The most famous Leo lady celebrity of course, is Jacqueline Kennedy Onassis, and everything about her reflects her Leonian astrological heritage: her commanding presence and queenly airs, her love of flattery and attention (typical of all Leos); her ambition for personal glory and a comfortable, well-cushioned throne; her stately bearing and her air for the dramatic—especially in the selection of her wardrobe and hairdos.

It is no secret that Mrs. Onassis has had a consuming passion for spending money on clothes. Nor is it any secret that for all the fortunes she's spent she has never made the grade as an elegantly dressed woman in high-fashion circles.

She did make it as Number 5 on Mr. Blackwell's ten "Worst Dressed" list for 1973, with the caustic comment: "If pants are IN . . . she will put them OUT."

Nevertheless, there is no denying that Jackie has the typical Leo's sense of showmanship and charisma, a magnetism that makes her stand out in a crowd, and an aura of eloquent pride and dignity when the occasion demands.

Who can ever forget that poignant picture of the beautiful young woman in widow's black firmly gripping her son's hand during the long televised funeral services of the late President John F. Kennedy? . . .

On the bizarre side of Leo there is Sydney's long-time favorite Leonian, Mae West, who still plays the queen of Hollywood filmdom and reigns over her own circle in fitting style—all in white. So far as I know, Miss West doesn't own a stitch of clothes—or anything else—that isn't white. Her evening gowns and furs are all white. Her apartment décor, from rugs to furnishings, is all white. She usually makes her dramatic appearance at public functions with a grand flourish of a white feather boa or ermine extravaganza. During the filming of that abominable bomb *Myra Breckinridge*, Miss West let out a real Leo-the-lioness roar when Raquel Welch walked onto the set one day dressed in a white gown—which the script called for. Queenie West was wearing all-white gowns in all her scenes. She wasn't about to be upstaged by a younger sex symbol in the same color.

Raquel walked out in a huff. Production was held up for days. I happened to be covering the movie's shooting at the time, which mostly meant watching everyone develop ulcers. Finally, Raquel's gown was sent out and dyed blue, La West languidly returned to the set, and shooting resumed.

VIRGO: Greta Garbo, Sophia Loren, Lauren Bacall, and Grandma Moses were born under Virgo. So were Maurice Chevalier and J. P. Morgan.

LIBRA: Helen Hayes, Deborah Kerr, and Brigitte Bardot were born under Libra. Among the men: George Gershwin, Thomas Wolfe, Dwight D. Eisenhower.

SCORPIO: Both Grace Kelly and Katharine Hepburn were born under Scorpio, but fashionwise they are at opposite ends of the pole. Hepburn is notoriously unorthodox in her dress, was wearing trousers long before pantsuits became popular, hasn't been seen in a skirt for years. But even in dungarees, sweatshirt, walking brogues, and bandanna, Miss Hepburn has more class than all the Best Dresseds put together.

SAGITTARIUS: Jane Fonda, Julie Harris, Mary Martin, and anthropologist Margaret Mead were all born under Sagittarius—and that's probably all they have in common. So were Socrates, Beethoven, Walt Disney, Noel Coward, Mark Twain, Winston Churchill, and Frank Sinatra.

CAPRICORN: Ava Gardner, Marlene Dietrich, and Ethel Merman were born under Capricorn. So was Joan of Arc. Men: Benjamin Franklin, Alexander Hamilton, Woodrow Wilson, Albert Schweitzer, Cary Grant, Edgar Allan Poe, and Richard Nixon.

AQUARIUS: Zsa Zsa Gabor and Kim Novak are Aquarians, and both exemplify the Aquarian's natural instinct for the unorthodox and unpredictable—both in temperament and in fashions. Zsa Zsa's tastes run rather a bit on the flamboyant side of elegance. Kim has never worked much at being a fashion plate, preferring to spend her time with her horses. In physical characteristics the influence of Aquarius often shows in remarkable nobility of feature, especially of profile. John Barrymore, known as "The Great Profile," was born under Aquarius, as were Clark Gable, Abraham Lincoln, and Franklin Delano Roosevelt.

PISCES: This is one of the most mystical and intriguing signs—Pisces the fishes, ruled by Neptune, a mutable, watery sign usually gentle, kind, sensitive, unlucky, and often melancholy. Also known as the sign of the poet or interpreter: Michelangelo, Chopin, and Einstein were born under the sign of Pisces. And so was Elizabeth Taylor, whom many consider to be the world's most beautiful woman. Certainly she has the world's most beautiful eyes. Curiously, although Neptune governs the feet, the most striking physical features of the Pisces person is the eyes. Liza Minnelli and Dinah Shore, both born under Pisces, have typical Piscean eyes.

Another sign, *ARIES*, as already noted, is closely associated with outstanding eyes (Bette Davis), but as Sydney explains it, "The Aries eyes are more direct than Pisces. There is usually an aura of mystery in Pisces eyes. Both Aries and Pisces eyes add to the general appearance of anyone born under those signs, but the classical Pisces eyes have a unique mystique of their own, a mystical quality that is difficult to define, an ethereal touch of sadness and poetry and songs unsung. . . ."

Perhaps no one exudes the sign of Pisces more than Elizabeth Taylor. The first time I saw her was during the filming of an atrocious movie, *Boom* (which bombed), on the island of Sardinia, in the Mediterranean. Her eyes and her mood matched the murky sea. The last time I saw her was at an Academy Awards banquet in

Beverly Hills, a Neptunian vision in a flowing, filmy gown of muted sea-green chiffon, and clearly frightened of the stampede around her.

She could never be mistaken for a Leo.

And anyone who has ever seen those incredible eyes close up, double-lashed, deep violet, and veiled in mystery, would know that they're the eyes of a Pisces.

Sydney refuses to get into the debate over the best-dressed or worst-dressed women and to what extent this may be influenced by the stars. He doesn't like to play favorites with the zodiacal signs, and he admits he is no fashion expert. He's willing to leave that to Mr. Blackwell, who incidentally has managed to compile a limited list of four "Well Dressed" ladies whom he calls "outrageously independent" according to fashion-industry standards.

"They are truly fashion independents, who know who they are and who dress for themselves, and that to me is being well dressed," he says.

They are Nancy Reagan, a Cancer; singer-actress Diana Ross, an Aries; actress-model Marissa Berenson, a Leo; and Princess Caroline of Monaco, an Aquarius.

"Liza Minnelli [Pisces] might almost make it someday," he added.

As Sydney points out, "Fashion trends change with the times and the years. Sometimes it's more fashionable to be flamboyant. At other times it's chic to be conservative."

Being a Leo himself, he is somewhat inclined to give Leos a slight edge in fashion awareness, although he is quick to add that writer Anaïs Nin, a classical Pisces, is one of the best-dressed women he has ever met.

He also feels that both Aries and Aquarius have certain qualities, such as a pioneering spirit and confidence in their own tastes, that lend luster to the Blackwell label of well-dressed "fashion independents."

But, more important, Sydney is not so much concerned with fashion labels as with how everyone, men and women, can improve their looks and their appearance by following a few helpful little astrological hints.

By now you have learned some of the simple and basic precepts of astrology, how certain signs are associated with various parts of the body and reflected in physical characteristics, movements, mood, and temperament; and you can play your own game of matching the signs to your favorite famous personalities.

Or take a tip from Sydney and match your own personality to the stars.

If you want to be astrologically aware in choosing your fashion wardrobe, here are Sydney's suggestions:

ARIES (sun in Aries, Aries rising, and Mars in first house) A dash of red is very important for both male and female. A man might wear a brown suit with a red pocket handkerchief. Headgear and eye makeup are very important for the woman; a cap or beret is very good on the man. Darker colors are becoming to both.

TAURUS (sun in Taurus, Taurus rising, and Venus in first house) An ascot or anything to do with neckgear is very important for the man. Also, scarves for the woman. She can do wonders with them. The shoulders are important to both; they should be accented in some way. Blue is very good for both man and woman. Both like to have a sensual appearance.

GEMINI (sun in Gemini, Gemini rising, and Mercury in first house) Gloves are important for the Gemini woman, and the man tends to have his nails impeccably manicured. Both like to use their hands in talking. They are very active, so must wear loose clothing, sports clothes that aren't binding and won't look messy as they move around. But a Gemini woman could wear a man's jacket and still look feminine.

CANCER (sun in Cancer, Cancer rising, and moon in first house) For the woman, emphasis is on the breasts. She is very conscious of her undergarments and wearing the right kind of breast support. For the man, there is emphasis on the belt or suspenders. Both love to eat, and they don't want to have to loosen belt or feel constricted. Since both have a tendency toward a moon face, turtlenecks are not good. Open-neck shirts and blouses are good for them. A Cancer woman is more aware of her décolletage than most women.

LEO (sun in Leo, Leo rising, and sun in first house) Gold is an important color. The Leo woman likes a flash of color such as burnt orange or gold. She would do well to wear a sash that stands out.

The Leo man needs a dash of color too—a brightly colored tie. The Leo man has to be very careful of his suit. He is difficult to fit, especially in the back.

VIRGO (sun in Virgo, Virgo rising, and Mercury in first house) The Virgo woman is very fastidious but also can be very glamorous. Clean lines are good for her, not sloppy ones. She is also very active and can wear a turban to keep her hair in place. The classic chic look is good for her. Also for the Virgo man. He is more clothes-conscious than most men and takes great pride in his neatness; likes to look clean and athletic.

LIBRA (sun in Libra, Libra rising, and Venus in first house) All clothes worn by the Libra woman seem to be pointing to the waist and culminate there. So a tight belt to accentuate the waist is good, or clothes that are indented at the waistline. This is a very gracious, feminine look but also allows her to move around easily. The Libra man is very concerned about blending into his surroundings, because he's a good listener. Flamboyant clothes are not for him. He's the type to wear an Eisenhower jacket (Ike was a Libra), but no frills or gimmicks for either the Libra man or the Libra woman. They like basic clothes.

SCORPIO (sun in Scorpio, Scorpio rising, and Pluto in first house) Intense but very sexy look for both of them. Dark green is very good for them. Clothes should be magnetic, but cool; sexy and sensuous come from that without trying. Should be an effortless way of dressing. The Scorpio man looks good in turtlenecks or sweaters. Both Scorpio men and Scorpio women have a dynamic magnetism and an animal-like quality.

SAGITTARIUS (sun in Sagittarius, Sagittarius rising, and Jupiter in first house) Both men and women are generally athletic, and this should be reflected in what they wear. The legs and thighs are very important, and a Sagittarius woman should be able to wear pants very well. The man is not afraid of new styles, but he's conservative, too. Clothes have a tendency to make him look heavier, and he can overcome this by wearing longer jackets.

CAPRICORN (sun in Capricorn, Capricorn rising, and Saturn in first house) Both male and female Capricorns have to be careful not to look morose. Should wear dashes of bright colors. Black is their basic color, as are other dark colors, but they should not be worn alone. A woman should add pearls or gold jewelry or a bright scarf. A man should wear a bright tie and matching pocket handkerchief. Dark is fine but not alone. Capricorns should not look foreboding.

AQUARIUS (sun in Aquarius, Aquarius rising, and Uranus in first house) Here we have a very unorthodox person who will try anything once, who likes the devil-may-care look but with humor, who likes to dare and to break tradition. Aquarians are the first to try anything new. The woman can wear clothing that changes looks in a second, when she changes her accessories. The man is daring but not so much so that people would lose confidence in him. Aquarians can be eccentric but never harebrained. They go for the unusual and like to create their own traditions. They are in tune with fashion, but they don't permit fashion to dictate to them. They have great confidence in their own taste.

PISCES (sun in Pisces, Pisces rising, and Neptune in first house) Shoes and feet are very important. The Pisces feet often hurt, so the woman may need to wear more comfortable shoes than she would like, and consequently more sporty clothes to go with them. But she can do more with slippers than most women can with expensive evening shoes. The man has to be very careful with his socks. He tends to wear them too short, should give more attention to this. The woman looks great in flimsy, filmy, flowing garments, nets and veils—the ethereal look. The man can achieve that ethereal look too. He can wear expensive clothes and wear them comfortably. Both Pisces men and Pisces women are at their best in that expensively chic, cool, and casual look.

Thus, if you're really overboard on astrology, you can use these certain colors, metals, and stones to co-ordinate your fashion wardrobe, accessories, interior décor, floral arrangements, or your dinner parties.

Each sign, as Sydney says, provides a valuable component, necessary to get any show on the road.

Sydney lives and breathes astrology and can find ways of applying it to virtually any conceivable aspect of everyday existence.

"I enjoy all of it," he says. "But I have to admit that I still wish the American public would be more interested in the weightier values of astrology rather than love and romance and food and fashions and all of that.

"However, I have to admit also that we certainly have come a long way from my early days in Philadelphia, when I felt like sort of hiding my astrology books under my coat while I was riding the trolley."

Coda…Number Nine… An End or a Beginning

Chapter 25
WHAT DOES THE FUTURE HOLD?

"The stars are there for us
to study and learn from them.
To be ignorant is to ignore
the poetry of our personal universe."

—SYDNEY OMARR

Sydney is optimistic about the future. He foresees a new age of enlightenment somewhere around the turn of the next century, which will herald a scientific awakening to the practical applications of astrology. He is confident that astrology will one day be used in the advancement of the biological and physical sciences, including medical knowledge.

He qualifies his optimism with one big important IF that tolls an ominous sound in the cosmos.

"IF we can survive the year 1984," Sydney warns. "This is the crucial year, 1984, the year we must prepare ourselves for and be ready to face, for it's another Pluto 22 year coming at us full force. And it's going to be far worse than 1975. I don't like to make predictions (I prefer to forecast trends and cycles), but if I were to predict a holocaust of the greatest magnitude, I fear that it would occur in the year 1984.

"That is the year that could usher in another major war or a catastrophic event that signifies wide-scale death and destruction.

"In a symbolic sense it may be a time of death for the entire world, a tearing down of the old to rebuild with the new. Not only physical and material things will be affected; but concepts, ideas, certain fundamental hypotheses, principles, and philosophies which are now commonly accepted may be utterly demolished."

Many months after I first typed these words from our original tape transcript, a wire-service news story caught my eyes.

It was headlined: SOCIAL, ECONOMIC DISRUPTION FORECAST.

The story, datelined Washington and carried in the Los Angeles *Times* (Monday, December 22, 1975), corroborated Sydney's dire forecast although it was not based on astrology but on a "Trend Analysis Program" of the life-insurance industry.

The report (prepared by the Institute of Life Insurance) was a computerized and specifically precise warning "to expect economic turbulence and social disruption during the next 20 years as the industrial era and its work ethic give ground to a slacker, somewhat different culture."

There was a frightening similarity in the main thrust of Sydney's forecast and the "Trend Analysis" report for life-insurance executives.

"The industrial era was ushered in on the strength of a particular set of philosophies, and there is much evidence that these have been weakening as new ones have arisen. . . . Whatever happens, the consensus seems to be that the odds are stacked against those who believe that our political system has seen in the Watergate affair the last of rough times."

The report concluded: "We may be somewhere in the middle of a turbulent transition to a new, or at least somewhat different, culture"—beginning about 1990.[1]

If Sydney's uncomputerized, astrological calculations are correct (as they usually are), and if 1984, the Pluto 22 year, ushers in the great holocaust or catastrophic event that signifies death and destruction, then it is conceivable that reconstruction, rebuilding, the "turbulent transition to a new, or at least somewhat different, culture" should begin about 1990.

Although he is reluctant to pinpoint political trouble spots, Syd-

[1] A more recent report as this goes to press: Nobel laureate Linus C. Pauling warns, "within 25 or 50 years there will occur the greatest catastrophe in the history of the world. . . . It might well be the result from a world war which could destroy civilization and might well be the end of the human race." Pauling, emeritus professor at Stanford University, received the Nobel Prize for chemistry in 1954 and the Nobel Peace Prize in 1962. He says he is "an optimist" and "the human race might survive." (From a speech at a meeting of the American Chemical Society in New York City, April 1976.)

ney ventures an intriguing comment that cannot be lightly dismissed in view of recent history in the Middle East:

"Whoever picked the birth date of the nation of Israel made a horrendous mistake. The leaders who created this nation should have had more knowledge of the planetary influences on the lives of men and nations. They should have tried to choose the correct time for a nation to be born, as Burma and other nations have done. If an astrologer had made such a mistake, he would have been laughed right out of the looney bin.

"I haven't personally cast a horoscope for Israel, but there can be no doubt that its chart is one of violence and aggressiveness that could engulf the whole world. I think the question of survival may depend on the rebirth of that nation.

"As individual human beings, we can't be reborn to suit the most favorable astrological aspects. But we can learn from history and help create and give birth or rebirth to governments of nations, utilizing certain well-established astrological trends and cycles and guidelines."

As Sydney says, "*If* we can survive the year 1984, then we can start rebuilding. From the ashes the phoenix will rise again, and with it the new age of enlightenment.

"All great thinkers have differed on many things, but not on this theme: that we are all subject to certain cosmic elements, particles, influences or forces as some call them, of the universe we inhabit. Who knows what hidden possibilities lie within man's reach when he properly investigates the realm of these higher horizons?" he asks.

The key to the proper investigation of astrology, he adds, lies in the magic word *funding*.

"If we should get a one- or two-million-dollar grant for research in astrology, the antiastrology scientists would go into reverse gear and jump in our boats fast. It's as simple as that," he says. "But astrologers don't get funding. Maybe someday we will. Then the scientists will give astrology a new name with a scientific status and try to find out how it works. I am not a scientist. I do not know how it works. I'm willing to admit that the more I know the less I know. But it seems to me that the true scientific yardstick is whether the thing works."

Sydney's good friend and mentor Carl Payne Tobey, who never

minces words on the subject, says, "So-called modern science is in a rut. It requires an awakening. We pay too much attention to theories while closing our eyes and minds to everything that we do not already believe. The word science originally meant a search for the truth. But it doesn't mean that today. It is heavy with dogma. We should stop trying to standardize the truth. It can't be done. We know so little about the whole that the disclosure of one new truth could change everything in so-called science today."

Indeed the disclosure of one new truth in recently modern times proved how far off base the priests of science can be in their controversy over "flying machines." A report issued by Harvard College Observatory in the 1890s stated flatly that no heavier-than-air machine would ever fly. It took a while to learn that heavier-than-air machines can fly off the ground, and from continent to continent, and even to the moon.

"Even scientists, like all of us, do make mistakes," says Sydney. "It would be nice if they paid attention to what Sir Francis Bacon once said to a colleague (a mathematician who was a violent opponent of astrology): 'I have practiced astrology. You have not. If I do not condemn it, how can you presume to do so?' "

Sydney has his own blueprint for the future scientific investigation of astrology. Its key word is Carl Jung's term: synchronicity.

"When scientists accept the fact that there is a synchronicity, a correlation, a correspondence or coincidence between the planetary patterns and events here on earth, this will be an important step in the progress of mankind," Sydney said. "As above, so below. The solar system is a giant clock. Its movements are the hands of the clock, regulating our own calendars and clocks and human activities. We respond to certain *times* of the solar clock.

"Scientists must begin their serious study of astrology with that mysterious but very real and dynamic element of *time*. They must begin to regard time as something real—like the ocean that holds up a ship or the air that holds up an airplane. There seems to be something about time that we do not understand. It remains the mysterious missing link in answers to the relationship between man and the universe. All you have to do is read the Bible to know this."

He quoted from Ecclesiastes: "To everything there is a season and a time to every purpose under the Heaven. A time to be born and a time to die.

"Maybe someday scientists will be able to computerize this," Sydney said. "I think astrology's greatest contribution to the future of mankind will be its role in the investigation and understanding of synchronicity, cosmic clocks, trends and cycles, and biological rhythms that are all based on timings of the great solar clock. I believe this will come in the dawn of our new age of enlightenment—that is, if we survive the crisis of 1984," he repeated with emphasis.

"You see, if we listened to the tickings of the great solar clock, if we heeded its hand movements that have been recorded throughout history, we might avert some of these great disasters—or at least be prepared for them. We have barely scratched the surface in our knowledge of *time*. When we begin to understand about time, we can by our own free will and action change the course of destiny. That's what astrology is all about."

Henry Miller puts it another way. "If everyone had a good, clear understanding of astrology, we would have a better world. Human beings are neither good nor bad but a mixture of both. The same is true for the twelve signs of the zodiac. We carry within us something of every sign. We cannot hope to achieve perfection, but we can hope to make the most of the qualities we were endowed with at birth.

"We can learn to accept ourselves for what we are and not look for miracles, to recognize our shortcomings and try to overcome them. The purpose of astrology is not to teach how to thwart destiny but how to live up to it, in accordance with it. In other words, to become aware, to know yourself better and realize your limitations.

"The whole world has this goddamned notion that any man can become what he wants to be. Balderdash! Every man has a destiny, and the sooner he learns what direction it is taking, the sooner he accommodates to the outrageous slings and arrows of fortune."

The controversial and outspoken author, known as that grand-old-man-cum-enfant-terrible of literature, was in one of his delightfully expansive and irrepressibly comic moods when I called on him at his home in the Pacific Palisades, a Los Angeles suburb by the sea. He lives not far from Sydney and is one of Sydney's greatest fans.

"When I am absolutely perplexed and bewildered," he told me, "I call on Sydney. People say I am an utter fool to do this, but I believe implicitly in what he tells me. People say a person of my prominence and stature shouldn't fall for this hocus-pocus. Me of all people. But they're ignorant. They don't know anything about astrology. The average man has no conception of what astrology is. Neither do I. But when I'm in a jam I consult the chart for help—medically, psychologically, logically, philosophically. Astrology is the total picture of any situation. Why is it so? That I cannot answer. But I know in general that what's wrong down here has something to do with what's going on up there, some planetary conjunction in my horoscope.

"You can't say I *believe* in astrology, but I accept it completely. It's like believing in doctors. Maybe 80 per cent of them are no goddamned good, but you need them in a crisis. I use astrology when I'm in a crisis, and most of the time I'm in tune with the stars."

He said he always consults Sydney when planning a trip, has canceled or postponed several trips to the Orient because the time wasn't propitious, and scheduled a date at the hospital for hip surgery on Sydney's advice.

But he disregarded it on his fifth, and last, marriage.

"He did our charts and he gave me a thousand and one reasons why I should not marry the girl. I am a Capricorn with Aries rising and three planets in conjunction, with a strong relationship to Scorpio.

"But when we're in love we don't live by our reason," Miller confessed, "and so I married her, though everything in our charts told us not to. Astrology was right; the marriage was wrong. We had it annulled in eleven days."

The walls of Miller's home are covered with books, Picasso posters, and his own surrealist watercolors—many of women nude from the waist down. A frail, gentle man with thinning white hair but a lusty zest for living, he said, "I'm eighty-two and I still adore women as a whole, even though I consider them a separate breed, a species apart. If the world were run by women, it would be a much better place. Men, in general, aren't worth the crap they're standing in. My five failures in marriage doesn't diminish my hunger or adoration of women.

"If I had paid attention to Sydney," he admitted, "I could have avoided some of the problems. Sydney is much more than an astrologer. He's a psychic, a mystic, a highly sensitive man with great intelligence and insight. Furthermore, as men go, he's a good, decent human being. Most men are no goddamned good. Take Picasso," he said, waving his arm toward the posters; "he was a sonofabitch. He was unquestionably a genius, but he wasn't a good man. I'd rather talk to a genuine idiot than a genius any time.

"Thank God, Sydney isn't a genius. But he's no idiot either. He can debate with the best of those goddamned intellectuals. His only trouble is that he's an idealist. He wants to help everyone. It hurts him to have people ignore his advice. He has to sit there and watch them destroy themselves when he knows he could have helped prevent it.

"I tell him that's not his problem. He's not their keeper. People have to help themselves."

If Henry Miller has such faith in Sydney, why did he ignore his advice on his fifth marriage?

"We are all human and we can't resist human impulses," he replied. "Astrologers are human, too; they're not God. But we expect them to produce miracles because we don't want to pay the price of our own sins. We expect them to get us out of the misery we have created for ourselves. Unfortunately, some of us cannot help committing the same kind of miseries all over again even when we know the astrological aspects are all wrong. The house of marriage has always been bad for me.

"But the house of love," he added quickly, "now, that house is still all right. Maybe ten or twenty more times and I might find the right one. . . . Remember what Carl Jung said: 'Astrology is deeply rooted in the human soul. The sight of the starry firmament has always made men dream.' "

It is mid-September as I write this. I stepped out on my patio and looked up at the starry firmament that has always made men dream.

There was a beautiful, bright full moon, and I remembered that this was the time when the fish bite better and the corn grows taller and certain forms of lunacy, or moon madness, are most likely to occur.

How much of it did I really believe?

But who would ever have believed that men would one day fly to that moon and actually walk on it?

The sky was a spectacular blaze of stars, but one star stood out in dazzling splendor above all the others. I recognized if from my childhood astronomy lessons as Venus, the most brilliant planet in the solar system. No one can miss Venus . . . the love planet . . . the Roman goddess of love and beauty . . . also known as the Greek goddess Aphrodite.

I gazed in wonder at the planet Venus twinkling away up there in all her glorious beauty. It wasn't clear to me why Venus, the planet of love, should rule over the sign of Taurus the bull.

But how much did I really know about it?

I searched the skies for some recognizable sign of the zodiacal signs: Aries the ram, Taurus the bull, Cancer the crab, Capricorn the goat, or even Scorpio the scorpion. Sydney had told me the signs and planets are there, for all to observe and interpret. I couldn't even find his own Leo the lion, or my Sagittarius the archer.

But I did locate the Big Dipper, the Little Dipper, Orion, and Cassiopeia's Chair, constellations I had learned in beginners' astronomy and mythology. I hadn't thought of them much since my early school days. There was a certain thrill in rediscovering them and even remembering fragments of the fascinating legends connected with them.

As I looked up at the moon and the millions of stars, I knew one thing I believed in for certain: it was a world of beauty beyond compare.

If the stars did nothing more than touch our lives with beauty, we would, indeed, as Henry Miller said, have a better world.

Is it really possible they can also give our lives meaning and direction and some form of abstract order?

Or is this all humbug? Is man an entity apart from the universe he lives in? Are we totally immune from the collective cosmic forces produced by the planets and all those millions of stars up there?

As I looked at them and thought about it, I found it much more absurd and impossible to believe this than to accept Sydney's and Carl Jung's word for it: "We are born at a given moment, in a given place and, like vintage years of wine, we have the qualities of the year and of the season in which we are born. Astrology does not lay claim to anything more."

"Astrology may do nothing more than to help us ask questions:

Why are we here? Where are we going? It may do nothing more than to make us understand ourselves better, but I think that's pretty important," says Sydney. "The stars are there for us to study and learn from them. To be ignorant is to ignore the poetry of our personal universe."

And therein, I think, lies the great gap between astrology and astronomy.

Astronomy has been called the most beautiful of all sciences, and justifiably so—until astrology is recognized as a science.

For, somewhere along the way, astronomy has lost the poetry of the universe. Modern astronomers, through their glass-chrome-steel-and-flint-eyed telescopic view of the stars, see only what can be measured by computerized mechanisms, not by human responses.

My own human response as I contemplated the stars was a sudden haunting memory of a line from an Elizabeth Barrett Browning love sonnet: "How do I love thee? Let me count the ways. . . ." I changed the words a little to fit them to the stars: "How do they touch me? Let me count the ways."

The computers have not come up with the answers yet. Maybe someday.

Meanwhile, if we are touched by even an infinitesimally small fraction of the beauty and poetry of the stars, our personal universe has been enriched.

The Symbolism of the Houses

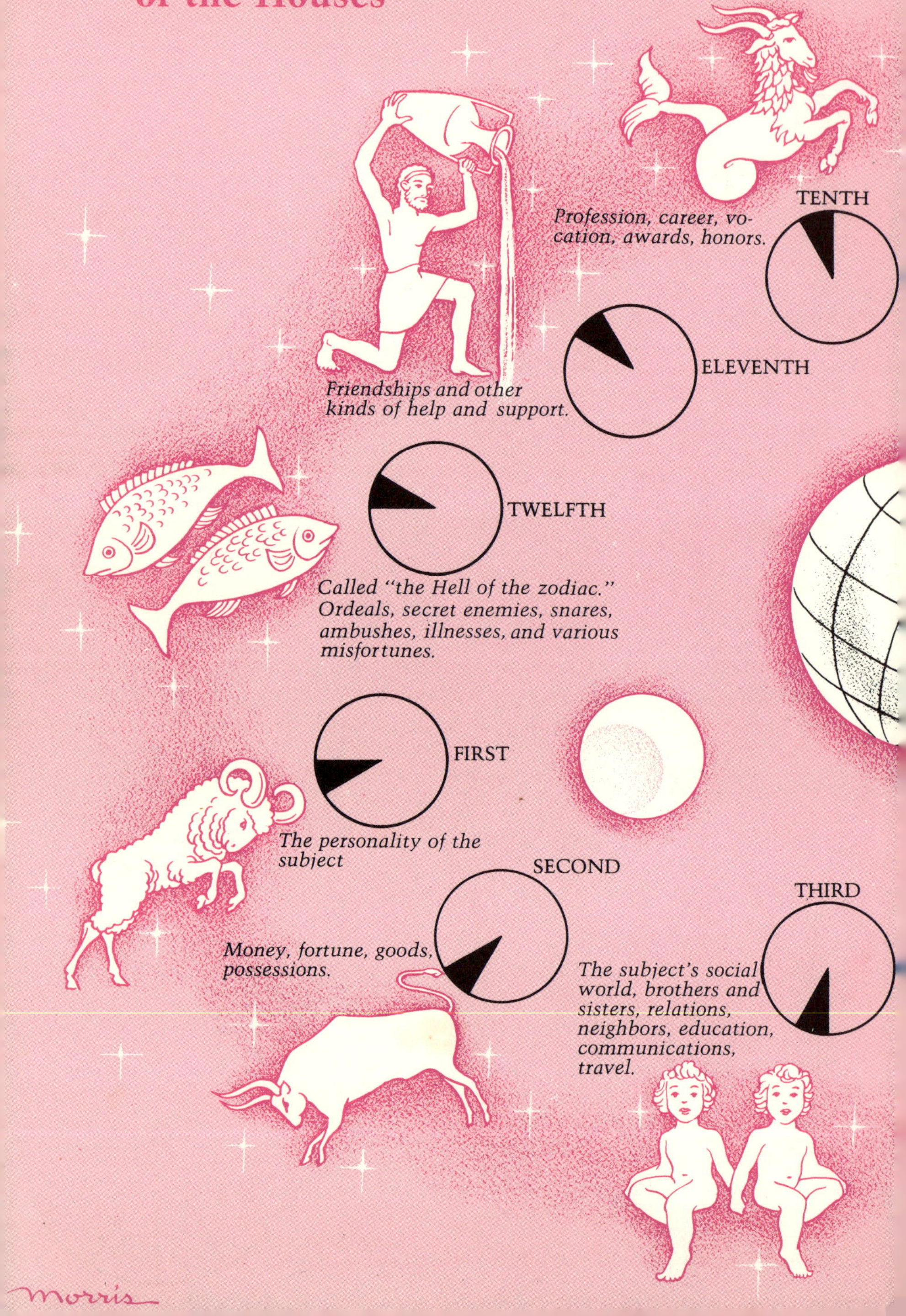